Acts of Enjoyment

Pittsburgh Series in Composition, Literacy, and Culture
Dave Bartholomae and Jean Ferguson Carr, Editors

ACTS OF ENJOYMENT

Rhetoric, Žižek, and the Return of the Subject

Thomas Rickert

UNIVERSITY OF PITTSBURGH PRESS

Published by the University of Pittsburgh Press, Pittsburgh, Pa., 15260
Copyright © 2007, University of Pittsburgh Press
All rights reserved
Manufactured in the United States of America
Printed on acid-free paper
10 9 8 7 6 5 4 3 2 1

Library of Congress Cataloging-in-Publication Data

Rickert, Thomas J. (Thomas Joseph), 1964–
Acts of enjoyment : rhetoric, Žižek, and the return of the subject / Thomas Rickert.
    p.   cm. — (Pittsburgh series in composition, literacy, and culture)
Includes bibliographical references and index.
ISBN-10: 0-8229-4333-6 (alk. paper)
ISBN-10: 0-8229-5962-3 (alk. paper)
ISBN-13: 978-0-8229-4333-4 (alk. paper)
ISBN-13: 978-0-8229-5962-5 (alk. paper)
1. Rhetoric — Study and teaching. I. Title.
P53.27.R53 2007
808.0071–dc22   2006039160

This book is for my father,
Thomas Robert Rickert

CONTENTS

ACKNOWLEDGMENTS

With so much discussion of "the Other" in this book, it is not surprising that I should acknowledge so many of the people who have helped me along the way. First, I would like to thank my mentor, Victor Vitanza, for his knowledge, guidance, and friendship; without him, this book could not have been written. I also wish to thank Luanne Frank and Hans Kellner, both of whom inspired me greatly and serve as ideals for what a teacher and scholar can be. Ben Agger, Collin Brooke, Jonikka Charlton, Lisa Coleman, John Muckelbauer, Jeff Rice, Dave Rieder, Geoffrey Sirc, Rajani Sudan, Pat Sullivan, and Lynn Worsham all helped me work through important issues; their wisdom and camaraderie sparked invaluable discussion and insight. Lynn deserves special mention for publishing my first essay, a longer version of which appears here as chapter 6. Janet Alsup, Janet Atwill, Samantha Blackmon, David Blakesley, Diane Davis, Jenny Edbauer, Byron Hawk, Dennis Lynch, and Michael Salvo provided feedback on various parts of the manuscript. They are brilliant people, and I am lucky to be able to count them as friends and colleagues. My graduate students in postmodernism and cultural studies classes at Purdue helped me work through many of the ideas presented here. I am grateful for their willingness to engage this material with me. Colin Charlton edited the whole manuscript and gave impressive amounts of feedback—I owe him so much more than the few bottles of Bordeaux I'll throw at him. My reviewers, Sharon Crowley and Michael Bernard-Donals, were very generous and supportive, as was my editor, Jean Carr. These three deserve much more than thanks. (And maybe Jean will take a chance on my next book, too.) Last, and most important, I thank Jenny Bay, who withstood my often torturous prose and read everything—more than once. That must be love! Her smart commentary and *jouissance*-infused attention to detail amazed and delighted me and made for a far better book.

I would also like to thank a different kind of Other by singling out the following bands and artists, who supplied my sound track for writing and from whom I derived many insights: Amon Düül II, Anubian Lights, Ash Ra Tempel, Black Sabbath, Bjork, Budgie, Kate Bush, Can, The Clash, The Doors, Echo & the Bunnymen, Brian Eno, Farflung, Funkadelic, Harmonia, Jon Hassell, Hawkwind, Bill Hicks, House of Love, Isis, Joy Division, Kyuss, Bob Marley, Massive Attack, The Melvins, Van Morrison, Neu!, New Order, Popol Vuh, A Primary Industry, Radiohead, Santana, The Sea and the Cake, The Sex Pistols, Shriekback, Sigur Rós, Sky Cries Mary, Stereolab, Sufjan Stevens, Talking Heads, Unida, War, Wilco, Yes, and Neil Young.

Acts of Enjoyment

Prospective

THE IDEAS ABOUT cultural criticism, rhetoric, and psychoanalysis underpinning this book emerged from my use of cultural studies in composition courses. More specifically, they arose from problems with cultural critique in the classroom that called for further inquiry. Unfortunately, no eureka moment occurred that would provide a richly loaded scenario allowing me to encapsulate with ease and simplicity the primary issues of this book. But perhaps this is more appropriate since I place so much stock in the processes of "working through." Indeed, "working through" is an accurate description of what brought these thoughts to mind. Sometime deep in the sixth inning of the 1990s, teaching my latest version of a cultural studies–oriented composition class, it struck me that something was awry. In retrospect, my unit on advertising seems particularly suspect. My students were becoming adept at picking apart ads and identifying their most pernicious features: the inducement to buy unnecessary, expensive items; the achievement of identity and modes of being through products; the reification of unjust class, race, and gender roles; and so forth. I faced little resistance from them, James Berlin and Company to the contrary. Or perhaps I should say their resistance appeared indirectly, in odd, hard to recognize, even symptomatic forms. Their adeptness led them to write competent, even excellent papers, but that was the extent of it. If there was any real change, it was in growing cynicism: "Yeah, I know I don't need these seventy-five-dollar designer blue jeans, but . . . " [spending ensues]. Where was the connection between what they were learning and their actual lives? If education, at least the humanities-based component, is in part predicated on the power of knowledge to enable a critically enlightened citizenry, what happens when we see a breakdown of this fundamental warrant? I became interested in this fault line between knowledge and action, not just as a problem of writing but as a larger problem of rhetoric that suggested, among other things, the limits of the narrative of false consciousness and its cure, enlightenment. Why was it that knowledge about oppressive, unjust, or disadvantageous practices, combined with grow-ing rhetorical savvy, led to . . . nothing, or at least nothing that could I see, beyond the ability to marshal such knowledge in writing papers that became, once again, classroom exercises with little potential for productively impact-ing student lives?

Perhaps it could simply be argued that I had stumbled upon a permuta-tion of the perennial conflict between philosophy and rhetoric, knowledge and persuasion. This, however, seems too simple and schematic. Rhetoric in most of its forms, going back to Aristotle, makes use of what is available, including philosophical and scientific knowledge and procedures. And phi-losophy stripped of rhetoric is impossibly arid or even, arguably, nonexistent. In short, philosophy and rhetoric are always in flux and intermingling, so highlighting the antagonism between the two elevates rarefied forms to an improbable causal status. It might still be objected that rhetoric accomplishes much of its work at other levels—across the lure of personality and credibility (*ethos*) and emotions (*pathos*). Could it not therefore be the case that what I observed were simply cultural forms of *ethos* and *pathos* at work? Wasn't this just a rhetorical war of positioning, à la Foucault, in which cultural rhetorics trumped classroom/academic rhetorics? In part, this is certainly true, but at the same time, other factors work to complicate this narrative. Two of these factors are fantasy and *jouissance*.

Fantasy is a common term for imagined scenes of wish fulfillment, but that is not how it is being used here; rather, *fantasy* refers to our largely un-conscious projections and constructions of other people and the world, thus underpinning how we come to see ourselves in the world. For instance, a feel-ing of ease upon entering a familiar coffee shop depends on an unconscious fantasy construction of the environs; should that fantasy frame shift (for a host of possible reasons that may have no direct relation to the coffee shop), our affective experience could well become one of unease, estrangement, even dislike. Fantasy such as this is an everyday and entirely pervasive part of experience, and in large part, we depend on it. It helps sustain (and, as we shall see, emerges from) human interactive bonding and unbonding. So fantasy is not a problem per se unless it helps sustain objectionable practices and beliefs. As I argue in later chapters, there are parallels—but also important differences—between fantasy and ideology. *Jouissance*, a French word customarily left untranslated, means enjoyment, but not in the traditional sense ("My, this 1995 La Louvière is an enjoyable glass of wine"). Instead, it refers to the, again, largely unconscious enjoyment one derives from habits, attitudes, beliefs, and activities. Nietzsche, for example, demonstrates that strict ascetics, who have seemingly renounced all pleasure, have merely redistributed their pleasures, setting up an alternate libidinal economy whereby they come to enjoy—to obtain *jouissance* from—their renouncements in part because they have a version of plausible deniability. Yet the *jouissance* is there, just as it is for martyrs, worrywarts, and anxiety addicts, not to mention my students . . . and academics, including, most assuredly, myself. Fantasy and *jouissance*, in other words, are neither arcane nor ephemeral.[1] They are part of our everyday doings and are integral to communities and communication.

What I slowly began to see in my classes was that, despite the problems I was having with cultural studies, I derived *jouissance* from teaching it, and my students, despite the acuity of their work, derived *jouissance* from those cultural artifacts and practices that they were critiquing, sometimes even those that were objectionable or unjust. Indeed, what I came to see is that critique itself could function as a source of *jouissance*, so that one could continue to enjoy behind the critical pose—another kind of plausible deniability. And, while the concepts of *ethos* and *pathos* certainly have bearing here, neither of them allowed me a sufficient grasp of these subtleties of criticism and enjoyment. Rhetoric's traditional conceptual constellation, I thought, needed augmentation, and so did contemporary rhetorical theory, which, while often friendly to French poststructuralist thought, seemed more leery of any post-Freudian psychoanalytic theory.

So while writing instruction is meant to produce sophisticated critical thinkers and writers, we are left with the important question of why training students to be attentive critics of texts, culture, and ideology so seldom induces real transformation in their lives. The question is simultaneously a practical one—what can we do to produce better citizens and rhetors?—and a theoretical one—can we develop rhetorical theories that surmount the insufficiencies of contemporary cultural studies? It so happens that at the time these questions first occurred to me I was reading the neo-Lacanian psychoanalytic work of Slavoj Žižek. Žižek presents theories of discourse, subjectivity, and ideology that can challenge and supplement our understanding of rhetoric and its workings. His psychoanalytic theories, attuned to the unconscious and other psychical factors such as fantasy and *jouissance*, are useful for providing more satisfying and complete explanations for individual and social conduct. Writing pedagogy thereby functions doubly here: it is the object of theoretical inquiry, but it also reflects back upon theory. This recursive, dynamic interchange grounds theory in praxis while simultaneously opening up new paths for exploration. Psychoanalytic theory helps explain why the critical hermeneutic motor driving cultural studies can advance but also impede educational development and rhetorical sophistication. Certainly, back in the 1990s, it helped me work through my own investments in cultural studies and the *jouissance* I derived from it (and sometimes still derive, I must admit). Critical hermeneutics, then, might very well address how it too may become complicit with social disadvantage and injustice, perhaps seeking as a complement to its negativity a focus on forms of transcritical, inventive production that are always present in individuals and groups.

Narratives of false consciousness and their flip side, projects of enlightenment, are aligned with the philosophical/scientific paradigm, but, more pertinently, they underestimate the power of human investment (including *jouissance*) in maintaining everyday life practices and beliefs. Psychoanalytic discourse is distinguished from cultural studies rhetorics and pedagogies on this point because it emphasizes the constitutive role of the individual in the production of social reality, and it provides sophisticated explanations about the complex (and still contested) relations between the personal and the social. Granted, most cultural studies modes of inquiry, especially those indebted to poststructuralism, have tended to emphasize the socially constructed nature of the subject. And while this focus has certainly been useful, it nevertheless obscures our understanding of the ways people are complicit with the forces, ideologies, and practices that contribute to social problems and injustices. Cultural studies pedagogies gravitate toward direct confrontation with these cultural issues, thereby asking students to change their beliefs, values, and practices based on what they learn and write in the classroom (Berlin and Vivion; Fitts and France). These kinds of pedagogies harbor approaches to persuasion that see students and other subjects as easily and consciously mutable.

Contrary to cultural studies in its practical application, psychoanalysis suggests that rationally based debate and structured conflict are rarely the sole or primary reasons for persuading others. The psychoanalytic concepts of desire, *jouissance*, and fantasy contribute to our understanding of the intricate relations between the social and the personal, the rational and the affective, while also demonstrating the insufficiencies of rhetorical approaches predicated on social constructivism and/or the rationalist apprehension of reality. Instead, the role of fantasy in human affairs suggests that reality is never present in its simple givenness, and the eruption of *jouissance* in our practices ensures that change can be difficult or perilous—even for practices that we might normally consider unpleasant or unjust. Therefore, even if much cultural studies work admits in theory the effects of nonrational factors, its rhetorical practice too often belies such acknowledgment, and nowhere so clearly as in its pedagogical expression.

In bringing the psychoanalytic perspective to the classroom, we can see that issues of power, fantasy, and desire complicate notions of unity, equity, or consensus, which are central values for cultural studies and social practice. Psychoanalysis further holds that language frustrates human attempts at mastery. That is, there is no possibility of achieving a meta-position or other absolute point that could claim to speak impartial, unmediated truth. The emphasis on immanence here opens up the question of rhetoric's antifoundational nature and its relation to (and definition of) truth and knowledge. This in turn leads to parallels between postmodernism and psychoanalysis.

While acknowledging and discussing the significant advances made by cultural studies rhetorics, I argue that these approaches typically rely on theories of discourse, subjectivity, and ideology that overemphasize factors of critical awareness, rationality, and autonomy. The result is that cultural studies pedagogies consistently fall short of achieving what they claim to produce: self-reflexively critical writers and thinkers. I argue for a contemporary rhetoric that builds on the social dimension opened up by cultural studies while taking full account of the nonrational, affective, and unconscious factors that shape human conduct. It may readily be conceded that unconscious motivations lead people to act in ways counter to what seems logical or best, but few forms of rhetoric or pedagogy can absorb the full implications of such a claim. It can be difficult to confront the *jouissance* that permeates human activities, especially the most problematic or reprehensible activities cultural studies seeks to change, because as educators, we tend to believe in the power of education. We risk much in doubting that power. My wager is that the risk is worth it, that we have much to gain in working through what appear as lapses, incapacities, or insufficiencies. Such working-through leads us to fundamental questions about writing and rhetoric. Thus, in engaging in such work, I am led to consider subtle entanglements of questions about language and its constitutive relation to subjectivity; the power of unconscious and libidinal elements in psychic and social activity; and the nature of writing—how we conceive, justify, and teach it in the postmodern academy.

I hold that writing cannot be presented as a simple skill or naive self-expression, divorced from larger social considerations or from the limitations we confront in our everyday affairs. Nor can it be considered only in its most obvious, conscious, and willed dimensions, as a simple tool for personal advancement. Writing is continuously shaping and being shaped by conscious and unconscious mechanisms and forces; in learning what these are and how they affect us, how they constrain and enable us, we increase the rhetorical sophistication we bring to writing and to the postmodern university classroom. This sophistication will include attention to limitations, and to seeing such limitations in a less negative and more affirmative manner than has been customary.

The challenges posed by psychoanalysis (and certain postmodern discourses) have specific consequences for our conceptions of the role of rhetoric in education and social affairs, suggesting that there are real limits to projects of educational, civic, and cultural transformation. Typically, these limitations are, if admitted at all, taken as obstacles to be overcome. Here, however, I take the stance that many such "limitations" are in fact mischaracterized, that they are actually integral to the achievement of social progress, and that they can be affirmatively rethought from the perspective of their positive, inventive dimensions. Thus, psychoanalysis should not be seen as the means to fulfill cultural studies or simply retool it to function more effectively. Rather, it should be seen as building out of cultural studies and its focus on critical hermeneutics toward forms of personal and social invention—which will also mean forms of production based on joy and desire, not guilt or *ressentiment*. It is only through such an affirmatively inventive approach that we can meet the challenges posed by the advent of the corporate university and forestall the pressure to reduce writing instruction, like other humanities disciplines, to the production of the student as the "minimally programmed unit" (Readings 87). If this book accomplishes little else, I would have it demonstrate that writing and rhetorical instruction implicitly call for more than such minimal programming.

I am left with one question that still needs answering: if this book is predominantly a critique of cultural studies, why not reject cultural studies entirely? In some ways, this is the path Richard Fulkerson takes in a 2005 article that attempts to chart a new topography of rhetoric and composition, accomplishing a skillful demolition of cultural studies in little more than three pages. Given the sharpness and economy of his critique, it might well be wondered, what is the justification for a book? Can't we just be done with it? My answer is, "No, we can't." Cultural studies still has much to offer us: a rich panoply of terms, ideas, methodologies, and foci that demonstrate the absolute importance of culture and the intricacies of its operations. Rhetoric and composition may still gain from such work. Indeed, I think this idea gets at the impetus behind the title of James Berlin's last book, *Rhetorics, Poetics, and Cultures*. Berlin opens the book by telling us that the discipline of English is in crisis, then goes on to argue that cultural studies provides the best way to reconceptualize and reinvigorate what he earlier called social-epistemic rhetoric. For Berlin, cultural studies is a new form of rhetorical practice that greatly updates classical rhetoric—certainly a necessary step—while also expanding the range of contemporary rhetoric. Given this, we should read Berlin's tripartite title as a Hegelian dialectical shift: rhetorics and poetics are thesis and antithesis, cultures the synthesis. Considered in this fashion, Berlin is tied to the same project that James Kinneavy attempts with *A Theory of Discourse*. Both scholars seek to reunite the different wings of English, Kinneavy through the communications triangle, Berlin through cultural studies. While I am far from sharing Berlin's faith in cultural studies as a means to renew the traditional rhetorical project of training an able and engaged citizenry, there may yet be possibilities in its take on culture for regrounding English studies and moving us away from the literature-rhetoric split. Note the qualifying "may" in the preceding sentence—it has to be said that other factors are also at work in this split, so that a cultural studies focus alone is likely inadequate for such institutional work. Other approaches, such as "third sophistics" (Vitanza), work on spatiality, eco-criticism, complexity theory, and institutional critique, suggest ways to reconnect literature and rhetoric, but most of this lies beyond the scope of this book.

Still, cultural studies does offer us much fertile ground for working through issues about how to reinvigorate the project of creating a critical citizenry. If my psychoanalytic critique of cultural studies points to its lapses, insufficiencies, and inelegancies; if it delves more into what has not yet been thought than into what has; if it aims toward a cultural studies shorn less of its political orientation than of its less than savvy political practices, still it aspires to retain cultural studies' tremendous advances in bringing theory, culture, rhetoric, and a belief in intervention to the academic table. Culture matters. Rhetoric must attend to culture; composition must attend to culture. I see psychoanalysis's critical transformation of cultural studies as preserving this focus on culture while advancing our understanding of the power of affective factors. My hope, too, is that we are reassured that seeming impediments are at the same time resources, ones that can help us lay the groundwork for more considered, sophistic, and inventive approaches to rhetorical life.

On Belatedness and the Return
of the Subject
Or, The View from What Will Have Been

P ERHAPS IT WAS inevitable that rhetoric and composition and cultural studies would eventually be combined. The explosion of work in the 1980s and early 1990s on poststructuralist and postmodern theory dovetailed with both the strong growth of rhetoric and composition and the development of cultural studies into a full-fledged interdisciplinary field. At the same time, books on postmodern theory proliferated, and arguments about postmodernism touched all areas of inquiry. From the perspective of this writing, however, it appears as if much of the earlier, more hyperbolic postmodern thought has run its course, at least in composition. Some radical ideas linger on in watered-down forms as lore, while many formerly heated debates have died out with the challenges they pose in limbo, unresolved. Michael Carter's return to Victor Vitanza's essay "Three Countertheses" is illuminating in this regard. In his 2003 book *Where Writing Begins*, Carter points out that Vitanza's critique of composition's status quo has largely been ignored (150, 230 n.1). Carter thinks that this avoidance is a mistake, and he accordingly undertakes a sustained engagement with Vitanza's work.

Carter's gambit is interesting because it has the earmarks of crisis and trauma. The avoidance he describes is a key marker that something traumatic has been registered. Customarily, after a period of avoidance comes an attempt to grapple with the trauma. Carter follows this pattern by delving back into postmodern debates that have lingered unresolved, especially in his lengthy challenge to each of Vitanza's three unanswered countertheses. By doing so, Carter hopes to surmount what he considers the debilitating effects of first-wave, or deconstructive, postmodernism, and thereby move us toward something he calls "reconstructive postmodernism" (151–55). Carter demonstrates that something significant happened with first-wave postmodernism, something so powerful that it cannot be ignored or left behind but instead requires a reconstructive return. Postmodernism's challenges have to be answered and thereby integrated into more secure, inhabitable narratives.

Carter is emblematic of two trends that are useful to my project: first, the perception that something traumatic happened to rhetoric and composition in the past; and second, the felt sense of crisis that necessitates a return to that traumatic event. Of course, the intervening years have had their effect, allowing for new understandings of the trauma that help make return possible. But my wager is that Carter returns to Vitanza because he is aware that the postmodern debates we left in limbo may be coming back to haunt us. Despite the fact that the modernist-minded liberal arts contingent saw postmodernism as an assault on treasured texts and values, from our perspective now we might well see academic postmodernism as an inventive resurgence of the liberal arts tradition, one that has pervaded nearly all wings of the university. But it seems that even this resurgence is facing challenges. Certainly, the advent of the corporate university, the downsizing besetting the liberal arts, and an emergent conservative vocationalism are registering in many circles as signs of a crisis, or at the very least as something traumatic. In short, I see Carter's return to Vitanza as an acknowledgment of the need to work through postmodern issues and debates that resonate with larger institutional transformations. Rather than these issues being seen as old hat, their return in traumatic form suggests that they are more relevant than ever. Their appearance as trauma also demonstrates the trace of a psychoanalytic narrative, the return of the repressed. If the repressed is returning, it requires reengagement and working-through. Thus, this book puts psychoanalytic theory and cultural studies into debate not simply to argue for the usefulness of psychoanalysis for rhetoric but also to contribute to a working-through of debates that we have let linger. Further, and perhaps as important, I see these arguments addressing larger concerns about the role of the liberal arts in the contemporary university.

At the very least, the large and growing number of books on the contemporary university bespeak a crisis, real or imagined.[1] Or, better, they create a felt sense of crisis that renders the difference between real and imagined moot. This crisis has long been in the wind, especially in the humanities, particularly in English.[2] Bill Readings's now-canonical book *The University in Ruins*, heavily indebted to Jean-François Lyotard's more general comments in *The Postmodern Condition*, declared the university to be a ruined albeit still thriving proposition; a couple of years earlier, James Berlin had asserted that all aspects of English were now in crisis (*Rhetorics* xi). In these and other end-of-the-millennium works on the beleaguered university, it was sometimes difficult to tell what was causing the crisis: changing external arrangements in the social and economic realms, the advent of new and challenging forms of inquiry labeled postmodernism, or some admixture of both (as suggested by Berlin). In *The Postmodern Condition*, Lyotard, responding in part to Jürgen Habermas, declared that the crisis of the university was one with the crisis of knowledge, narrative, and legitimation and was therefore to be characterized as part of the ongoing "postmodern condition." However, this argument and others like it met with widely divergent reactions, many of them quite resistant. In composition studies, postmodernism was seldom embraced, Victor Vitanza being an early, notable exception. More characteristic were scholars like Lester Faigley, who connected postmodern theory itself with crisis and warned against its hyperbolic excesses (*Fragments* 21). Intriguingly, and elevating the sense of crisis, Faigley presented under the cloak of ambivalence his own hyperboles about postmodernism, such as likening its effects to the detonation of a "terrorist bomb" (44).[3]

Of particular interest to Faigley, Berlin, and others was the issue of subjectivity, especially the decentering or fragmentation of the subject, which was held to jeopardize political and rhetorical agency; but of equal interest was the constructed nature of the subject, an insight that led Faigley to argue that disagreements in composition and rhetoric were largely over competing versions of subjectivity (16–17; see also Crowley, *Composition* 8–10; S. Miller, *Textual* 2–3). Scholars like Vitanza and D. Diane Davis in turn explored the implications for the dissolution of the subject, pointing out that subjectivity was itself a key (modernist) problem (see Vitanza, "Three" 152–57; D. Davis, *Breaking* 21–68). But these debates and complications have done little to ameliorate the felt sense of crisis and, if Sharon Crowley's polemics about writing instruction in *Composition in the University* are any indication, may have exacerbated it. Composition seems ill-equipped to handle larger issues concerning its emplacement in the university or contemporary culture, thereby fulfilling its always-present disciplinary insecurities. Indeed, Crowley even contends that composition's keystone course, first-year writing, might best be abolished as a universal requirement (*Composition* 241).

Whatever one's stance on this issue, it should still strike us as peculiar that this polemic has such a cynical edge. First-year writing has so fallen, Crowley points out, that it runs primarily on institutional momentum rather than according to any large-scale standard of success, such as furthering the goals of rhetorical education, and it further propagates systemic, unfair employment practices. As Crowley demonstrates with considerable acumen, composition predominantly serves to produce the proper kinds of (universal) student subjectivity, to reify ideological notions of correctness, and to exploit workers (*Composition* 8–10, 231–32, 241). She acknowledges that workers, howsoever exploited, nevertheless want to keep their jobs and would probably suffer if the number of classes offered were reduced. In this regard, then, for all her argumentative sophistication and attention to the disenfranchised, Crowley essentially gives us a cynical shrug. Since little may be done that does not further objectionable interests and reproduce the existent order, she seems to say, let us just relinquish the requirement—the course really is not that important anyway. I find this to be symptomatic. Faced with institutional/educational contamination, writing instruction is compromised, and Crowley's response is to reject it as a requirement.[4] There is something cynical about this move, but what is interesting is that the cynicism does not in the least challenge her argument; rather, as a dominant tone resonating in our contemporary zeitgeist, this cynicism harmonizes well with all aspects of her work, making it even richer, more compelling.

CYNICAL PROBLEMS

This leads us to German scholar Peter Sloterdijk, whose early 1980s bestseller *Critique of Cynical Reason* acutely diagnosed our contemporary malaise as a problem of cynicism. In terms of education, Sloterdijk charges that "basically, no one believes anymore that today's learning solves tomorrow's 'problems'; it is almost certain rather that it causes them" (xxix). For Sloterdijk, this means that education as the pursuit of enlightenment is at an end, just as the goals of modernist enlightenment—exemplified in Kant's call to throw off the shackles of self-imposed immaturity and dare to use one's own reason—are themselves jeopardized.[5] Although scholars such as Faigley want to attribute the crisis *to* postmodernism, others, such as Sloterdijk and Lyotard, show that the crisis concerning modernist goals, reflected in all arenas of existence including the economic, *is* postmodernist. From this perspective, Nietzsche stands as the first great diagnostician of the fact that the knowledge brought forth in modernism, coupled with power (as in the slogan "knowledge is power"), was already on the road to nihilism, and Sloterdijk further suggests that such thoughts are harbingers of today's widespread cynicism. If in *Dialectic of*

Enlightenment Max Horkheimer and Theodor Adorno successfully retool Nietzsche to demonstrate that enlightenment was doomed to fall back into myth and barbarity, they are less successful in revitalizing a kind of critical knowledge that would not be indebted to power or would refuse to collaborate. This becomes the crux of a problem that has haunted enlightenment, and by extension critique, ever since. And so we get Sloterdijk's pithy explanation of our contemporary cynical state: "Cynicism is *enlightened false consciousness*. It is that modernized, unhappy consciousness, on which enlightenment has labored both successfully and in vain. It has learned its lessons in enlightenment, but it has not, and probably was not able to, put them into practice. Well-off and miserable at the same time, this consciousness no longer feels affected by any critique of ideology; its falseness is already reflexively buffered" (5). If Kenneth Burke famously claimed that we are rotten with perfection, Sloterdijk seems to suggest that we are rotten with knowledge — not, however, knowledge in itself, in isolation. We are rendered cynical by the collision of knowledge with the "schoolings of reality," or the inducements to accommodate ourselves to given circumstances (6). Thus, it is the reflexivity that is crucial: "always a bit unsettled and irritable, collaborating consciousness looks around for its lost naïveté, to which there is no way back, because consciousness-raising is irreversible" (6–7). Cynicism is reflexively defensive, the very product of the knowledge generated in the attempt to teach or transform. Cynicism, then, springs from the bad faith of knowledge compromised by accommodation.

In English studies today, and composition and rhetoric in particular, we can link Sloterdijk's notion of consciousness-raising to a proliferation of scholarly and pedagogical approaches, including liberatory or critical pedagogy, social-epistemic rhetoric, and most pertinently here, cultural studies. The large anthology *Cultural Studies*, edited by Lawrence Grossberg, Cary Nelson, and Paula Treichler, a foundational text for American cultural studies, describes cultural studies not simply as the study of cultural change but "as an active intervention in it" (5). Cultural studies scholars are thereby urged to consider any and all aspects of culture, with an eye to the moral evaluation of society and the pursuit of working-class or other "progressive" values and traditions, and to see themselves as politically engaged participants (5). Such ideas have had wide influence. Berlin, arguably the key proponent in composition for melding rhetorical theory and cultural studies, has flatly stated that transforming student consciousness is the only worthy goal for education ("Rhetoric and Ideology" 492). While not everyone is so programmatic — and indeed, Berlin's later statements in *Rhetorics, Poetics, and Cultures* are less strident — many composition scholars have taken up the challenge to transform or at least critically engage student subjectivities, as well as the contested notion of what subjectivity is and how it is constructed discursively and ideologically (Harkin and Schilb; Faigley; Crowley).

In the field of rhetoric and composition, theorists such as Patricia Bizzell, John Trimbur, Alan France, Linda Brodkey, and especially Berlin were quick to see the importance of cultural studies for rhetoric and the writing classroom. They began adapting cultural studies to the socially oriented poststructuralist and antifoundationalist theories of discourse that had emerged in the 1980s. These teacher-scholars explored what happens when the subject is seen as constructed socially in language; in retrospect, it seems obvious that they would find much value in exploring this question through cultural studies. By the mid-1990s, several rhetoric and composition collections had emerged to address the intersection of poststructuralist-becoming-postmodernist and cultural studies thinking.[6] Essays in these collections argued about the political relevance and necessity of poststructuralism and cultural studies from a wide variety of perspectives (not all of them favorable) and included detailed descriptions of (and some accusations about) what was going on in writing classrooms—teaching, assignments, activities, and writing itself. What these scholars tended to hold in common is the idea that critical thinking, cultural analytics, and rhetorical skill can all be combined to promote social change for the better, or at the least get students to question their received ideological beliefs concerning race, class, gender, and politics. Cultural studies pedagogies were criticized, of course, from a number of perspectives. Conservative critiques, such as Maxine Hairston's, accused cultural studies of an overtly leftist political bias. Radical critiques, such as Vitanza's, noted that cultural studies remained invested in modernist, and dangerous, liberatory narratives. However, Vitanza's challenge—that cultural studies writing pedagogies demonstrate proof of their claims for achieving student empowerment—went unanswered.[7] Marshall Alcorn notes that the project of challenging or transforming students' ideas often fails, a fact probably already well-known to most teachers, but he adds that an argumentative exchange such as that between Vitanza and Julie Drew reinforces the point that the attempt to "enlighten" students can also lead to cynicism (*English Class* 39).

Such critiques have done little to stem the progress of cultural studies, however, and perhaps serve primarily as a pretext for more discourse about it. Nevertheless, the interweaving themes of critique, social betterment, and subjective transformation have emerged as far more complicated matters than they at first appeared, as attested by the sheer volume of material generated on these issues. At the very least, cultural studies is of rhetorical interest insofar as it is attendant to how language is used, how it uses us, and how it informs and is informed by culture. There is a sense, that is, that cultural studies is but the latest wrinkle in a liberal arts–minded rhetorical education. Some might object, as Walter Beale does, that rhetoric and cultural studies are at odds: rhetoric accommodates, while cultural studies critiques; one is ameliorative, the other oppositional (1–2). However, this suggested conflict between the goals of cultural studies and rhetoric is sutured by the idea that being critical or oppositional is one of the keys to personal success and social progress. Indeed, this is one of the argumentative moves implicit in Terry Eagleton's resurrection of rhetoric for literary and cultural critique in his 1984 classic *Literary Theory* (205–7). The ability to critique and resist current ideological discourses enables one to work toward a better, more humane future, while also equipping one to deal adequately with the complexities of postmodern life (mass media, pluralism, commodification, consumerism, and the like). For these reasons and others, while there exist competing versions of what rhetoric is or could be, the dominant institutional articulation of rhetoric in composition classrooms remains heavily oriented toward "critical thinking," and even if the more overtly political pedagogies are now disfavored, an emphasis remains on the "empowerment" of students through their critical apprehension of the cultural discourses that construct them.[8]

We have thereby returned, by a somewhat circuitous route, to where we began, for one of the primary contentions of this book is that "empowerment" (and, by association, what passes for critical thinking), for all its potential seductiveness, is a keenly problematic goal, one tied precisely to the enlightenment goals Sloterdijk so eloquently diagnoses as generating cynicism. More precisely, we have yet to inquire rigorously enough into the nature of "empowerment" if, as Sloterdijk suggests, the equation of power and knowledge is a key factor in the onset of postmodern cynicism and the felt sense of crisis.

What I want to discuss next is the idea that cynicism and crisis have a temporal dimension and that this temporality is integral to how we conceive subjectivity. That is to say, what we see here are relations to a past, and specific comportments toward that past. If, as Nietzsche suggests in "On the Uses and Disadvantages of History for Life," a focus on the past forestalls a creative invention that requires an affirmative forgetting, it is also the case that cynicism—including the problematics of decision making exacerbated by cynicism—and crisis are *temporal* symptoms. As we shall see, however, the temporal dimensions of subjectivity present further complications that block any easy alleviation of these symptoms and can even exacerbate them insofar as they contribute to the further dispersion and instability of subjectivity. In a nutshell: subjective transformation is a rhetorical issue, hinging on our notions of persuasion, language, and subjectivity itself, but it is crucially threaded through temporality, which demarcates a series of complex questions about relations to the past, the emergence of a split or fissured subject structured by time, and decision making. Subjectivity and time, knowledge and power, body and place, language and world all come together here in an intricate rhetorical knot. While these terms are of course abstractions, the investigations that follow should show how concrete the stakes ultimately are.

Sloterdijk's attention to what the past has brought forward to us today, formerly as the modernist sign of hope, now as a postmodern cynical malaise, dovetails with the critical enterprise of cultural studies, which is also finely attuned to the past. Indeed, it is of more than ironic interest that while so much of this material seems to focus on the present and future, it nevertheless remains firmly grounded in past happenings. If one of the primary impetuses grounding cultural studies pedagogies is opposition to "what is," and thereby to the good life offered through the dominant cultural forms, then in a sense the future is already inscribed within or charted by this structuring orientation. The future glimpsed through a cultural studies pedagogy is keyed to an opposition structured by the past. Because of this, much cultural studies work remains caught up to an impressive degree with belatedness, a temporal structure that has as much to do with writing as it does critique, and as much to do with subjectivity as it does knowledge of what to do. Indeed, we see emerge here a tight connection between disparate notions of the subject. Teachers, students, and rhetoric and composition as a field are gathered together insofar as they are structured as ongoing processes of anticipations (of the future) and reconstructions of past events. Meaning, critical or otherwise, emerges after the fact. The symbolic significance of an act registers belatedly; the necessity of delay is "built in." We might go so far as to say that what we mean by subjectivity is precisely its return—what Freud referred to as *Nachträglichkeit*, sometimes rendered in English as "deferred action," other times as "belatedness." As I will explain later, this understanding of the subject—fissured, decentered, and dispersed as it is—is crucial for Slavoj Žižek's Lacanian theory of subjectivity.

Hegel, Freud, Lacan, and Derrida have in different ways taken up the connections among knowledge, writing, and belatedness, suggesting that they have great bearing on the constitution of the subject and the nature of writing. As Hal Foster remarks, *Nachträglichkeit* poses serious questions for our commonplace notions of repetition, difference, and deferral; and of causality, temporality, and narrativity (32). Yet of further relevance is that this structure of belatedness nevertheless remains tethered to what we might call the "nexus of the crisis": the fact that one still has decisions to make. Indeed, is this not the ultimate promise of rhetorical education: the practical ability to make effective rhetorical acts in public spaces? But what happens to this practical ability, assumed to be a teachable and therefore realizable goal, when we think it through the alternate forms of causality and temporality suggested by a structure of belatedness? We should keep in mind here Lyotard's commentary on *Nachträglichkeit*: that it is an "unconscious affect" that does not affect the pragmatic realm but the "physics of the speaker" (*Heidegger* 12). By this Lyotard means that subjects are silently—the silence emerging from the perspective of consciousness, the realm of pragmatics—constituted by such affects, the material consequences of which will not show up until some unspecified later time. What happens, then, to the critical capacity brought to the table by cultural studies, or similar critical work tied to the realms of knowledge, pragmatics, and consciousness, if belatedness presents structural complications to cultural studies' ostensibly progressive goals?

THE PROBLEM OF THE PREFACE AND THE MOMENT OF DECISION

Near the beginning of his career, Hegel spent a substantial portion of the preface to *Phenomenology of Spirit* discussing the nature of prefaces. He found that in actuality a preface is always wanting; it is "superfluous," or even "inappropriate and misleading" (1). The preface makes a pretense of explaining the work, when the "work" proper can only be explained in terms of time and movement—the time of writing it, thinking it, reading it; and the movement that takes place through these activities. As Hegel sees it, there can be no substitution, summary, or retelling of the work that would fulfill the actual psychical and material movements in time and space that occur as one reads the work. Understanding the work is inseparable from the act of working through it. Each journey through the text is irreducibly unique, and no such journey can be shortened or recaptured by a preface or any other attempt at replication. At the same time, this makes of the preface something unique in itself. Since it is comprised of remarks preparing us for what the working-through will accomplish, in one sense the entire work, which is leading up to the ostensible fulfillment of the final passages, is also prefatory. Insofar as a preface is written after the work is completed, then, the work in actuality prepares us for the preface.

Jacques Derrida takes up this theme in *Dissemination*, stating, "time is the time of the preface; space—whose time *will have been* the Truth—is the space of the preface. The preface would thus occupy the entire location and duration of the book" (13). The preface figures the impossibility of achieving a full presence of meaning; thus, the book itself is always prefatory when considered in relation to the repleteness of meaning that it offers. This gesture of repleteness can never be realized. What will have been the Truth is never quite the same as the fulsomeness that is offered, but is instead a Truth constructed retroactively, one different from what the work offers. For Derrida, this difference marks the belatedness of any working-through in relation to the work itself. Likewise, toward the end of his career, Hegel again takes up the issue of the temporal—an issue that, in truth, he never stopped working through—in *Philosophy of Right*, stating that for philosophy, "the owl of Minerva spreads its wings only with the falling of the dusk" (13). Wisdom comes, if and when it comes, if it is to come, belatedly. Wisdom is marked by the "what will have been" and in this sense is also retroactive. But this retroactiveness, or belatedness, marked by Hegel's imagery of a falling and a coming darkness, and described by Derrida in terms of the Truth that will have been, carries with it a certain tragedy tempered by an accompanying sense of fait accompli. It is late, perhaps too late, but nevertheless, this is, this will have been, our truth.

Derrida, like Hegel, is haunted by this notion of belated truth. This haunting manifests itself in several of Derrida's texts, including *Of Spirit* and *Spectres of Marx*. In *Of Spirit*, Derrida announces that he is going to speak of ghost, flame, and ashes (1), then, near the end of this lengthy, originally oral presentation, returns again to the intertwined themes of Hegel and ghosts, suggesting that he is neither in the proper place nor has adequate time to bring up all the ghosts flapping in the wings of the alchemical theater of his lecture. His rationale is that it is, finally, "too late" (99). This is arguably not only a reference to the lecture, which has gone on too long or, perhaps, has gotten well out of hand. Instead, what is evoked is nothing less than the belatedness of knowledge and wisdom. *Of Spirit* arises from the flame, the ash, the ruin of Heidegger, and is both an indictment and a salvation, an attempt to work in and out of Heidegger (for) something good. But along with the question concerning timeliness, or *kairos*, we are left with the trace of another issue. If wisdom is belated, if it, indeed, is always "too late," what good remains to or in it?

The question of the good has from the earliest times haunted thinking, and it haunts us today. Still, I want to suggest that perhaps our time, at the dawn of a new millennium, feels the belatedness of knowledge with a keener edge than in past eras (and certainly this is one of the ideas haunting Sloterdijk's work). In a 1997 work of literary criticism, *Singularities: Extremes of Theory in the Twentieth Century*, Thomas Pepper states immediately that "this book is not written to help anybody" (xi). This statement ostensibly lets us know that his book will not provide a clear road map or "mini-manual" for the difficult authors he writes about, which is quite sensible given his careful, considered approach. But there is nevertheless something odd about the statement. As the very first line of the book, its declamatory force must be noted. As I argue below, writing is largely a matter of recovery from the first line. In Pepper's case, I am dubious of the recovery and see instead a striking example of postmodern cynicism, cloaked in learned sensibility and even realism. But the statement encapsulates issues every writer must face at some point, ones that I face now: Why am I doing what I am doing? What purpose does my work serve? Is it, finally, oriented toward something good, and what could that "good" possibly be? It is obvious that these questions haunted Pepper: a page after stating that his writing is not meant to help anyone, he castigates the postmodern age as "a time of massive cynicism and universal lying, in which all qualities have been devalued, or rather suspended, in a wave of reactive consumer populism that seems both inescapable and never-ending" (xii). Pepper's discontent with the postmodern age—as if any other age were somehow better—is one with his statement that his book is not written to help anybody. He thereby comes to embody the very cynicism about which he complains. In an era when Lou Reed's lament that it is "so hard to be good" is more true than ever, when the good has become well-nigh impossible to define, much less to enact, when the aspiration to the good underpins much of the greatest evil ever perpetrated, it is perfectly understandable that one might just say: stop. Stop trying to do good; stop trying to help. Pepper may have his truth here, I concede, and I applaud his willingness to face up to the issue so elegantly. At the same time, I must add that it is, ultimately, too late to do anyone any good. Pepper's awareness of this may be one of the reasons for his opening stance: not necessarily to be unhelpful, but certainly to offer no help. Or, perhaps even more significantly, to foreground that he is offering no help, a move that appears radically and self-reflexively defensive, that seeks to remove all grounds for a retroactive assignment of accountability. "If this hurts you," Pepper's text suggests, "it is your responsibility; I offered nothing, suggested nothing. The responsibility is yours and yours alone."

Why is Pepper's truth belated? Avital Ronell reminds us that helpful or not, for good or ill, decisions will necessarily have been made. Faced with the withdrawal of certitude, decisions will be made in spite of any insecurity or risk; this will have been the space for what Ronell, in *Crack Wars*, calls the "ethics of decision" (46). Knowledge, truth, wisdom—these may all be belated, but that in no way lets us off the hook. We will have to decide. If evil follows our actions, we can palliate the pang of responsibility by saying, "We never meant to hurt anyone," or, more cynically, "We never meant to suggest we could help anyone and therefore will accept no responsibility in the matter." Whether we offer help or not when we write, we take up the possibility that such an offer will have been one of our tasks regardless of our intentions, a point most notably underscored as the effects of actions and words on others.

Indeed, this possibility arises as an assignment we receive in spite of what we write. We do not choose this; it is chosen for us. This is a crucial point for understanding the "ethics of decision": a decision does not occur in a vacuum, nor is it merely a chosen act initiated by an autonomous agent. We will have been decided, so that the notion of self-willed decision becomes something akin to a perspective illusion that allows for our accommodation of this radical dispersion of agency.[9] Temporality also emerges here. As Ronell argues, "The relationship to a past that, never behind us, is hounding and calling up to us, on good days friendly and populated, implicates nothing less than an ethics" (*Dictations* xviii).

In what follows, I try to keep in mind the idea that we will have to decide, or take up the "having been decided": there can be no easy relinquishing of the relationship to the past or the perspective illusion of decisive agency. As Paul Mann says, there is "no choice but to choose" (258)—which also amounts to acknowledging that we will have to act and that our actions will have been understood in the form of "I acted," not in the form of "it acted through me" nor in terms of a "forced choice." But as we shall see, just as we cannot evade our socio-symbolic assignments, so too we cannot evade how the Other (as language, culture, law, the past, and so forth) works through and wills us. For those scholars and teachers in rhetoric and composition, very often actions come in the forms of writing, in and for the field, and pedagogy, in which students are taught to write and think in specified ways. In the work of scholars and teachers influenced by social-epistemic rhetoric, poststructuralist theory, and cultural studies, the question of acting, writing, and thinking in socially responsible ways comes to the fore. While such questions more directly address rhetorics and knowledge, they also continually evoke ethics and responsibility. Such calls require interrogation. In this regard, we should emphasize the use of the word *responsibility* and would do well to keep in mind that, as Ronell states, "responsibility is monstrous" (D. Davis, "Confessions" 270). The minute someone says that s/he has acted responsibly, the minute someone relinquishes the specter of doubt, the space of irresponsibility is opened. Going further, what we have here are two senses of irresponsibility—the irresponsibility that comes with setting aside an ethical demand, thus relinquishing one's social bonds with the Other; and the irresponsibility that takes on the Nietzschean sense of, in Ronell's words, "being nonconformist" (D. Davis, "Confessions" 271). What Ronell does not address is the question of how we decide between these two senses of irresponsibility. Are we, even in deciding this—or, just as plausibly, in having it decided for or through us— thrown back into the domain of an "ethics of decision"?

One thing my project objects to, then, is the motivated surety that underlies the opening of the space of irresponsibility—or, put differently, the assumption of correctness that would deny the decisive alterity of the Other. Social-epistemic and cultural studies–based pedagogies too often fall into the mode of a motivated surety that denies the alterity of the student or that willfully neglects those who desire to speak or act otherwise. And it does so in the names of enlightenment, empowerment, knowledge, and critique. While it will not do to castigate these goals uniformly (as if that would be possible), it certainly is upon us to inquire into the ways they are deployed, institutionally and professionally articulated, commodified, or made into commonplaces standing for the universal good. When I later examine questions concerning discourse, subjectivity, ideology, law, cynicism, violence, and action, underlying these often disparate issues is the idea that foreclosing on a certain, healthy doubt—concerning knowledge, critique, decisions, subjectivities—is coterminous with foreclosing on the possibility of an ethics for the postmodern age. Furthermore, doubt is one of the modalities that can lead us beyond critique toward, on the one hand, forms of working-through in which one develops sophisticated, comprehensive interpretative and productive approaches to texts and, on the other, forms of critical, ethical invention where skill greets a capacity for innovation, or even transgression. This is not to suggest that I am concerned with ethics or resistance in any direct manner, but only that any stance one takes on these issues invokes the dimension of the ethical and the possibility of doing something otherwise than one is institutionally or socially induced to do. Such concerns should not be ignored: ultimately one will have to write, to teach, to act, based on one's relations to language and to others.

Questions concerning the ethical are thereby thoroughly implicated within the social, which, as Berlin repeatedly argues, also implies the rhetorical. And this means that another aspect of the "return of the subject" refers to rhetorical and material practice limned by the necessity of making ethical choices that are entangled with different and contradictory knowledges of the Other. This includes the assumption of responsibility—already a kind of subjectivization—for what was chosen for or acted through oneself. Such practice is itself structured by a sense of belatedness but is complicated, even jeopardized, by the eruption of *jouissance*. *Jouissance*, again, is not so much simple enjoyment or pleasure, but its excess, even to the point at which it can turn into something else (i.e., pleasure from the nonpleasurable). *Jouissance* is akin to glue: it is sticky, suffusing all of our rhetorical, personal, and social activities; guiding, motivating, driving us onward; or, perversely, locking us down, trimming our orbits. *Jouissance* makes everything we do worthwhile, yet it also makes us less amenable to change than most rhetorical theories of persuasion would have us believe, generating conflicts that defeat the noblest goals of the just society. *Jouissance*, I am saying, may not contribute as helpfully as many would like to the great project of "neighbor love." As Žižek waggishly quips, "Love Thy Neighbor? No, Thanks!" (*Plague* 45). And so the complications accrue. We act *as if* we have chosen, regardless of the extent to which we were already willed or acted through, and find ourselves caught up in the *jouissance* that suffuses such subjectivization, a *jouissance* the return of which we seek continuously, addictively, perversely.

Clearly, the substantial degree to which I utilize psychoanalytic theories of discourse and subjectivity situates the book along a psychoanalytic versus post-structuralist axis. Psychoanalytic accounts, whatever their limitations, provide us with theoretical resources unavailable elsewhere that can aid us in thinking about our relations with language, others, and society. If we take seriously the idea that postmodernism has initiated a far-reaching sea change in cultural formations and practices, including transformations in our understanding of the constitution of human subjectivity, then psychoanalysis, with its empha-sis on theorizing the ways in which language, psyches, and society combine with and coconstitute each other, has advantages over other fields of intellec-tual inquiry for revealing our unique modalities of possibility and limitation, freedom and subjection. It opens avenues for thinking through the intermin-gling of psyche and body, affect and language, and bringing into our discur-sive considerations the reciprocal, recursive relations among them. It suggests concrete ways for grappling with embodiment and affect; while psychoanaly-sis cannot be said to have closed the book on these subjects, what is there re-mains productive. In this regard, I agree with Barbara Biesecker's claim that Lacan, especially as he shows up in the work of contemporary neo-Lacanians like Žižek, Renata Salecl, and Joan Copjec, "will have already been the great theorist of rhetoric for the twenty-first century" (222).

NACHTRÄGLICHKEIT: BELATEDNESS AS SUBJECTIVITY

As I have intimated, psychoanalytic thought shares with Hegel (and Derrida) an awareness of the belatedness of knowledge. Indeed, even the subject's sense of identity is belated, being a retroactive achievement that effaces itself as the finger of time moves forward. If, as Ronell claims, responsibility is monstrous, how can we not also see identity as in some sense monstrous, too? The minute one has said who one is, the realization will follow that, ultimately, that is not who one is. This is another form of belated knowledge. Every identity is provi-sional, a patchwork woven of the moment for the moment and unraveling just as quickly as it was made. And yet, these provisional identities are necessary, and like it or not, we are subjected to them, incessantly, continuously. Even if they do us no good. But this also suggests that for psychoanalysis, subjectivity is not to be explained away as an epiphenomenon or as something dispersed, as in so much poststructuralist and cultural studies thought. Rather, psychoanalysis emphasizes the indispensability of the subject, in spite of pronouncements about the death of the subject (Fink, *Lacanian* xi; see also Laclau 20–22). The notion of the subject returns to haunt us, and even if, or perhaps because, subjectivity is a problematic and contested notion, it remains fruitful. Nevertheless, the psychoanalytic subject is not the autonomous, choosing subject of modernism. In this sense, there is some affinity between psychoanalytic and postmodern conceptions of the subject, despite the fact that stronger versions of postmodernism seek the dissolution of the subject. For this project, the psychoanalytic subject is of import for being an uncannily composed albeit fissured entity, a dynamic presence traced by a kind of after-the-factness, that remains useful for scholarly inquiry.

Furthermore, the belatedness of the subject is integral to conceptions of writing. This is exemplified most keenly through the phenomenon of *Nachträglichkeit*, or deferred action, which is crucial to Freud's analysis of the Wolf Man, outlined in "From the History of an Infantile Neurosis." *Nachträglichkeit* is among other things a tremendous "act" of asubjective invention; by *asubjective*, I refer to the fissuring across which such invention occurs (temporal, conscious/unconscious), a fissuring that precludes the understanding of an act solely as that of a conscious, willing agent. In his write-up of the case, Freud tells us that the analysis of the Wolf Man went on for years but that the most important dream for the analysis actually came early.[10] As a child of four, the Wolf Man had dreams about silent white wolves, six or seven of them sitting in a tree outside his window, and always awoke in a fright. During the analysis some twenty years later, it was revealed that the patient's neurosis was keyed to this dream he had when he was four; however, the dream itself was the result of a scene of *coitus a tergo* he had witnessed when he was one and a half. Even though he was now in his twenties, Freud tells us, the Wolf Man's reaction to this primal scene, over eighteen years in the past, was as fresh as if it had happened yesterday. For that reason, Freud is not best served by the word *recollection*, as the *Standard Edition* translates him, but rather *activation*. Here is how Freud explains the process: "This is simply another instance of *deferred action*. At the age of one and a half the child receives an impression to which he is unable to react adequately; he is only able to understand it and to be moved by it when the impression is revived in him at the age of four; and only twenty years later, during the analysis, is he able to grasp with his conscious mental processes what was then going on in him. The patient justifiably disregards the three periods of time, and puts his present ego into the situation which is so long past" ("History" 47). What is particularly important here is the idea that this is not simply *delayed* action. A traumatic event did not simply lay buried for twenty-odd years before manifesting itself anew as neurosis. Instead, there was a *deferral*, temporality itself becoming integral to the production of the neurosis. At the age of one and a half, the spectacle of parental coitus means nothing and cannot produce trauma. Only later, at the age of four, is the memory, long forgotten, reactivated by means of some unconscious association or other traumatic event and introduced to consciousness through the transposition of the dream work. As Jean Laplanche remarks, it takes two traumas to create a trauma (88).

This aspect of temporality is central to psychoanalytic thinking, and it clearly demarcates some differences from previous understandings of temporality. For Freud, past and present become intermixable, or rather, the past can be activated in the present and produce life-changing effects. Not only is time collapsible, but the passage of time itself generates the conditions of possibility for what-will-be-trauma to actualize itself as consciously experienced trauma. We might say that Freud is suggesting an alternate clock system, one in which the unconscious is time-less, meaning that time does not pass in the same way as conscious subjective experience. Indeed, as W. H. Newton-Smith explains, the selection of a preferred clock system "is intimately bound up with the choice of physical theories" (qtd. in Mullarkey 16). I take this to mean that a clock system, a way of defining and measuring time, comes to shape our experience of self and world. This notion is not really a new one, as thinkers like Henri Bergson and Martin Heidegger grounded their philosophical enterprises in temporality. I will not be rehearsing their ideas here, but I do want to take from them the basic notion that "subjectivity is temporality" (Mensch 5). Such a notion can seem simultaneously obvious and abstract. But in actuality, it is an all too common insight, if seldom unpacked. Perhaps a concrete example can be illuminating here.

I went running one winter afternoon. It was the end of February in Indiana, and we were having a surprisingly pleasant day. The sun was shining, and it was warm enough to wear shorts and a T-shirt. The surprising thrill of the weather, the pleasure of exercising outdoors in the sun, and the CD playing in my Discman jogged my memory, and I recalled a visit to one of my brothers in Seattle ten years earlier. I was struck not only by the feelings evoked by the memory but also, in a metadiscursive moment, by their relevance to this introduction. How so? *Nachträglichkeit* describes a structure whereby an event occurs, is forgotten or remembered in a particularly benign manner, and remains as such until a later time, when, through the accumulation of new memories and understandings that reach a tipping point, the earlier memory resurfaces. But it does not return in the same way; it is now transformed through time and movement into a new arrangement, so that we inhabit our memories differently. Such was the case with this memory. First, I had first heard the CD I was playing during that forgotten visit to my brother, in a pool hall where we had drinks and conversation and camaraderie. So the music was itself associated with a happy time, and that happy time merged with the happiness I was experiencing during my run—an unexpected warm sunny day, the pleasure of exercise outdoors. But it is also true that of late—for reasons I will omit—my brother and I have had a falling-out, which has caused me distress.[11] So the pleasant memory, which had long been buried (not repressed; we should recall that for Freud at least repression plays a far stronger role), resurfaced and mattered in a new way, showed up as a special moment now gone, because of this turn in our relationship. This, then, is the structure of *Nachträglichkeit*, in which memories resurface and force subjective revisions, but recursively so. The older memory is transformed as it is reframed and resituated through the accumulation of new experiences, feelings, memories, which amounts to the achievement of a new sense of self.

We can say, then, that the structure of *Nachträglichkeit* describes a particular notion of subjective composition. This has similarities to Foucault's notion of power as productive, but it adds emphasis to subjective agency in a manner Foucault does not. As Copjec and Žižek argue, Foucault tends to fall into a narrative of subjectivization, in which production is seen as a force *on* the subject—that "subjects" the subject—whereas *Nachträglichkeit* can be located neither at the pole of external force nor at that of internal agency. Going further, we can also claim that it does not occur in a middle ground either. By emphasizing the radical recursivity of these many forces, all poles/positions are scrambled, and agency emerges precisely *there*: at the subjective point through which one's own singular and dynamic network is threaded.

This leads us to Lacan's point that a sentence is dependent on the passage of time for its meaning, as the last word of the sentence retroactively makes sense of the words leading up to it ("Position" 267). The same is true for us because as subjects, who we are is but the continual and anticipatory process of recalling and narrativizing the past—personal, local, cultural, global. This process of subjective composition is ceaseless, ongoing year to year, week to week, moment to moment. In sum, Lacan's theory of subjectivity emerges from these two aspects of temporality: first, the retro-formation of the subject; and second, the intersubjective beyond that emerges when subjects attempt to identify with the barred Other, to anticipate or come to know what the Other will feel, think, or do. Both these aspects of subjectivity have as their primary impetus the bringing of the past into the living present, in order to prepare for the oncoming future. That is, while subjectivity is temporality, this temporality emphasizes the past as a primary modality.

The crucial role of the past emerges less as a concrete valuation that people choose than as an effect implicit to the theoretical structure itself. Lyotard tells us that in this sense *Nachträglichkeit* marks the unconscious's permanent threat to consciousness, in which the time of the past, buried in the unconscious, is looming, ready at any moment to deliver its blow to consciousness (*Heidegger* 17). How we respond remains the always-open question; the decision whether we are "to analyze, to write, to historicize, is made according to different stakes, to be sure, but it is taken, in each case, against this formless mass," against this nebulous threat of the blow from the unconscious, from the past made present (Lyotard, *Heidegger* 17). The threat remains nebulous because it is caught up with the problem of remembering, which is also to say forgetting. In either case, consciousness has a limited purview of the matter, and it remains primarily an unconscious affair—an affair of the Other. But this in no way absolves people or cultures from confronting the necessity of trying to come to grips with and explain this "stranger in the house" of consciousness, culture, and language (Lyotard, *Heidegger* 17). The allusion to Heidegger serves to remind us that language is not only the "house of being" but the mark of an uncanny stranger in the house, a lurker who looms spectrally, a someone or something constitutive of our sense of not-being-at-home (*unheimlich*) (see Heidegger, *Being* 232–35). Time in the tense of *Nachträglichkeit* manifests the appearance of this stranger, a spectral, lurking past.

It is in this precise sense that we should listen again to what Freud tells us. In the analytic scene, *Nachträglichkeit* is an activation, not a recollection. The past comes forward as trauma because of the passage of time. When Lyotard discusses *Nachträglichkeit*, he does so in the context of the Heidegger scandal, Nazism, and the Holocaust, all of which reinscribe us within scenes of repressed affiliation, of remembered horror, of belated explanation—attempts to grapple with the unspeakable, events after which we cannot, as Adorno would remind us, write poetry (although we can apparently still write criticism). However, from a psychoanalytic perspective, this critical discourse runs backward in time (Forrester 203). Thus, *Nachträglichkeit* is not just an activation, as Freud claims. It is a *retro*activation. Within this structure, all knowledge takes on a character of belatedness, which, as discussed above, Hegel relates in *Philosophy of Right*. Philosophy cannot in the end give instruction about what the world ought to be because it always comes on the scene too late. Thus, Hegel says, "When philosophy paints its grey in grey, then has a shape of life grown cold. By philosophy's grey and grey it cannot be rejuvenated but only understood. The owl of Minerva spreads its wings only with the falling of dusk" (*Philosophy* 13).[12] Cultural criticism today may be driven by the desire to achieve political or moral intervention, and of course it can do so, but it nevertheless still works within a trajectory of belatedness, a sense that its insights, no matter how au courant, are always only dead on time. This structure of belatedness is coincident with positionality. As Brian Massumi argues, this amounts to a "tendency to arrest," to making the stasis of the position primary over the dynamics of movement (8). The political or moral intervention of cultural studies remains tethered to the past, which it constantly tries to overcome but also bears. This is its belatedness, a structure it never surmounts. In a sense, cultural studies, for all its radical political desire, remains enmeshed in what it wants to get beyond and can never make the leap into postcritical, joyous invention.

REVISIONARY WRITING

I have been arguing that *Nachträglichkeit* is a crucial concept for thinking about subjectivity, narrativization, and critical thought. The attempt to think of subjectivity in the present, as something that emerges immanently from the play of productive forces, misses the temporal delay that is equally constitutive of the subject. If the subject is not simply the positioning that occurs within the field of power, in effect the subject is a composition. Or, more accurately, subjectivity is *composing*. The subject's return is repetition, but every repetition is a recomposition. As Foster remarks, "we come to be who we are only in deferred action" (29). Or, as Žižek states, "when [an event] erupts for the first time it is experienced as a contingent trauma, as an intrusion of a certain nonsymbolized Real; only through repetition is this event recognized in its symbolic necessity" (*Sublime* 61). A key aspect of the return of the subject is this form of composition. The subject comes into being as what it is through this continually ongoing process of bringing the past into the present or the anticipated future. This further means that in our understanding of subjectivity we can no longer let ourselves be beguiled by the lure of immanence and contingency. Even if in its enactment every physical or rhetorical act is contingent, its symbolic integration necessitates delay. At the same time, we must be aware of the problem that arises when we seek social transformation, as cultural studies does. While it can certainly acknowledge the delay necessary for the symbolic articulation of an event, cultural studies tends to gloss over the ongoing compositional nature of that delay. As mentioned above, Massumi's charge against the bulk of cultural criticism is that it neglects movement, which necessarily includes the continual comings-to-be and passings-away that mark forms of change that cannot be captured through grids and other theoretical apparatuses that determinately map people, culture, and world. We might say that for cultural studies, the past is to be rewritten for the sake of the future right now in the present, but in so doing, it neglects the extent to which the past is already being rewritten as a condition of the present. Subjectivity is not only composition, then; it is revision-in-movement, the combinatory woof and warp of singular, emergent events and belated, symbolic integrations.

Stephen King, the horror novelist, once stated that all writing is recovery from the first line, suggesting that the event of the first line is something traumatic. It is like a blow or a coup that leaves us off balance and from which the rest of the text works to stave off the damage or regain equilibrium. I do not imagine that we consider this aspect of writing much when we ask our students to write and revise. Perhaps we do not often think this way about our own writing. But lately I have been thinking about what King might have meant as I work through my own writing, as I pursue the continual work of drafting and revising. What I am most struck with, working on this first chapter and its webs of psychoanalytic thought, is the strange (*unheimlich*) resonance that emerges from the idea of revision. We all know the mundane version of revision from the process movement, almost as a mantra: after drafting, revision. Less obvious is the psychoanalytic idea of revision as part of the dream work described by Freud in *The Interpretation of Dreams*. The dream work consists of condensation, displacement, and secondary revision, a tripartite and belated process of making unconscious, traumatic material acceptable to shy and flighty consciousness. In revising a text, I am making it better, yes, in accordance with sound writerly principles. But from another perspective, I am only making what is traumatic in the initial draft acceptable to myself. What is traumatic? Any number of things: errors of arrangement and syntax, tangents and gaps, and so on, with all the mechanical and organizational elements that apply. But it is important to keep in mind that such items, sometimes trivial in themselves, take on traumatic qualities because of their connection to or resonance with other, less specifiable forces. For example, simple errors undercut such crucial symbolic work as evoking the proper sense of authority, of "getting the unmasterable" right, or of making an argument saleable to fellow academics and publishing venues. But the stakes go higher still when we think of how writing confronts us with the vertiginous and the sublime, the uncanny and the perverse, the limit and the abyss. These seem like innocent and abstract metaphors, but they are anything but, invoking all that haunts us about writing—our own incapacity, insufficiency, failure, finitude. Faced with the blank page or screen, we are hailed by the call to say it all, a stark impossibility that haunts whatever we do say, jeopardizing it, perhaps mocking it. And for all that, for all the trauma that comes forth with writing, there also comes an affirmation, a visceral, sometimes even sublime thrill—perhaps more difficult for some than others to experience, but nevertheless there—and who can say we could divorce it from the traumatic? All this, yes: but in particular it should be emphasized that writing brings its own *jouissance*.

In keeping with the structure of belatedness, then, I am staged doubly in doing revisions. I confront who I was as originally laid out in a text, whether months, weeks, or even minutes ago, and I confront anew the very same nest of problems that initially set my text in motion. And those problems, if I follow Žižek's arguments, admit of no ultimate solution, only further condensations, displacements, and revisions, further working-through. Writing and subjectivity thereby resonate together. So perhaps, as writers, scholars, and teachers, we are all just writing our own escapes and thereby writing ourselves.[13] Revision merely greases the wheels for us. Writing will never really get us to the great good place, the place where trauma could be resolved and not just palliated. And it is in this precise sense that I think again about King's statement that all writing is recovery from the first line. We as writers are all caught in this recovery, and the first line is but the trace of a fundamental core of antagonisms that return again and again in spite of all our best efforts, or maybe because of them. (Is this writing's eternal return?) Writing is salve, not salvation, a recovery from the opening blow, with all the discomfiting mucky-muck revised away for ease of presentation to the waking, enlightened world—and the fragile, writerly self.

I do not find a reason for despair, much less cynicism, in this way of thinking. For me, this approach gets at the heart of rhetoric: it is not just a means of reading or producing—rhetoric is fundamentally attuned to action. And every action hinges on a decision, albeit in the broader conception of decision discussed above. Like a first line, every action, every de/cision, is a "cut" marking out a space within which we come to exist and hence from which we are recovering. We could also say, from which we are inventing. The existential irony of all this is that we reach to rhetoric—to writing and speaking and imaging—to aid us further in the recovery, only to have to recover yet again from our previous recovery, and so on. The circle of repetitions is endless. It is, as revealed in the old Indian fable about what ultimately supports the world, turtles all the way down.

But is it only endless, circular repetition? Of course not. We cannot forget the Other. This is one of the lessons I take from Lacan and Žižek. However, long before I ever read psychoanalytic theory, I gained an inkling of this insight from Jim Morrison's enigmatic lines in "An American Prayer":

Words got me the wound
And will get me well again
If you believe it

The shift in the last line from first to second person, to the "you" who is our Other, confronts us with a traumatic and irreducible truth. We have words, and they are *pharmakons*, the ancient Greek word indicating something that is both cure and poison. But words alone cannot suffice, for they matter insofar as they create the possibility for relations. This extends the notion of "communication" into the realms of the transsymbolic, the incommunicable, and affect, and it extends the notion of "relations" far beyond simple notions of communicative agreement or communities of consensus. Words become social relations, and social relations become words. No transcendence would allow us to escape this endless reflexivity and intersubjectivity. The immanent practice that most directly faces this truth is rhetoric. Rhetoric is thus not just words, not just information, not just communication. Rhetoric is bound up with the intransigent psychic glue that dis/joins us to each other in an infinity of possible relations, offering everything but the transcendence that would rescind the offer.

So, if we are only ever in recovery from the first line, from the first text, and we are only seeking escape in our revision, only revising a more acceptable version of the text for presentation, we can nevertheless keep sight of the fact that this is precisely what is most precious about rhetoric—that it offers us more words and that these words are what create us within communities and thus help make everything that *is* possible. If I am often critical of cultural studies rhetorics, it remains important to recall that theorists like Berlin believed strongly in the power of rhetoric, and, I hasten to say, I share that belief. Perhaps I just wish that he and others like him had a keener sense of the tragic to accompany such great hopes. Mann suggests that, faced with a decision, wrestling with possible courses of action, "I cannot foresee that I will discover I never arrived at the point of decision at all. The moment my future appeared, I was already past it, with all its consequences still to come" (269). This emphasizes the temporal modality of what Ronell calls the "crucible of undecidability" (D. Davis, "Confessions" 244). The act of deciding is itself rendered uncertain, not just in terms of its consequences or futurity but in terms of retroactivation. Our moment of decision shows up afterward, and even then, it may be less the active decision we might have hoped. As Mann concludes, "Oedipus chooses what he will discover, in the end, will never have been a choice" (270). Oedipus thinks he has made a choice, but after the fact, he will learn that his act was not a choice. This is the tragic dimension, certainly, and perhaps also fatalistic in its tenor. Mann notes, however, that this emphasis on the inevitability of human error and being overmastered (in Oedipus's case, by the gods) is for Nietzsche "a profoundly affirmative action" (252). Such affirmations, and the meanings and practices that stem from them, remain for us a profound collective challenge.

COMPOSING THE RETURN OF THE SUBJECT

Subjectivity, then, is to be understood as the return of the subject considered compositionally, and the emphasis on return lets us know that such ongoing compositions are structured belatedly. The subject is thus in motion. It is not a static subjective position, nor even a mobile positionality, but literally a dynamic, ongoing activity. As I discuss later, this is precisely how we should understand Lacan's sketch of the subject across the graph of desire, especially as it has been reworked by Žižek. Not only is the subject dynamic in this sense, but it includes unconscious, libidinal, and other affective factors left underdeveloped in too much cultural studies discourse and pedagogical scholarship. Because of this, such insights are especially important as regards teaching and scholarship, and we must work productively to extend them further. When we ask ourselves or our students to take a position, to be critical, or to act, we are setting out to form knowledges and identities. What psychoanalysis offers us—to a scandalous degree, perhaps, when pushed to its limits—is not only the insight that such knowledges and identities are provisional at best, or what Lacan and Žižek characterize as phantasmatic, but the notion that even to arrive at the *telos* of knowledge or identity is already to pass through Ronell's "crucible of undecidability" (D. Davis, "Confessions" 269). Since such constructions are belated and retroactive, bringing them into being means opening up spaces for constructing them otherwise. The crucible of undecidability grinds up certitude as easily as it grinds up the autonomous, choosing subject of liberal humanism. D. Diane Davis suggests that for Ronell, all ontological questions are ultimately tied to the Other because of a structure of dependency. As she puts it, "the subject who acts is always, in advance, under the influence of something/someone" ("Confessions" 244). Our choice, then, is not one of opting to work within the structure of dependency or not—over this we have no control. Our choice is a forced choice: we can choose freely to accept this structure of dependency that will have been in place regardless of our choice.

The field of composition has been and continues to be fascinated if not preoccupied with forms of control (see Vitanza, "Three"; D. Davis, *Breaking Up*). The lesson of the crucible of undecidability is that such control will never be forthcoming. Of course, this lesson in no way releases us from the obligation to write and to act, another form of the forced choice to which we will in some way have to accommodate ourselves. This is one aspect of what Nietzsche meant when he presented the concept of the eternal return. I ultimately think of Ronell's "ethics of decision" in terms of the eternal return, which means that there is no time when a decision can be made at a metalevel. The eternal return invokes the same as the repetition of risk, opening the void of the impossibility of a decisive foundation.

That no decision can be made at a metalevel is one of the key ideas running throughout Žižek's work, specifically in his argument concerning the Real, which is to be distinguished from reality by the fact that it cannot be represented. In this sense, the Real is foreclosed from direct apprehension in reality. But continuing further, Žižek reminds us that what is foreclosed always returns, just not in any direct form of representation. The Real returns in the form of gaps, errors, symptoms, slips, and other behavior idioms. This foreclosure marks an acknowledgment of the fundamental human condition as being out of joint, abyssal, and excessive (*Ticklish* 16). No metalevel exists at which a subject can operate that is not also caught up in some mundane, tragic, or miserable piece of the Real. We might say that the eternal return of the same is akin to the eternal return of the Real. And at the level of action, the Real returns as the condition Ronell describes as passing through the crucible of undecidability. We never reach the point at which actions speak for themselves, and there is no necessary mode of symbolization for an action (*Sublime* 97). Thus, our acts elude us even as we mis/recognize them as our own, and they also return to us, although, again, unrecognizably so. Like the Real, such undecidability is also foreclosed from the symbolic, even as it emerges there in uncanny, unlooked-for guises. We see here an uncanny form of the logic of the subject as return.

What is the good of this belated knowledge? In the end, we can only know what this good will have been through the process of having read, thought, written, and acted. The good, if it is to come, is only achieved through recognitions that cannot be coerced or controlled. This is, I think, the implication of the argument I develop at the end of this book concerning the Act: asking students to attempt a form of writing that will be an Act is linked to the idea that whatever good is to come of teaching and writing will come from them and will be for them. This has to be one of the crucial ways in which we attend to the alterity of students. Instead of immersing them in the "gray on gray" of critical hermeneutics thoroughly caught up in a structure of belatedness, we might transpose this desire to overcome the past into affirmative forms of contemporary invention. Ultimately, what the Act describes is a particularly potent form of invention, or an unleashing of the eventual within the ongoing, belated processes of symbolic integration. It is not so much personal as social, or rather, the two must come together across the Act. This is so because an Act is transformative—in its bringing forth of the evental, it produces change in our socio-symbolic networks. Such transformation is far more likely to come from a sense of joy or desire than from guilt, obligation, or depression (see Sirc, "Difficult").

The Act cannot be aligned with the overcoming of social antagonism or with the achievement of the great good place because Acts emerge within and through the muckiness of social complexity, without direct promises of betterment or liberation, and as the productive expression of *jouissance*. If an Act remains caught to some degree in the structure of belatedness, since subjectivity is itself constituted retroactively, still the Act is not predicated on the desire to overcome or seek revenge on the past. In this sense, the Act moves beyond critique, which, as Mann argues, "is driven by obscure identifications, attachments, revulsions, by forces of desire and aggression that its various representations always conceal and displace" (24). The Act resonates less with critique and more with productive, cultural—which is also to say social and rhetorical—engagement. The Act is an event. This also suggests that there is no purity to an Act, no transcendence to a higher plane. Further, the social dimension of such in(ter)vention is also its ethical limit; the actions and inventiveness of the Other will always emerge as the correction for Acts that go awry. It is in this sense that attending to the alterity of the Other takes on its full ethical implication; it is not solely alterity in itself but the implicit difference that it offers that holds the highest importance. Social dissensus is at least the equal of consensus as a resource for hope and as a valued guarantee that the structure of belatedness infusing critical hermeneutics can be engaged. Yes, we will have to decide, and social dissensus remains necessary to ensure that even if things go badly, still differences will emerge. While consensus will also emerge, and holds a rightful and necessary place that rhetorical thought has long valued, dissensus remains as its limit, not as a problem to be surmounted nor even as a tragic condition to which we must accommodate ourselves. Rather, dissensus is something to be affirmed. It is to be transvalued. This of course is difficult, and no more so than when, through writing and teaching, one wants to be persuasive. To be right. To be recognized. But this desire should not mitigate the larger cultural responsibility of affirming rhetorical dissensus and, just as important, of making dissensus not an empty term to rally around but a series of multivalent practices that are not merely critical but productive, joyous, and inventive.

Toward a Neo-Lacanian Theory
of Discourse

Work on discourse, then, is itself not neutral. The questions it poses concerning the historical and material existence of ideologies, discourses and their meanings concerning the ways in which individuals are constructed as subjects, and concerning the relations between theory and practice involved in "speaking for others," are questions that some would prefer never to raise. For there stand, behind the work on discourse that emerged and developed at the end of the sixties and in the seventies, the ultimately political questions of how and how far the society in which we live can be changed.

—Diane Macdonell, *Theories of Discourse*

Here we can see clearly how fantasy is on the side of reality, how it sustains the subject's "sense of reality": when the phantasmatic frame disintegrates, the subject undergoes a "loss of reality" and starts to perceive reality as an "irreal" nightmarish universe with no firm ontological foundation; this nightmarish universe is not "pure fantasy" but, on the contrary, *that which remains of reality after reality is deprived of its support in fantasy.*

—Slavoj Žižek, *The Plague of Fantasies*

Communication does not take place through subjects but through affects.

—Slavoj Žižek, *Tarrying with the Negative*

THE STUDY OF DISCOURSE as it has emerged in the last fifty years is strikingly diverse and interdisciplinary. It includes, according to Deborah Schiffrin's taxonomy, speech act theory, interactional sociolinguistics, ethnographies of communication, pragmatics, conversation analysis, and variationist discourse analysis (we could also add critical discourse analysis, narrative analysis, discursive psychology, and more) and ranges from philosophy to linguistics to anthropology, and everywhere in between (6–11; cf. Jaworski and Coupland 14–35). Such a wide range of approaches indicates that the notion of discourse is itself quite broad. This may also suggest why discourse has emerged as a special interest in the past few decades—the fact that diverse fields find the study of discourse useful indicates larger cultural and episte-mological shifts. This is the argument Adam Jaworski and Nikolas Coupland make in their overview of discourse theory. Looking to Foucault, they argue that the interest in discourse stems from an ongoing transformation in how knowledge is understood to be constituted. We can connect this insight to the generalized "validity crisis" concerning knowledge taken up in the work of Habermas and Lyotard, in which it is suggested that the formerly secure foun-dations that legitimate science and knowledge production are threatened. So while the reference to Foucault is certainly apt, Jaworski and Coupland might have just as easily addressed postmodernism itself and the debates that have sprung up concerning the imbrications of knowledge and discourse in the work of innumerable theorists. Certainly, such work has in various ways ad-dressed Jaworski and Coupland's definition of discourse as "language use rela-tive to social, political, and cultural formations" and "language use reflecting social order but also language shaping social order, and shaping individuals' interaction with society" (3).

Jaworski and Coupland address only sparingly these various postmodern thinkers and debates, preferring to focus primarily on work in the linguistic tradition. The work they give the most weight approaches discourse primar-ily at the sentence level, similar to that in *Discourse Studies in Composition*, a collection edited by Ellen Barton and Gail Stygall, in which linguistics and sentence-level analysis play a major role. I should say at the outset that this is not the approach to discourse I am developing here. While the linguistic tradition has great value, especially as it is combined with poststructuralist so-cial theory to produce critical hybrids like discourse analysis (see Fairclough), I am interested in what psychoanalytic theory can offer that is not available in linguistics-based analyses, especially in terms of developing a rhetorical understanding of discourse. Nevertheless, although my particular focus is on the conjunction of psychoanalytic theory and rhetoric, my wager is that, in general, nonlinguistic fields of study still have much to offer discourse theory; indeed, the emergence of critical discourse analysis itself attests to the fruitful conjoinment of linguistics and poststructuralist social theory.

In the following, then, I use psychoanalysis to inflect and extend rhetori-cal theory on discourse. Psychoanalysis attends to our inner affective states, positing useful and inventive concepts for understanding how we as affective subjects are constituted and threaded through language and social systems. Concepts like desire, fantasy, and *jouissance* demonstrate that the entrance into language and the resultant emergence of the subject are transformative events for human beings. As a consequence, a theory of discourse cannot just be an abstract account of linguistic functionings; rather, a theory of discourse already takes part in an understanding of what it means to be human and to have a life. Accordingly, it is profitable to consider how this is so by means of contrast with other theories of discourse. One point that will emerge rather soon is that a communications-based model of rhetorical transaction is woefully inadequate for understanding the intricacies of human interaction. A rhetoric that limits itself solely to the most direct, intended aspects of communicative interaction is a rhetoric impoverished. Psychoanalytic theory provides an early but quite sophisticated attempt to theorize how affective factors structure communication in ways we are only partially aware of at any given moment. Although poststructuralist thought has made great inroads on this issue, and indeed has much overlap with psychoanalysis, its engagement with the problem of the affective constitution of human being and human interaction is less acute than it could be.[1]

Poststructuralist thought, especially in the work of Foucault, has directly concerned itself with discourse, and it has done so in ways distinguished by attention to social, epistemological, and institutional dimensions. This point is crystallized in Diane Macdonell's mid-1980s monograph *Theories of Discourse*. Covering Foucault, Althusser, Pêcheux, and Hindess and Hirst, Macdonell argues that while it is a commonplace that discourse is social, cultural studies work on discourse has (from the time of her writing) been limited in its attention to issues such as class; the advantage of the work of the poststructuralist writers she covers, she states, is their extension of discourse to an area previously considered neutral: knowledge itself (2). Macdonell captures a primary impetus in work on discourse as it emerges in poststructuralist thought when she notes that in general it attempts to "write the history of those forces which shape our thinking and our knowledge" (2).

Expanding on Macdonell, we might say that poststructuralist thought attends to the tight connection made between discourse and our construction/ perception of the world, or, better, how that world is always mediated through discourse and thereby accords us particular ways of being and acting within it. Lacan, Derrida, and Foucault, for example, all give priority to the place of language in the world, especially in the formation of subjectivity and the conduct of human affairs: Lacan emphasizes the dialectic of assuming a signifier that cannot provide the satisfaction of identity or expression implied by its fulsome promise; Derrida argues that "writing," as the play of *différance*, undermines the myth of presence or any other assumption of closure and centering; and Foucault theorizes the workings of power in terms of the disciplinary and productive effects of discourse. All three are concerned with the decentering, constitutive capacities of language that disrupt previous linguistic conceptions founded on identity, generality, representation, and homogeneity. In short, theories that move beyond our previous linguistic conceptions initiate a sea change, a shift to a concern with discourse. Thus, in *New Theories of Discourse: Laclau, Mouffe, and Žižek*, a book that picks up where Macdonell's leaves off, Jacob Torfing notes that after the break with "the conception of such a linguistic system as a closed and centred totality, it has been common to refer to it [language] as discourse" (3). We can extend the scope of this statement to include speech, writing, multimedia, and other forms of textual and image-based sign production.

The field of rhetoric and composition has also devoted attention to theories of discourse—poststructuralist, neo-Aristotelian, and others—with an eye to how such theories can inform writing and pedagogy. James Kinneavy and James Berlin offer differing theories of discourse that nevertheless have in common the idea that discourse is tightly bound up with our sense of reality. Kinneavy, whose early to midperiod work appeared prior to the influx of poststructuralist thought in America, favored a formalist approach to discourse modeled on the communications triangle, which he understood to be derived from the work of Aristotle (*Theory* 18–19). In his later works, he acknowledged and utilized poststructuralist theory without, however, deviating far from his initial neo-Aristotelian stance. Even when he delved into German hermeneutics—Heidegger and Gadamer in particular—Kinneavy retained a representationalist understanding of communication still commensurate with the communications/semiotic triangle, even though Heidegger's thoughts on language, developing out of his existential analytic, were quite at odds with representational thought and the metaphysical tradition from which it arose.[2] Berlin, heavily influenced by poststructuralist thought, shifts the theoretical emphasis from the discernment of an objective, formalist model of discourse to an acknowledgment of the constitutive and decentering capacities of language; in such a view, discourse is seen as always contingent and situated, which means, among other things, that there can be no universal, objective theoretical undertakings not understood as having concrete social, political, and historical motivations. This view has consequences for our understanding of history, intersubjective relations, and reality and also for theories of truth. The latter is worth highlighting because poststructuralist and cultural studies rhetorics emphasize the constructed nature of truth, often reducing it to a "story" or a "fiction." In contrast, neo-Lacanian psychoanalysis suggests another dimension to truth that avoids the fictionalizing move, while refusing to fall back into naive realism or a positivistic account of objective truth.

Lacan, for example, rejects any simple positivistic truth claims but neverthe-less holds that science grants a form of access to the Real that produces truth-ful knowledge.

Kinneavy's model of discourse may have sufficed for awhile, but after the discursive turn and the influx of poststructuralist thought, it became clear that it needed emendation. However, even as this work proceeded, the more radi-cal dimensions of poststructuralist and postmodern thought on discourse were deflected in many composition scholars' work, as evident when we examine how these radical dimensions were streamlined to fit a model of discourse still indebted to the communications triangle. In other words, poststructural-ist thought was used to shore up rather than challenge Kinneavy's triangle. What I am attempting here, then, is the development of a third model of discourse derived from Lacanian and neo-Lacanian psychoanalytic theory. Using Lacan's graph of desire in a somewhat loose fashion, the differences among these three theories of discourse become clear, as does the redefi-nition of the four elements of the triangle (expressor, receptor, reality, and language) by poststructuralist and psychoanalytic theories of discourse. Two related ideas are key here: that discourse constructs the human subject, and the subject it constructs is not just decentered but fissured; and that certain consequences of this fissuring apply to human interaction and, more spe-cifically, to how we conceive rhetoric. That is, the disjunction of the sub-ject in discourse, which includes the subject's nonjustification in the larger socio-symbolic field (what Lacan calls the big Other), gives rise to *jouissance*, fantasy, and other affective, nonrational (but not irrational) phenomena that suffuse and shape human affairs. Such affective phenomena preclude the possibility of simple, direct communication, which in turn impacts our un-derstandings of truth and persuasion.

KINNEAVY AND THE COMMUNICATIONS TRIANGLE

In 1971, Kinneavy published *A Theory of Discourse: The Aims of Discourse*, in which he introduced the communications triangle as a model of discourse derived from classical sources (Aristotle) and modern language theory (Karl Bühler, Roman Jakobson, and others).[3] Kinneavy tells us that his aim is to bring discursive order to the chaos of composition theory (*Theory* 1), a state-ment that dovetails with Timothy Crusius's summation of Kinneavy's essen-tial project as *"the retrieval of the liberal arts tradition within a semiotic frame-work with practical intent"* ("James" 352). Crusius understands Kinneavy as bringing history, theory, and practice together under the auspices of semiotic and structuralist thinking. Nevertheless, even though Kinneavy himself is re-garded as one of the preeminent figures in the consolidation of rhetoric and composition as a unique discipline, the influence of his theory of discourse is still in dispute. In 2000, Thomas P. Miller noted that A *Theory of Discourse* is "often cited but too little used" (316). However, only in 1984, Richard P. Fulkerson had charted a substantial number of articles and books commenting or drawing on Kinneavy's work, also citing a good number of critiques, many of them directly concerned with the communications triangle ("Kinneavy" 54– 55 nn.1–4).[4] All in all, Crusius tells us, approximately fifty articles, books, and dissertations tackle Kinneavy's work, most of them directed toward A *Theory of Discourse* ("James" 355).

Nevertheless, all dispute and criticism aside, the communications triangle remains an important model for understanding discourse, showing up in rhetoric and composition, communications, sociology, and other fields. Crusius points out that the longevity of A *Theory of Discourse* is largely attributable to the triangle. It is a "memorable, easily graspable schema . . . capable of almost endless application," which, Crusius surmises, will outlive the theory Kinneavy based on it—"rhetorical thought has always employed the triangle," he states, consciously or not ("James" 356). Presumably, rhetorical thought always will. Certainly, the triangle shows up regularly in first-year composition textbooks, a clear sign of populist acceptance.

Kinneavy's goal for the triangle is to present something foundational around which the whole discipline of English can be structured. He writes: "The foundation for a structure of English study should be fairly solid. It may be stating the obvious to say that the foundations must be grounded in the very nature of the language process itself. No imported metaphysic of structure would seem as applicable as the nature of the language act. Consequently, one sound foundation for the discipline would be the so-called communications triangle, i.e., the inter-relationships of expressor, receptor, and language signs as referring to reality" (*Theory* 18). The communications triangle posits a version of reality grounded in language, which Kinneavy argues provides a

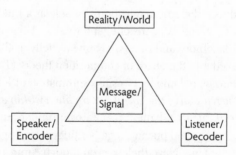

Fig. 1. The Communications Triangle

TOWARD A NEO-LACANIAN THEORY OF DISCOURSE

sound foundation for the discipline. By this he means, in part, that the triangle is able to account for the differing uses to which an English Department puts language. Indeed, the four elements are, in Kinneavy's view, "basic to all uses of language" (*Theory* 19). They are the compass points that serve as a "total framework" for a theory of discourse (*Theory* 17). From these four basic elements, Kinneavy spins out a complex and supple theory that encompasses the aims of discourse, stemming from the emphasis placed on each of the four elements. An emphasis on reality will produce referential discourse; on audience (receptor), persuasive discourse; on language, literary discourse; and on the author (expressor), expressive discourse. In this way, too, rhetoric and literary study find common ground, being but different expressions of the four ultimately shared aims of discourse.

THE TROUBLE WITH TRIANGLES

It is a commonplace criticism of the triangle that the four elements are essentialist, being reductive abstractions from the vibrant heterogeneity of discourse. Crusius is typical in this regard when he charges that the triangle is "classically structuralist in that it is composed of timeless, placeless, nearly contentless elements" (*Discourse* 20). Given that this ground is sufficiently covered by Crusius and others, I will devote little time to it. I do want to note, however, that Kinneavy anticipates this charge, defending himself with an argument for the value of scientific abstraction, claiming that the isolated object of investigation can be "reinserted into the stream of life, more intelligible for its academic isolation" (*Theory* 24). Too, Crusius grants Kinneavy this defense by acknowledging that we are all structuralists and essentialists when we name something, but with the proviso that we counter the structuralist moment with a poststructuralist one that seeks to deessentialize and rehistoricize (*Discourse* 21).

A somewhat different critique is launched by Charles Bazerman, who argues that we can move beyond the static qualities of the triangle by stretching it into a pyramid, adding a fourth vertex he calls the "intertext," or the symbolic field (108). This is a useful suggestion. However, it is interesting to compare Bazerman's ideas to Kinneavy's. In an interview with Fredric G. Gale and Michael W. Kleine, "Speaking of Rhetoric: A Conversation with James Kinneavy," Kinneavy himself discussed how the triangle could be stretched into a graphically three-dimensional pyramid to provide a place "for all kinds of approximations, and more than a continuity" (33–34).

Kinneavy's attempt to add greater nuance to the triangle seems to stem more from a concern with students than from criticism, yet a good portion of this criticism points out the triangle's unwieldiness. In "Two Propositions," Vitanza contrasts Kinneavy's typology of discourse (referential, persuasive, literary, and expressivist), as derived from the triangle, with Lacan's quite different list of the four types of discourse: the Academic, the Master, the Psychoanalyst, and the Hysteric.[5] Vitanza notes that locating Lacan's Hysteric discourse on the communications triangle would necessarily make it a form of "*abnormal* (self-) expressive discourse" ("Two" 58). Hysteric discourse, because it moves among various positions, none of which can be decisive, opens up meaning and disrupts identity. Vitanza's point is that utilizing the triangle as a total framework for understanding discourse will necessarily exclude and/or distort nonsystematic — and in particular non-Aristotelian — forms of discourse ("Two" 58). Further, Vitanza's arguments, and his use of Lacan, Kristeva, Lyotard, and other poststructuralist theorists, suggest that poststructuralist and postmodern theories of discourse are better idioms for understanding and re-including forms of discourse that have been excluded by the triangle.[6]

Despite these criticisms and the alternate proposed discursive theories, the attempt to build on or away from Kinneavy's theory of discourse returns all too frequently to the same four elements, with all the attendant limitations this imposes. James Berlin's project is illustrative in this regard. Berlin attempts to incorporate poststructuralist and Marxist theory into his understanding of rhetoric, but he nevertheless remains engaged with the basic categories outlined by Kinneavy. In his early essay "Contemporary Composition: The Major Pedagogical Theories," Berlin retains the four elements of the triangle (writer, reality, audience, language) but argues that language must be made primary: "Rather than truth being prior to language, language is prior to truth and determines what shapes truth can take. Language does not correspond to the 'real world.' It creates the 'real world' by organizing it, by determining what will be perceived and not perceived, by indicating what has meaning and what is meaningless" (775). Berlin is typical of many composition and rhetoric scholars responding to the influx of poststructuralist thought. Putting the matter schematically, we can say that for Berlin and like-minded others, poststructuralist theories emphasize the social, historical, relational, antiessentialist, decentered, and constructivist aspects of discourse.[7] These ideas have contributed to the view that discourse is not only social but political. Thus, in his 1988 essay "Rhetoric and Ideology in the Writing Class," Berlin classifies a strikingly diverse group of rhetorical theorists under the rubric of social-epistemic rhetoric because "they share a notion of rhetoric as a political act involving a dialectical interaction engaging the material, the social, and the individual writer, with language as the agency of mediation" (488).

Poststructuralist theories — and the postmodern politics that in part stems from them — are often centered on the function and play of discourse in the social realm. These theories emphasize the preeminence of language in the construction of reality, power relations, and subjectivity. As Lester Faigley puts it in *Fragments of Rationality*, "Postmodern theory decisively rejects the primacy of consciousness and instead has consciousness originating in language, thus arguing that the subject is an effect rather than a cause of discourse" (9). Statements such as this assimilate the model of reality proffered by the communications triangle with the insights of poststructuralist theory. In each case, the various elements of the triangle are mediated and/or constructed by discourse. As a result, the static elements of the triangle are updated for an audience that understands discourse as constructed, constructing, and perpetually reconstructing.

We see here that the impact of poststructuralist and postmodern thought transforms how we conceive the communications triangle without in fact displacing its fundamental role in understanding discourse. Linda Brodkey's useful distillation of postmodern discourse theory in *Writing Permitted in Designated Areas Only* is illuminating on this point. Brodkey sees herself as a theorist trying to develop "a method that assumes language, thought, and reality to be *interdependent*" (11). Insofar as poststructuralist theory can be useful for such a development, she sees that the poststructuralist project tries to "demystify the part [discourse] plays in our constructions of self, other, and reality" (13). She clarifies this properly critical aspect of poststructuralist discourse theory through her explication and use of the concept of articulation, which allows a researcher "to coordinate a writer's representations of self, other, and reality in a text with readers' responses to these representations" (15). For Brodkey, discourse retains its representational capacity, and even though she also emphasizes its constitutive role, that role is still anchored to the ever-present elements of the triangle—self, other, and reality.

The pervasiveness of the communications triangle in theories that attempt to mine poststructuralist thought for social and political transformation is even more explicit in the work of Berlin, who, in addition to politicizing discourse theory by placing language and the social at the forefront, also constructs a taxonomy of the composition and rhetoric field based on the triangle. Although he kept working on his taxonomy throughout his career, its basic categories were in place even prior to his first major article in *College English*, "Contemporary Composition: The Major Pedagogical Theories," which made his taxonomy more generally known.[8] In "Contemporary Composition," Berlin states that he is in accord with the four fundamental categories that other compositionists had used to describe the composing process—all corresponding to the four elements of the triangle. His disagreement, which is primarily directed at Fulkerson's "Four Philosophies of Composition," is one of definition/conception versus degree/distribution. Rather than simply shift emphases among the four universally defined elements, Berlin claims that we must re-envision the very definition of these elements. As he puts it, "Rhetorical theories differ from each other in the way writer, reality, audience, and language are conceived—both as separate units and in the way the units relate to each other" ("Contemporary" 766). Like Brodkey, Berlin does not question the units themselves or the fourfold way they structure reality.

My purpose here is to build on and away from what Berlin initiates. Berlin argues that "to teach writing is to argue for a version of reality" and that there-fore it is necessary to attend to the ways in which our composition pedagogies delineate "what can be known, how it can be known, and how it can be com-municated" ("Contemporary" 766). Each composition pedagogy comprises particular and uniquely defined matrices of reality, writer, audience, and lan-guage, an arrangement that Berlin terms an "epistemic complex" ("Contem-porary" 766). What we see here is a tension between his argument that a particular "epistemic complex" produces a particular notion of reality—with which I agree—and his assumption that the four elements of the communi-cations triangle inflected by the insights of poststructuralist theory can ad-equately map that reality. Indeed, if we push Berlin's thought a notch or two further, we can only conclude that his use of the four elements of the triangle produces a particular and troubling epistemological orientation. Even rede-fined or reconceptualized, the trace of Kinneavy's original neo-Aristotelian categorization remains. Consider, for example, Berlin's reliance on the trian-gle to divide up the various factions in the field of rhetoric and composition. It would be difficult to map the field differently than Berlin suggests—Classi-cists (corresponding to audience/persuasion), Current-Traditionalists (reality), Expressionists (writer), and New Rhetoricians (language)—if one adhered to the elements of the triangle.[9] This point underscores the connection between a theory of discourse and the production of knowledge. Accordingly, a differ-ent theory of discourse would necessarily produce a very different map of the field.

In *Teaching Composition as a Social Process*, Bruce McComiskey essays just such a project. The exigency for his project emerged in his graduate semi-nar introducing students to rhetoric and composition theory and practice, in which McComiskey taught Fulkerson's map of the field and Berlin's revi-sion of it. He asked his graduate students to use these maps to schematize the books and articles they read throughout the course. However, the students resisted the cartographic commonplaces. McComiskey states, "They did not want to 'camp out'; they wanted to 'forage'; the result tended to be hyphen-ated compounds: 'I'm a rhetorical-expressivist'" (6). McComiskey notes that

Berlin himself thought that his field map had begun breaking down around 1975, and the experience McComiskey had with his students convinced him that a new map was needed. He proposes one that illuminates commonalities, unlike those of Berlin and Fulkerson, both of which create distinct, dichotomous positions, one clearly favored over all the others (e.g., Berlin was a tireless advocate of social-epistemic, then cultural studies rhetoric). McComiskey retains the basic language as derived from the triangle, but instead of divvying up the categories, he combines them into layers: the textual, rhetorical, and discursive (6). We can single out a layer, but only with the understanding that we are actually using all three simultaneously (6–7).

I would argue that the problems McComiskey and his students had with Fulkerson's and Berlin's maps emerge from the triangle itself, not just from the particular uses they made of it. Arguments that the triangle abstracts and essentializes categories are demonstrably correct, insofar as such categorizing enables and underwrites Berlin's and Fulkerson's tactics. The triangle allows one to isolate and value one position at the expense of the others—hence the "My social-epistemic pedagogy can beat up your expressivist pedagogy" battles of the 1990s. McComiskey, like his students, and like many in the field, desires a more sophisticated, complex map. But one wonders what is retained in the movement to levels, when the levels themselves still correspond to the communications triangle: the textual = language, the rhetorical = audience, and the discursive = reality/world. McComiskey's advance, ultimately, is simply to disperse the weighted value more widely throughout the triangle, not to challenge the way the triangle structures discourse and world.

The point here is not to wage map wars as much as it is to underscore the limitations of the triangle (without denying its usefulness) in its continued manifestation in rhetoric and composition, no matter how transformed and updated with the latest theoretical insights. What the triangle impedes is greater insight into the categories it upholds as natural and essential to thought and action—that is, how those categories themselves have emerged. We get precious little insight, for example, into the dynamics of inside/outside. By what processes do social and economic forces "condition our very identities as writers" (McComiskey, *Teaching* 6–7)? Can these processes be mapped in accordance with the categories of the triangle? If not—and I am arguing that they do fall short—it behooves us to develop further our understanding of what the triangle both allows and disallows in terms of a theory of discourse.

OUT OF THE TRIANGLE, INTO THE FISSURE

The above discussion should make clear the extent to which composition and rhetoric scholars have accommodated poststructuralist thought to the elements of the triangle without an attendant questioning of the discursive model of reality proffered through the triangle. Taking our cues from Berlin's own suggestion that the teaching of writing implicitly makes a case for a particular version of reality, we should say that our theories of discourse do the same. A comparison between the communications triangle and Lacan's theory of discourse, then, does more than simply make a case for one theory of discourse over another. It also demonstrates what notions of reality are implicit in the triangle, regardless of the particular content of the four elements or what values they privilege. One need not get caught up in arguing that one model of discourse is somehow essentially better than another, either. It is enough to demonstrate and explore limits—in this case, of the triangle—in order that other discursive models may be productively employed or that a space and need for them may be generated.

A psychoanalytically inflected theory of discourse, grounded in Lacanian or neo-Lacanian thought, provides substantially different conceptions of discourse, subjectivity, and reality. First, such a theory provides concrete explanations for relating what is language to what is not language. Similarly, and to use psychoanalysis's own terminology, it provides an articulation of the circular interrelations between the Symbolic and the Real. Indeed, it is the emphasis on linking between such disparate phenomena that makes a psychoanalytic theory so useful for theorizing discourse. Any understanding of discourse and the writing process should be able to account for the ways in which language interacts with and affects our psyches, and vice versa—what I refer to above as the dynamics of inside/outside. What must be further accounted for is the properly constitutive role that discourse plays.[10] A disadvantage of the triangle is its limitation for describing how language constructs us and our world and for thereby disallowing how such constructions are inherently political. Updating the triangle with poststructuralist theory, however, does constitute an advance because of its emphasis on discourse as constitutive and its acknowledgment of the roles of ideology, power, and identity.

A Lacanian theory of discourse shares with poststructuralism this challenge to the representationalist paradigm implicit in the triangle. As mentioned earlier, Lacan and neo-Lacanians like Žižek have a constitutive view of language. It is important to stress that this position is not a form of linguistic idealism, as Lacan retains throughout his oeuvre a sophisticated notion of the Real. In fact, this notion of the Real came to be a point of impasse between Lacanian and Foucauldian theories of discourse, a discussion I take up later. For now, it is enough to get a clearer sense of what it means to uphold a constitutive understanding of discourse. This will also help underscore what psychoanalytic and poststructuralist thought have in common, not just what their differences are.

We can begin with Žižek's critical appropriation and extension of Ernesto Laclau and Chantal Mouffe's discursive theory as explained in *Hegemony and Socialist Strategy: Towards a Radical Democratic Politics.* In brief, Laclau and Mouffe deny the possibility of any discursive totality or essence: discourse is to be understood as conflicted, open, and incomplete. Temporary articulations are possible, but they are always contingent and unstable, incomplete and open to new articulations.[11] Poststructuralist theories of discourse (especially Derrida's), on which Laclau and Mouffe rely, share this understanding of always open and incomplete totalities. Note that this conception of discourse already initiates a rupture with the totalizing discourse model of the triangle, but it also suggests why it has been so easy to accommodate the triangle to poststructuralism. Even though the triangle posits a discursive totality, the Derridean insight developed by Laclau and Mouffe that a totality is always compromised—always different and deferred—can still be captured by way of negation. One simply suggests that all the elements of the triangle are unstable and open to rearticulation. The structural relations remain. However, as Torfing explains in *New Theories of Discourse*, there is a difference between conceiving the social as a totality that always falls short of closure and conceiving it as something already fundamentally split or fissured that we try and fail to conceive as a totality (52). This is the point at which Žižek parts company with Laclau and Mouffe. While he retains notions such as chains of signifiers and a discursive field open to rearticulations, he theorizes the discursive field in terms of a fundamental fissure, not simply as something nontotalizable.

From Žižek's perspective, the social is better understood in terms of a fundamental antagonism that prevents any closure, rather than as a Derridean field of signifiers whose incompleteness stems from the signifier's free play in the absence of any organizing, totalizing center. It is thus a question of whether substitution or antagonism is primary in the operations of discourse. The advantage of the neo-Lacanian conception is not just that totality is prevented, but that the failure of the possibility of totality is its *positive* condition (in the mathematical sense of being a negation of a negation). This failure to achieve closure is the positive, constitutive moment of a discursive field, and it functions at every social level. All the elements brought together in the triangle—writer, audience, language, and reality—would be understood as particular articulations covering over their existential impossibilities and in that sense just as prey to disarticulation and rearticulation as anything else that is discursively constituted. Further, the relations assumed in the triangle can also break down here. Lacan's notion of the big Other, for example, collapses audience and language together into an integrated (although still fissured) socio-symbolic entity.

What these elements in particular do not form is a fundamental structure (Kinneavy) or a group of variably defined elements with clearly structured relations (Berlin). However, the most important difference comes down to this: the fissure, or fundamental antagonism, suggests that some of the most important forces working in and on discourse drop out of our conscious apprehension. That is, nondiscursive elements are caught up with and suffuse discourse, even as they evade direct or easy translation into discourse. Nevertheless, we can chart their effects; describe their structural roles; and, perhaps most important, theorize how they are integral to understanding the relations of discourse to human constitution. Among the most important of these nondiscursive elements are fantasy, *jouissance*, and desire. It may be useful to think of these not simply as nondiscursive phenomena but as a human being's various affective modalities for integrating language and world.

Although I have been emphasizing the differences between neo-Lacanian and poststructuralist thought, these perspectives should not be seen in terms of mutual exclusion or either/or. Thus, one point psychoanalytic and poststructuralist theories continue to hold in common is an emphasis on theorizing how language constitutes social reality. As Lacan states in *L'envers de la psychanalyse,* "what dominates society is the practice of language"; "it is on discourse that every determination of the subject depends" (qtd. in Bracher et al., *Lacanian* 107, 108). In rhetoric and composition, as in other fields of humanistic inquiry, this idea has become a commonplace. Where neo-Lacanian theory and poststructuralism begin to part company, however, is regarding the precise relation between language and reality. For Lacan and Žižek, reality is formulated as "the Real," those things that are foreclosed from the symbolic and that return as errors, gaps, and misrecognitions. In plainest terms, this means that language fails to capture the Real; the Real always exceeds what can be conveyed by means of the symbolic. The dual nature of the Real can be slippery to grasp. The Real refers in part to the real world—its fulsome materiality—which Lacan and Žižek see as always having a surplus above and beyond whatever symbol or knowledge we bring to things. Thus, the body itself is of the Real insofar as we acknowledge that aspects of the body exceed our conscious apprehension and cannot be made coterminous with its production in social systems and culture. These aspects include bodily chemistry, involuntary reactions, sensations, and so on, as well the surplus of meaning, or overdetermination, that emerges in discursive activity but is not equivalent per se to such activity. Discourse and the socius do impact and shape our understanding of these things, but the point is that our understanding cannot exhaust them. This further serves to point to the very limits of consciousness. From another perspective, the Real can also be glimpsed in language's spectacular limits (I use the word *spectacular* to emphasize the aspect of spectacle, as something "to be seen/heard/noticed"). Errors, gaps, and misrecognitions are meaning effects emerging from the ways language goes awry.

Our notion of "meaning," then, is best understood not in terms of an encoder/decoder model (Kinneavy), nor as a function of a particular sociohistorical positioning (poststructuralism/Berlin), but rather as a relational effect produced retroactively by a subject entangled or enmeshed with the big Other, which is for Lacan the social/symbolic edifice. As I explained earlier, this retroactivity marks the spot of the subject, which otherwise does not exist insofar as having any positive, essential content; the subject manifests itself discursively through effects only—through its failure to achieve symbolization, through its processes of retroactive recognition and meaning production, and the like. In plainer terms, we can say that psychoanalytic theory accounts for the subject as an empty place, or X, in the symbolic order prior to the effects of subjectivization, whereas poststructuralism tends to see the subject *as* these fictionalized, shifting subject positions. Discursive production for neo-Lacanian psychoanalytic theory retains this trace of the subject in order to account for that ultimate, uncanny X that defines a particular individual. Unlike much poststructuralist theory, however, the uncanny X marking the place of the subject cannot be symbolized, which also means it cannot be positioned. In the end, the subject cannot be reduced to discourse or the mechanisms of subjectivization initiated by means of discourse.

Each of the components utilized by Žižek to outline his theory of discourse—the Real, the retroactive production of meaning, fantasy, *jouissance*, the big Other—revolves around a common theme: the fissuring of the symbolic order. Such fissuring has effects, among the most important of which is the way the symbolic introduces lack into human subjects.[12] Lack in this sense has very particular meanings. The radical contingency of all the signifiers in the symbolic realm precludes the possibility of any meaningful order that is not also subject to dissolution. As Žižek argues, an irreducible gap separates the Real from its modes of symbolization. This is one modality of what Žižek calls a "fundamental antagonism" that precludes the possibility of achieving any ultimate harmony or stability in subjects, societies, or discourses. I should note here, because this issue arises again later, that while *fundamental* refers to a kind of universal, essential limit, it does not have any particular, historical content; rather, the limit is expressed in endlessly different variations.

This understanding of discourse theory is substantially different from the one implicit in the communications triangle, which still retains some vision of wholeness: the four elements model the world as being consistent and meaningful. In contradistinction to the communications triangle, Žižek explains that symbolization itself is already made possible because the radically contingent nature of the field of signifiers has been preorganized in the form of chains of signifiers tied to a few dominant terms. These dominant terms, what Lacan calls Master Signifiers, capture and organize the desires of individual subjects and society. Another way of putting this point is that discourse cannot be theorized apart from discourse's own constitutive role in the formation of worlds and subjects and nondiscursive but discursively constituted elements such as desire and fantasy, which have a dialectically corresponding role in shaping the purposes and types of language use. For Žižek, Master Signifiers are integral for understanding the role of the political in discourse, providing the link between his theory of discourse and his theory of ideology.

LACAN IS NOT A POSTSTRUCTURALIST

In spite of their differences, Žižek's theory of discourse and poststructuralist-informed cultural studies accounts still have much in common. In "Postmodernism, Politics, and Histories of Rhetoric," Berlin explains how language is understood differently in postmodern theory than in modernist conceptions: "Language instead is taken to be a complex system of signifying practices that constructs realities rather than simply representing them. Our conceptions of material and social conditions then are fabrications of language, the products of culturally coded linguistic acts. Language does not reflect experience, it constitutes it" (171). The priority given to language and its productive role in human affairs also serves to destabilize essentialist notions of the subject and upset foundational truths and metanarratives. The capacity for language to fold back on itself, to refer not to some reality but only to other signifiers, destabilizes all concepts that require a centering, foundational, or transcendental signifier. As Berlin summarizes, a sign "has meaning by virtue of its relation to other signs, not externally verifiable certainties" ("Postmodernism" 172). There is no metaposition or foundational signifier that will suffice to ground the symbolic order. In this way, another common point is established among Lacan, poststructuralism, and other currents of contemporary thought. Žižek notes, for instance, that the phrase "There is no metalanguage" is a "commonplace found not only in Lacan's psychoanalysis and in poststructuralism (Derrida) but also in contemporary hermeneutics (Gadamer)" (*Sublime* 153).

These poststructuralist attacks on metanarratives and the stable subject have been perceived as useful for a politics that sets itself against institutions and practices of social injustice, but as a hindrance for the practice of actual political acts. If no stable subjects survive, agency must be reconceived; if no metanarratives survive, not only are foundational truths challenged, but so are the truths that would be deployed to unseat those foundations. Accordingly, poststructuralist and postmodern theories have been given a mixed reception by those who are politically minded. In *Fragments of Rationality*, Faigley remarks that this "power to fold language back on itself makes postmodern theory . . . an extremely powerful means for exposing the political investments of foundational concepts, but the same power prevents postmodern theorists from making claims of truth or emancipatory value for this activity. Postmodern theory can resemble a terrorist bomb that demolishes bystanders and even its maker as well as the target" (43–44). This constitutes what Faigley calls the "impasse of postmodern theory," and he states that it has been around long enough for the self-questioning of postmodern theory to begin (20).

I think that this impasse is a false one. It depends on an idea that continues to suffuse rhetorical theory and cultural studies—the idea that agency requires critical distance and a substantive theory of the subject (see Muckelbauer). This is a common but problematic reading of poststructuralism, even showing up in proponents of psychoanalytic thought. In his essay "The Subject of Discourse: Reading Lacan through (and beyond) Poststructuralist Contexts," Marshall Alcorn Jr. asserts that "poststructuralists and Freudians hold quite different assumptions about the 'subject of discourse'" (19). Alcorn argues: "There is a repeated 'identity' pattern in poststructuralist thought that works to erase the human subject, to make 'the subject of discourse' an entity composed, contained, derived from, and imprisoned by language. . . . The subject thus fades back, without a residue, into its constitutive element, language. The subject of discourse becomes a subject *of discourse*" (26). The point for Alcorn is that language "contains" the subject in poststructuralist accounts; this position is often attributed to Lacan as well.[13] Alcorn suggests instead that the subject of discourse cannot be theorized as something constituted exclusively by language; instead, the subject exists in a dialectical relationship with language, so that neither one can be understood as containing the other. From this perspective, the subject does not entirely contain language as the modernist traditions would have it, but neither does language entirely contain the subject. As Alcorn states, relations between discourse and subjects are two-sided: "The subject operates upon discourse, and discourse operates upon the subject" (27). In other words, as Biesecker contends, neo-Lacanian thought helps us understand the symbolic and its functioning without reducing all understanding to the symbolic and its positive relations (227; cf. Copjec).

Žižek also argues that Lacan is not a poststructuralist. Poststructuralist and psychoanalytic positions differ not only in their notions of what constitutes the subject but also on the issue of metanarratives. Faigley, as noted above, points out what he sees as the impasse of postmodern theory: the fact that no metanarrative is possible is both a useful tool of critique and a dire hindrance to effective political action that requires truth claims. Žižek reminds us, however, that "we usually lose from view how Lacan's theory treats this proposition [that there is no metanarrative] in a way that is completely incompatible with poststructuralism, as well as hermeneutics" (*Sublime* 153). Žižek claims that the poststructuralist position is too "theoretical"; by this he means that it is "a theory which excludes the truth-dimension; that is, which does not affect the place from which we speak" (*Sublime* 155). This is another way of saying that the proposition that "no utterance can mean precisely what it intends to say and the process of enunciation will always subvert the utterance" is "*the position of metalanguage* in its purest, most radical form" (*Sublime* 155). Žižek's argument is less a polemic than a radical extension of the poststructuralist *telos*. Not only will the process of enunciation subvert all possible enunciations, but we must extend this insight to include the proposition itself, so that the position from which the enunciation originates produces a concomitant excess of meaning signifying the impossible absurdity of occupying such a metaposition. For poststructuralists, "there is no metalanguage" means that the signifier is in some sense always rebounding from its literal meaning, its object. However, in Lacan, "there is no metalanguage" must be taken literally to mean that "all language is in a way an object-language: *there is no language without an object*. Even when the language is apparently caught in a web of self-referential movement, even when it is apparently speaking only about itself, there is an objective, non-signifying 'reference' to this movement" (*Sublime* 158). In this manner the value of the object, heretofore devalued in the poststructuralist spin of endless semiosis, is returned to the object, and returned to it through language. Furthermore, by returning to discourse its object status, we can avoid the impasse implicit in much poststructuralist thought of making claims denying the possibility of truth that paradoxically claim truth status. In other words, poststructuralist theories of discourse tend to operate by means of discursive positionality and thereby often conflate the specific utterance with its referential content. This understanding of how language operates is fully consonant with the understanding of discourse offered by the communications triangle. Implicit in both is a certain pragmatic directionality, even if in the case of poststructuralism that directionality is largely self-referential. What a neo-Lacanian theory of discourse offers is a way of understanding a constitutive gap in discursive operations that avoids the impasse of endless self-referentiality.

It is important to realize that the object thus reconstituted in Žižek is transformed. Žižek is not proffering the kind of object that corresponds oppositionally to the subject, wherein the status of the object is achieved through the reestablishment of the subject-object split. Instead, the object takes form as an exclusion internal to language. We can understand this through Žižek's example of the painting *Lenin in Warsaw*. The painting depicts Lenin's wife, Nadezhda Krupskaya, in bed with a young member of the Komsomol. Žižek explains that the typical response of a visitor viewing the picture is to ask, "Where is Lenin?" The proper response, on the other hand, is to recognize that Lenin, though absent from the field of representation, *is* the object of the picture. Žižek writes: "If we put aside Lenin's position as the absent Third, the bearer of the prohibition of the sexual relationship, we could say that 'Lenin in Warsaw' is, in a strict Lacanian sense, the object of this picture. The title names the object which is lacking in the field of what is depicted. That is to say, in this joke, the trap in which the visitor was caught could be defined precisely as the metalanguage trap. The visitor's mistake is to establish the same distance between the picture and the title as between the sign and the denoted object, as if the title is speaking *about* the picture from a kind of 'objective distance,' and then to look for its positive correspondence in the picture" (*Sublime* 159). If Lenin were not away, the sexual liaison depicted in the painting would not be possible. "The field of representation," explains Žižek, "is the field of what is positively depicted, but the problem is that everything cannot be depicted" (159). That is to say, every field of signifiers must necessarily exclude an element that would correspond to an objective, nonsignifying reference to the self-referential movement of language (158). The mistake of the typical observer of the painting is to assume that the title operates from a metalinguistic position, as if it achieves its meaning through a direct correspondence between the picture title and the pictorial content. What the painting does instead is invite the viewer in as a participant in its truth; it puts us into the eventual truth that is the condition of possibility for the liaison.

In a manner akin to a Möbius strip, the frame is thus framed by part of its content. Every discursive element that aspires to function as a transcendental signifier is nevertheless only materialized, or given positive form, as just another element within the phenomenological or discursive field. This is one of several manifestations of what Žižek calls a fundamental antagonism that can never be overcome. And while the antagonism is irreducible, its permutations are innumerable. Furthermore, the manner in which these antagonisms are articulated and negotiated by individuals and society has direct bearing on language and the formation of subjectivity. In this way, a neo-Lacanian theory of discourse foregrounds the political dimension. A particular discourse can be considered not only according to its socio-historical position (poststructuralism) but also as a negotiation, from that socio-historical position, of a fundamental aspect of human existence that deflects any form of representation that would be adequate to it. The truth value of direct representation thereby gives way to the truth value inherent in the failure of any direct representation—in the way truth emerges as the collapsing of an observer into a participant or as a reframing of a privileged (referential) frame.

This insight must be extended to theories of discourse themselves. The truth of the theory of discourse offered by the communications triangle (as utilized by Kinneavy, Crusius, and others) or an updated triangle inflected by poststructuralist thought (Berlin, Faigley, Brodkey, McComiskey, and so on) is precisely the more or less accurate description of the purposes and categories of discourse. Inherent in all these theories, no matter how ultimately self-reflexively aware they may be, is the attempt to describe how it is that discourse really functions for us. We can see this drive at work even in those understandings of discourse that are the most self-reflexive. Brodkey and Susan Miller, for example, share a poststructuralist understanding of discourse that they convey through metaphors of fictionality. Brodkey calls the theories of Lacan and Foucault "stories," while Miller opens *Textual Carnivals: The Politics of Composition* by claiming that her study is "blatantly a fiction" (1). The irony of their position is well captured by the title of Miller's final chapter, "On Seeing Things for What They Are" (177). Miller and Brodkey, like many other theorists in composition and rhetoric, find themselves in the dubious position of having to acknowledge the constructed and artificial nature of discourse and theory while simultaneously attempting to make truth claims from such fictions. I find this to be an untenable position, although I harbor no nostalgia for a return to an understanding of discourse as truthfully referential. Instead, I want to read productively the impasse that Brodkey and Miller attempt to navigate and to see in their negotiations not a failure to theorize discourse adequately but something "essential" about discourse itself.[14]

That said, it should be added that a neo-Lacanian theory of discourse does not escape from the will to provide an accurate description of things any more than poststructuralist theory. However, it does maintain one key difference. As Žižek's project suggests, any theory of discourse should include an understanding of the ways in which discourse fails to represent the excess that is reality, or, to put it otherwise, how reality in all its fulsomeness exceeds the representative and expressive capacities of language. But it is not enough to stop there. Instead, we must take one further step and acknowledge how this failure is itself productive. In other words, the positive truth content of discourse, and especially of a theory of discourse, arises from the retroactive recognition of (1) an excess that eludes discourse, which (2) nevertheless exists in and through discourse, so that (3) this perceived lack in discourse is reunderstood and redescribed as the traumatic excess of discourse.[15] Integral to a neo-Lacanian theory of discourse is the notion that the success of such a theory is not predicated solely on its ability to accurately describe discourse. Instead, the goal is to understand discourse as something that can never achieve such an accurate representation of itself or anything else and to theorize how the purposes and categories of discourse are in large part determined by this incapacity. By inscribing such partiality and finitude into the workings of discourse itself, neo-Lacanian discourse theory thereby also realigns our understanding of truth.

THE REAL AND THE EMERGENCE OF TRUTH

In the neo-Aristotelian conception of the communications triangle, reality is theorized as something to which we can gain access through language. As Kinneavy asserts, "it is possible to consider the signals of a language as representing or referring to reality" (*Theory* 20). The question becomes, however, what is reality in this formulation? Postmodern thought has challenged any simple correspondence between signifier and referent, while also demonstrating how language mediates experience and constructs reality. In "Poststructuralism, Cultural Studies, and the Composition Classroom," Berlin reminds the contemporary rhetorician that s/he must be aware that the subject (producer) of discourse "is a construction, a fabrication, established through the devices of signifying practices. . . . But if the subject, the sender, is a construct of signifying practices in social-epistemic rhetoric, so are the material conditions to which the subject responds, the prime constituents of the message of discourse" (21). Although reality is linguistically mediated, the full consequences of this position are deflected in favor of a simple view of rhetorical conflict that ignores the wider implications of how rhetorical conflict is also bifurcated between content and form. Not only is the social-discursive field structured by differential and conflictual contexts, but discourse itself, in its functioning, is already structured by conflict. Lacan refers to this fundamental conflict as one modality of the Real. (The other modality, I should add, is the world itself in its symbolic inexhaustibility, that is, as it exists beyond language.) Let us, however, consider Berlin's statement that "signifying practices are always at the center of conflict and contention. . . . In the effort to name experience, different groups are constantly vying for supremacy, for ownership, and control of the terms and their meanings in any discourse situation" (21). For Berlin, the roles of ideology, hegemony, power, and rhetoric all become crucial in articulating the relations between signifying practices and the realities to which they refer. Reality itself, however, remains knowable, communicable, and understandable, a Whole that invites differing interpretations and perspectives that interact and conflict within the social totality.

Berlin unwittingly falls into the metalinguistic trap, and he does so in a manner useful for examining the concept of the Real in Lacan. We must ask, from what position can Berlin assert that all conceptions of reality are contested fabrications? Implicit in Berlin's very argument is the position of objectivity that would discern the truth about how discourse really functions for us. Can we avoid the conclusion that Berlin's argument is also a fabrication? We can do so, I suggest, not because he is involved in logical contradiction (his statement that reality is a linguistic construct purports to be the truth of the matter that is itself *not* a construct but the way things really are) but because his argument misses the truth-dimension invoked by his own statement. That is, the argument does not affect the place from which it speaks. We see here an example of the charge Žižek makes that statements taking this kind of inadvertent metalinguistic position constitute "a barely hidden acknowledgement of the fact that [the argument] is speaking from a safe position, a position not menaced by the decentered textual process" (*Sublime* 155).

The trick is to reread Berlin's statement, which is typical of global assessments that attempt to navigate the postmodern moratorium on metanarratives qua overarching truth statements, with an eye toward how it *could* invoke the truth-dimension. Thus, rather than understand Berlin's statement as either (1) a truth claim describing the really existing state of affairs or (2) a fabrication that is contradictory as regards its implicit claim to be true, we should opt for (3) a statement that invokes the Lacanian Real, a position that is paradoxically impossible to occupy. But as Žižek points out, it is also impossible to avoid: "One cannot *attain* it [metalanguage], but one also cannot *escape* it. That is why the only way to avoid the Real is to produce an utterance of pure metalanguage which, by its patent absurdity, materializes its own impossibility: that is, a paradoxical element which, in its very identity, embodies absolute otherness, the irreparable gap that makes it impossible to occupy a metalinguistic position" (*Sublime* 156). We might read Berlin's statement, then, as a truth statement that, by way of its very "error," brings us to the truth of the Real as unsymbolizable deadlock. The irreparable gap sundering the position of universality (a statement claiming that this is the way the world *is*) from the position of a particular perspective (a statement claiming that this is the way the world is *for me*) is an index for the fundamental antagonism that eludes signification. Nonetheless, this gap produces structural effects in the socio-symbolic order. In short, the epistemological break between the universal and the particular invokes the order of the Real as an impossible deadlock that can be neither dissolved nor symbolized. Berlin's statement, then, falls too short, even though we cannot say that it is simply in error. Instead, we should again invoke the necessity of reading his claim speculatively to see in his stopping short already a kind of truth. The impossibility of not falling into a metalinguistic position that is itself necessarily false (or not all, limited, partial) indicates the extent to which the social can never be grasped as an "objective" totality. As Žižek puts it, the "traumatic Real is thus that which, precisely, prevents us from assuming a neutral-objective view of reality, a stain which blurs our clear perception of it" (*Plague* 215). Thus, we retain a notion of truth, but we lose any notion of transparent access to truth.

As a preview to upcoming arguments about ideology, I would like to point out that we can also see one reason for cultural studies' allure here. When cultural studies gets pulled into composition in the work of Berlin, Patricia Bizzell, Alan W. France, and others, it brings with it this poststructuralist understanding of reality as a decentered, resignifiable Whole. This includes the elusive metalinguistic position making possible the belief that the critical insights achieved through cultural studies are truthful enough to initiate change. The knowledge produced through cultural critique palliates its potentially corrosive self-reflexivity by acknowledging its partiality or fictionality, even while it continues to operate from a privileged metalinguistic position. We might recognize the admission that the cultural studies frame could be reframed, but the collective investment in its critical knowledge precludes any actual reframing. Indeed, this is precisely the bait and switch that will allow Berlin to reformulate social-epistemic rhetoric *as* cultural studies and to see them as somehow the same and equally productive of rhetorical truth, no matter how tempered by claims to self-critical reflexivity.

To return to where we were: this predicament about the status of truth has served to introduce us to the Lacanian order of the Real as something both preceding and resisting symbolization. Thus, no signifier suffices to convey the Real's rich fullness. Additionally, not only is the Real what precedes and resists symbolization, but it is also the leftover produced by symbolization. We are familiar with this in our everyday life. Errors, slips of the tongue, accidents, and other such phenomena whereby more is said than intended, or where the unconscious makes itself heard, constitute a form of excess or surplus signification that returns through the symbolic. Although nothing is actually lacking in the Real, the effect of symbolization is to introduce lack into all aspects of human affairs. From our perspective as symbolic beings, then, reality is characterized by lack: it does not have "it," that which would ultimately satisfy our desire or express the essential truth of our subjective being. Furthermore, the

Real is in some sense unbearable; its rich fullness also includes an accompanying terror that requires palliation. This suggests that while the Real and reality are enmeshed, they are not the same. Thus, in comparison to the Real, Žižek defines reality as "the minimum of idealization necessary for the subject to sustain the horror of the Real" (*Plague* 66).[16] This "minimum of idealization" is correlative with the role of fantasy in sustaining human existence in the face of the Real and providing the sense of Wholeness and Meaning necessary for maintaining social bonds. It also suggests that we do not have pure access to the world—its meaning and symbolic relations, within which we exist, are caught up with our own unconscious suppositions. Errors and slippages are the way the Real emerges in everyday reality to prick us, to remind us of our partiality and finitude.

MASTER SIGNIFIERS AND THE BIG OTHER

In the communications triangle, audience (receptor) and language are given their own categories, indicating their status as separate and distinct entities. However, for Lacan and Žižek, enough overlap exists between them to justify their inclusion under one umbrella term, the big Other. As Žižek explains in *For They Know Not What They Do: Enjoyment as a Political Factor*, the big Other is on the one hand the impersonal order of symbolization in general but on the other hand also designates the radical alterity of the other person beyond our mirroring (199). Our attempts to find a signifier or form of identification that would express who we are in our essence find their limit in the Other, from whom we are fundamentally severed. Furthermore, the communications triangle mystifies the relation between language and receptor that the Lacanian concept of the big Other clarifies. Language and Other (subjects) are united in the misperception that they are both whole, seamless entities when in fact they are not. Just like the subject, the big Other is fissured. Thus, the perception that the Other is whole and plentiful is an elementary gesture of fantasy, and such fantasy is one of the mechanisms by which the subject defines itself in its ongoing, constitutive dialectic with the big Other. Especially crucial here is the way the communications triangle presents a model of reality that would efface this constitutive dependence in favor of relations between semiautonomous entities, albeit linguistically based ones. As we will see, what is obscured is the way signifiers become the terrain of rhetoric. Signifiers, Biesecker states, have "ontic clout" (223). The big Other points not only to how we invest language but to how language equally invests us. One way to conceive of rhetoric is as the playing out of these coinvestments in socio-symbolic spaces.

Žižek, alluding to the work of Laclau and Mouffe, describes language as a heterogeneous mass of free-floating signifiers, an understanding that is similar to poststructuralist theories of language. Unlike poststructuralist accounts, however, Žižek's Lacanian argument is that a consistent field of meaning emerges only when a Master Signifier also emerges. The formerly dispersed field of signifiers is linked and bound together, or quilted, by the Master Signifier. This action retroactively structures the field of meaning so that it appears that it had always been aligned just so. We might then ask why a Master Signifier is necessary and, if it is necessary, from whence it arises. Žižek explains that such a signifier emerges out of the contradictory nature of the symbolic order. On the one hand, the symbolic field is finite, being both contingent and limited, never able to achieve adequate representation of the impossible fullness of the Real. On the other hand, the field of representation is infinite in that there is nothing outside the text: everything can be told, there is no external viewpoint from which the limits of language can be judged (*Enjoy* 102; cf. Derrida, *Grammatology*). This inherent tension necessitates that a paradoxical element within the symbolic field stand in for what eludes symbolization. As Žižek puts it, always at least one element "functions as the signifier of the very lack of a signifier," and this element is the Master Signifier (*Enjoy* 102–3). Another way of putting this is that the inherent tension of the symbolic order develops from the limits of the signifier. The sliding of signifiers that can never quite express the Real in its impossible plentitude can only be halted by the signifier of this very impossibility, a signifier that founds itself in the very act of its enunciation.

In the neo-Lacanian view of language, then, every discursive field has an element that must drop out of the field and, in so doing, retroactively reorganize that field to create the appearance of consistency. A useful way of visualizing this is in terms of a sliding tile puzzle or Rubik's Cube. One tile or element must be absent so that a space is open to allow the movement of the other pieces, and a new order to be generated. In this sense, absence is productive, demonstrating analogically the larger Lacanian point that a given system cannot be reduced solely to its immanent, positive elements. Again, this is substantially different from poststructuralist accounts of discourse, which remain at the level of immanent, free-floating signifiers structured more or less directly by social and material practices.

This is not to say that Žižek is arguing for a transcendental conception of discourse. The Master Signifier functions in a manner akin to a transcendental signifier, except that it is strictly internal to language. For this reason, Lacan claimed that the Master (as a signifier, symbol, or person) is an imposter. Žižek explains: "The Master is somebody who, upon finding himself at the place of the constitutive lack in the structure, acts as if he holds the reins

of that surplus, of the mysterious X which eludes the grasp of the structure
. . . yet the *place* occupied by him—the place of the lack in the structure—
cannot be abolished, since the very finitude of every discursive field imposes
its structural necessity" (*Enjoy* 103). Discourse, being paradoxically finite and
infinite, is structured by this constitutive lack, which is signified by a corresponding paradoxical element that retroactively provides coherence to the
field of signifiers. The confusion arises when the structural effect is conflated
with the particular content or a particular Master Signifier. Discourse may
structurally presuppose an authority (what in philosophy would be called a
transcendent element), but that authoritative function is formal, not particular, and relational, not essential.

Žižek explains that this conception of the presuppositions of discourse
is radically different from that proposed by Habermas, who conceives the
goal of communication to be centered on rational discussion free of constraints (see *Communicative*). Impediments to this goal are distortions to be
overcome. For Lacan, the presupposition of discourse is not free and equal
discussion, but discourse as something authoritarian and agonistic. The Master Signifier emerges from the constitutive contradictions of discourse itself
as an empty signifier quilting the dispersed field of signifiers, with the result
that "the infinite chain of causes ('knowledge') is interrupted with an abyssal,
nonfounded, founding act of violence" (*Enjoy* 103). Whereas for Habermas
distortion blocks the achievement of free and open discourse between rational subjects, for Lacan distortion is fundamental for the discursive field. Re-
moving the distortion would cause the field of meaning to collapse. Because
of this, the logic of unmasking the Master Signifier—of demonstrating the
falsity of its organization of the discursive field—necessarily fails to abolish
the place it occupies. The structural effects remain implicit. This further suggests why cultural studies pedagogies that ask students to critique a discursive
formation organized by a Master Signifier—political, sexual, religious, and
so forth—typically induce little or no change. Critiques of TV programs or
advertisements that leave unchallenged students' comportment toward these
things are typical and common examples. I am arguing that a structural component to the discourse remains operational regardless of the specific, contingent content of its dominant, organizing term. To the extent that critique does
not address the structural absence and concentrates solely on the positivity of
the given elements, it will be of limited effectiveness.

WELCOME TO FANTASY ISLAND

The standard definition of fantasy involves the hallucinatory satisfaction of
a wish. Daydreams or reveries about accomplishing some deed or obtain-

ing some valuable object are characteristic of this understanding of fantasy. Psychoanalysis, however, theorizes fantasy differently, as an idealizing framework that functions in support of reality and that should accordingly be understood as constituted a priori through subjective and unconscious forces. Žižek states: "We can see clearly how fantasy is on the side of reality, how it sustains the subject's 'sense of reality': when the phantasmic frame disintegrates, the subject undergoes a 'loss of reality' and starts to perceive reality as an 'irreal' nightmarish universe with no firm ontological foundation; this nightmarish universe is not 'pure fantasy' but, on the contrary, *that which remains of reality after reality is deprived of its support in fantasy*" (*Plague* 66). Fantasy's endless permutations give to reality the particular consistency we require. Since one aspect of the Real is that it pertains to a fundamental antagonism or inconsistency that remains unsymbolizable yet operational in the symbolic order, we can understand fantasy as providing the necessary screen allowing us to live with this inconsistency. Žižek takes this concept even further by pointing out that fantasy structures the entire array of human experience; it is "the frame through which we experience the world as consistent and meaningful" (*Sublime* 123).

A shift in the fantasy frame structuring our experiential reality can be traumatic. For example, most of us have had the experience of being with a group of friends, laughing, talking, and socializing, when all of a sudden we have the sense that we are all alone, that our friends are far away from us, which in turn gives rise to other feelings of unease and disassociation. What has happened is that the fantasy frame undergirding the friendly intersubjective network has been wrenched, and now, without that support, our perception of "reality" has radically changed. Such events occur on the larger social level as well. A famous example may be found in Yeats's poem "The Second Coming." In the first stanza, the speaker laments the transformations the world is undergoing, the lack of a center, the sense that chaos is rushing in to despoil innocence: "Things fall apart; the center cannot hold; / Mere anarchy is loosed upon the world." Of course, Yeats's poem means more than I am suggesting here, but it is not hard to hear in the stirring notice "Surely some revelation is at hand; / Surely the Second Coming is at hand" the sense of despair-ridden fait accompli that comes from dashed dreams of social harmony and justice. However, what is essential here is that the stability and order that Yeats laments were artificial from the beginning. Žižek's locution for this idea is that "society does not exist." The idea that society is an ordered, stable whole is only possible within the frame of fantasy. The Real of the social is that it is a radically dispersed mass of heterogeneous elements. Yeats's poem is arguably more effective because of its evocative portrayal of the effects of the dissolution of a constitutive fantasy frame than because of any provable loss of the old, supposedly stable traditions (e.g., where is the great trauma of the Industrial Revolution?).

Fantasy also serves to cover over the lack in the Other. Žižek writes that fantasy appears "as an answer to '*Che vuoi?*', to the unbearable enigma of the desire of the Other, of the lack in the Other; but it is at the same time fantasy itself which, so to speak, provides the co-ordinates of our desire—which constructs the frame enabling us to desire something" (*Sublime* 118). "Che vuoi?" (What do you want?) is the difficult and ambiguous question with which the big Other confronts us. Žižek explains that the "subject is always fastened, pinned, to a signifier which represents him for the other, and through this pinning he is loaded with a symbolic mandate, he is given a place in the intersubjective network of symbolic relations" (*Sublime* 113). However, this mandate is arbitrary with regard to the actual characteristics of the subject; there is no way to account for it by reference to some essential truth of the subject. For this reason, a fundamental discrepancy always exists between who one is for others and who one is for oneself. We may reasonably ask, why am I what you are saying that I am?, but there can be no ultimate answer or justification. This is not to say that an answer cannot be offered, but the catch is that such answers do not suffice. Something always escapes, and this excessiveness generates a sense that rationales are slippery and unsteady. One remains unjustified in the big Other. The unjustness of being pinned on a signifier is ultimately an arbitrary and purely structural effect that deflects canalization.

It is at this point that fantasy once again enters. It is not the fantasy scene itself that serves as the goal of fantasy, but the gaze that is viewing it. Of course, that gaze is in a sense impossible, as it is pure conjecture on the part of the subject—there is no way to bridge the gap between the subject and the Other's desire. This illuminates another of Lacan's famous locutions, that "desire is always the desire of the other." Žižek explains how this idea functions in fantasy:

What we encounter in the very core of fantasy is the relationship to the desire of the Other, to the latter's opacity: *the desire staged in fantasy is not mine but the desire of the Other*. Fantasy is a way for the subject to answer the question of what object he is in the eyes of the Other, in the Other's desire—that is, what does the Other see in him, what role does he play in the Other's desire? A child, for example, endeavors to dissolve, by means of his fantasy, the enigma of the role he plays as the medium of the interactions between his mother and his father, the enigma of how mother and father fight their battles and settle their accounts through him. In short, fantasy is the highest proof of the fact that the subject's desire is the desire of the Other. (*Metastases* 177)

The subject is forced to extrapolate from the given situation what the desire of the Other is, and fantasy arises as the "solution" to this impossible position (impossible because a subject cannot occupy it). In this way also, the gap sundering the subject from the Other is reconceived; no longer an obstacle, this gap becomes the motor driving subjectivity and social interaction. Thus, fantasy again functions on the side of reality, bringing together disparate elements and providing the necessary framework for their interaction in intersubjective and socio-symbolic space.

Earlier, I discussed the poststructuralist tendency to explain discursive formations in terms of the contingency of their socio-historic elements. Such a theory of discourse seeks explanations in the positive relations (such as relations of power) among all elements. As Joan Copjec points out, this is the logic of Foucault's panopticon: the subject is produced in the confluence of multiple discourses on the body. As Copjec puts it, what is produced in Foucauldian theory is "a *determinate* thing or position, but, in addition, knowledge and power are conceived as the overall effect of the relation among the various conflicting positions and discourses" (18). As is apparent, Lacanian theory proceeds differently. A subject position is not achieved solely by the direct agglomeration of positive forces. We need also to attend to incompleteness, to the fact that subjects, discourses, and the big Other are barred or fissured. Thus, rather than seeing discourses as functioning directly to construct the subject, neo-Lacanian theory adds a further wrinkle: the subject's incompleteness is threaded through the incompleteness of the big Other. For Foucault, the gaze of the Other in the panopticon is what is internalized by the subject, and this internalization induces the proper, docile comportment. There is a direct mirroring of the gaze that allows for the emergence of the disciplined body in accord with power. For Lacan, however, the production of a disciplined subject is not this simple. Instead, the subject, rather than mirroring via internalization of and compliance with the productive gaze of power, posits a beyond to that gaze (Copjec 34). This is the opening of the space of fantasy. It is not that there actually *is* something beyond the discursive field; rather, the subject is called to *suppose* such a beyond. Thus, the subject is again caught in the fantasy scenario of the "Che vuoi?": What is wanted from me? What is being concealed from me? Who am I supposed to be for you?

Fantasy, then, is integral to the way discourse invests and produces subjectivity, not solely as the positivity of given relations but in conjunction with the subject's projection in and through discourse of a nonexistent beyond to discourse. As Copjec distills it, for Foucault, discourse functions as a mirror: we are produced, mirrorlike, in the play of disciplining power. In Lacan, however, discourse functions as a screen: the subject shows up as a function of its projections of a beyond to discourse. In this way, subject and discourse coinvest in each other as two intersecting triangles—the point from which the subject looks out on the world and the point (phantasmatic, supposed) from which the world in turn looks back into us (Copjec 33). Fantasy, it seems, cannot be diagrammed on the communications triangle, except insofar as we posit a second triangle that would fissure and decomplete the first.

FANTASY AND *JOUISSANCE*

Not only does fantasy emerge as a crucial component of a subject's comportment to reality and other people, but it coordinates a subject's own enjoyment of these coping strategies. As Žižek states, fantasy is "an entity that is exceedingly traumatic: it articulates the subject's relationship towards enjoyment, towards the traumatic kernel of his being, towards something that the subject is never able to acknowledge fully, to become familiar with, to integrate into his symbolic universe" (*Metastases* 178). Enjoyment (*jouissance*) is a paradoxical form of pleasure that is derived from unpleasure, pain, and trauma. Through fantasy, one's enjoyment is centered in particular objects, habits, and actions. Žižek writes: "Someone may be happily married, with a good job and many friends, fully satisfied with his life, and yet absolutely hooked on some specific formation (sinthom) of *jouissance*, ready to put everything at risk rather than renounce *that* (drugs, tobacco, drink, a particular sexual perversion . . .). Although his symbolic universe may be nicely set up, this absolutely meaningless intrusion, this *clinamen*, upsets everything, and there is nothing to be done, since it is only in this 'sinthom' that the subject encounters the density of his being—when he is deprived of it, his universe is empty" (*Plague* 49). Fantasy operates as the frame that orients, or situates, the subject's *jouissance* in a particular symbolic ensemble. I discussed above how the symbolic is defined in relation to the subject by its inability to supply the needed signifiers that would express the essence of the subject or overcome its fundamental disharmony—which is to say that the symbolic and the subject are both characterized by a certain lack. However, it is also the case that the symbolic, in the form of Master Signifiers, laws, cultural codes, associations, and the like, organizes, regulates, proscribes, and authorizes various kinds of identifications, actions, beliefs, and affiliations. The price for this, however, is that *jouissance* is evacuated from the body. Žižek explains that this is "the great Lacanian motif of symbolization as a process which mortifies, drains off, empties, carves the fullness of the Real of the living body"; but of course the Real is doubly articulated, so that the Real is also "the product, remainder, leftover, scraps of this process of symbolization, the remnants, the excess which escapes symbolization and is as such produced by the symbolization itself" (*Sublime* 169). Desire is the effort to regain what was lost through the process of symbolization; hence, desire is on the side of the symbolic. Desire seeks satisfaction in the Other—through words, signs, people, objects. It is an attempt to recapture the Thing, the piece of the Real that embodies the *jouissance* that would make up for what has been lost. Fantasy is the framework through which desire operates or is given its orientation. The object of fantasy, which can be understood as the stand-in object for the lost *jouissance*, is the *objet petit a*. Mark Bracher explains that this precious object "figures in discourse as the return of the being or *jouissance* that is excluded by the master signifiers" (*Lacan* 41).

The subject is decentered not only in its being (the "I" that thinks is not the same as the "I" that is the object of perception of the thing that thinks) and in the symbolic but in relation to *jouissance* as well. "Much more radical and elementary than the decentrement of the subject with regard to the 'big Other,'" claims Žižek, "is the decentrement with regard to the traumatic Thing-*jouissance* which the subject can never 'subjectivize,' assume, integrate" (*Plague* 49). The subject is caught in a process of ceaseless questioning with regard to this object, a wondering not only if the object is *it* but if, in identifying with it, s/he is also *that*? We see, then, how desire and fantasy shift and flow as Master Signifiers and the chains of signifiers they organize also shift and flow in metonymic and metaphoric flux, at the individual level and the social level. When we encounter other human beings, or when we reflect on ourselves, signifiers function as our representatives, so that in any encounter the makeup of the subject is at stake. Bracher explains further that to have an effect, "a discourse does not have to engage *directly* a master signifier, image, or fantasy; such engagement can also be indirect, for negotiations among signifiers do not take place merely among these primary representatives but also—to pursue the diplomatic analogy—among members of the staffs of representatives. Such lower-level negotiations are, in fact, where the real work gets done, for the position of a primary representative is held in place by its numerous alliances and oppositions to lesser signifiers, and without undoing ties of this sort and instituting new ties, the position of the primary representative remains unaltered" (*Lacan* 49). With regard to the communications triangle, we see the importance of recognizing the extent to which language and audience (the receptor) may be combined when we consider discursive aims. If it is through signifiers that function not so much as *representations* of the world and people but as their *representatives*, then the relations between language and audience are mystified each time we isolate the two as separate entities.

The signifiers, images, and objects that circulate in socio-symbolic space, however, are never neutral in regard to our comportment toward them. Above

and beyond the mechanism of identification, they are continuously pene-
trated or suffused with *jouissance*. Wherever subjects are, whatever they are
doing, *jouissance* arises and permeates activity and interaction. For example,
when someone renounces some pleasure—sweets, perhaps, or sexual activity—*jouissance* reemerges to provide a strange pleasure in the renunciation.
Yet this *jouissance* also represents the limit of interpretation; it cannot be symbolized or grasped, and thus it is also traumatic for the subject. Žižek states
that all we can say about *jouissance* as it is incarnated in a Thing is that "the
Thing is 'itself,' 'the real Thing,' 'what it is really about,' etc." (*Tarrying* 201).
Nor is *jouissance* restricted to the subjective level. The Thing functions significantly within socio-political life, serving to organize and bind communities. Žižek suggests that "the Thing is present in that elusive entity called 'our
way of life.' All we can do is enumerate disconnected fragments of the way our
community organizes its feasts, its rituals of mating, its initiation ceremonies,
in short, all the details by which is made visible the unique way a community
organizes its enjoyment" (*Tarrying* 201). These features, however, exist in a
manner that transcends any specific ritual or other manifestation of the "way
of life." Whether we are speaking of the organization of enjoyment on the individual or the national level, something about it is more "it" than itself. Not
only can enjoyment not be reduced to any specific entity, but it also produces
effects above and beyond its concrete material practice. This is also true for
large-scale communities, like nations, where ineffable and immaterial effects
help maintain investments in organizational stability. Žižek explains, "Nation
exists only as long as its specific *enjoyment* continues to be materialized in a
set of social practices and transmitted through national myths that structure
these practices" (*Tarrying* 202). It is at this point that another problem with
the discourse theory modeled by the communications triangle becomes apparent. Even if we grant that language has priority in constructing or mediat-
ing subjects and phenomena, as the communications triangle suggests, there
remains no way to account within this model for the unsymbolizable kernel
of *jouissance* that remains as a constitutive factor in individuals and larger
groups, including nations. It is not enough to reduce them to being contingent discursive constructions. As Žižek argues, "such an emphasis overlooks
the remainder of some *real*, nondiscursive kernel of enjoyment which must
be present for the Nation qua discursive entity-effect to achieve its ontological
consistency" (*Tarrying* 202).

REMARKS ON DISCURSIVE CONCEPTS

In the above discussion, I have presented aspects of neo-Lacanian theory
that support an understanding of discourse that is substantially different from

that modeled in the communications triangle as described by Kinneavy or amended by Berlin and other rhetoricians using poststructuralist theories. I want to conclude with a brief discussion about discursive concepts that will illustrate concretely some of the points I have made. A commonsense, traditional understanding of a "concept" can be defined according to the characteristics that are claimed to adhere to it in an essentialist manner. The concept of "democracy," then, could be given an essentialist definition listing the primary features of a democracy—perhaps that the citizenry has the right to cast votes that play a part in determining governmental policies, and so on. Such a definition has as its goal an accurate representation of what democracy or some other concept essentially is, and this understanding of the concept would more or less correspond to Kinneavy's original, neo-Aristotelian theory of discourse, as well as to the four elements of his triangle. As amended by poststructuralist theory, however, the concept of democracy would not be granted any totalizing, essential characteristics. Instead, democracy would be defined as a concept that is always open and situated within concrete social, political, economic, and historical forces. In this sense, the definition of democracy is plural and open to contestation. Certainly, this understanding foregrounds the socio-political element, corresponding to the theories offered by scholars such as Laclau and Mouffe, Berlin, Bizzell, France, and more.

Neo-Lacanian discourse theory, however, understands concepts differently than either of these two approaches. Instead of having essentialist features, or negotiating in the social realm for control over various shifting positions, the concept of democracy would be said "not to exist." Democracy is not to be conceived as a positive concept, even as a slippery and ultimately indefinable one. Democracy, like other concepts, is to be considered as structured by a fundamental antagonism or split that prevents it from ever showing up with any conclusively positive features. Democracy does not exist except insofar as we might apply that label to an existing system of government. In other words, it is in the process of naming itself, in the conceptual designation by a signifier and the rhetorical weight the designation comes to hold, that certain meanings accrue. But the signifier itself is empty of meaning except to the extent that it separates itself from what is not democratic. As in poststructuralist theories of discourse, this process of separation involves social and political negotiation. This underscores the fact that while in theory the term *democracy* might be applied willy-nilly, in practice this is obviously not the case. Substantive shifts are possible but seem to require as accompaniment a catalyst such as a large social realignment. To continue, rather than being conceived as the socio-political play of shifting identities, democracy would in this model be conceived as pure difference itself—which is to say, a symbolic nothing—

misrecognized as an identity with positive characteristics. This is the phantasmatic element integral to the concept. And it is precisely at the level of misrecognition that neo-Lacanian discourse theory introduces the subject for the achievement of definition and identity, along with all the psychical forces, conscious and unconscious, that go with the subject.

To take these thoughts to their logical conclusion, would we then have to say that none of the four elements of the triangle "really exists" either, except insofar as there exists a certain political hegemony that allows us to designate them by the assigned signifiers and a concomitant *jouissance* in the phantasmatic order the triangle offers us? Transformations in meaning and content, the achievement of socio-political identity, and the effect of persuasion, then, are not merely a matter of contestation and articulation in the social arena but are already inherent in what discourse is and how it functions and must be taken to include partiality and incompleteness, on the one hand, and the phantasmatic suppositions of the subject, on the other. Rhetoric is one way to describe the emergent discourse of these entwined interplays because it works to shift fantasy frames, treat with (and evoke) *jouissance*, and ply the seams of metalinguistic positionality. That these aspects of rhetorical work elude fully conscious control, go awry, impede success, or present other difficulties is no argument against them. Rather, rhetoric and its workings remain complex, which shows, quite clearly, how much more we still must learn about the field, and that we cannot rest on classical and modernist laurels.

3

In the Funhouse
Mirroring Subjects and Objects

Foucault's work on the fields of discourse, on institutions, etc., and on their multifold interrelations with the construction and exercise of forms of social power is, of course, important. Still, his is work which provides no explanation, so far as I can tell, of the way in which discourses actually intersect with and in the "subject." . . . It may sound surprising to say this, especially since Foucault is frequently praised for emphasizing *both* the dominatory and the enabling function of power. However, it seems that Foucault's "subject" is more incapable than not of becoming an agent of large social change and that the supposedly enabling moments of power relations are subsumed under the "subject's" subjection.

—Paul Smith, *Discerning the Subject*

You think you're yourself, but there are other persons in you. Ambrose gets hard when Ambrose doesn't want to, and *obversely*. Ambrose watches them disagree; Ambrose watches them watch. In the funhouse mirror-room you can't see yourself go on forever, because no matter how you stand, your head gets in the way.

—John Barth, *Lost in the Funhouse*

ARLIER, I PROPOSED that subjectivity is temporal, meaning that it is constituted by the ongoing dynamics of retroactivity. Here I extend that discussion to include other forms of reflexivity pertaining to subjectivity as it emerges at the intersections of cultural studies, psychoanalysis, and rhetorical theory. I am especially interested in the ways poststructuralist accounts of subjectivity have been appropriated to politicize composition both in the classroom and as a discipline. Integral to these approaches is the idea that subjectivities are culturally produced, not naturally given, and that the production of subjectivities involves the deployment of power for social and political ends. In other words, the process of subjectivization is not an innocent one; at all times, various interests are being served in some capacity. The increased emphasis on the subject as something that is produced has resulted in a concomitant anxiety about the ways subjects can successfully wage resistance or achieve some measure of autonomy. Oftentimes, poststructuralist theories of the subject are equated with a loss of agency; since the subject is "produced," the argument goes, nothing remains of the subject that gives it the means to act outside of the various forces of production. As the quote above shows, Paul Smith takes his impetus from this debate, claiming that theories that privilege the process of subjectivization undermine the possibility for resistance (xxxi).

I want to look closely at the ways social-epistemic rhetoric and cultural studies work out this equation of the subject with the subjectivizing forces that produce it. Although the Lacanian subject is also produced through discourse, it is never reduced to or made equivalent with the subjectivizing forces of power and knowledge. The kind of agency that emerges from this perspective is in excess of a given contextual juncture. There is leeway in psychoanalytic thought between the subject and its symbolization/subjectivization that is not present in poststructuralist thought, especially of the Foucauldian variety. Indeed, it is precisely this absence of leeway that accounts for much of the criticism leveled at Foucault that he fails to provide a theory of agency (see Macdonell; Smith). However, such criticisms of Foucault work out of a preunderstood definition of agency marked by profound investments. Thus, the problem is not that Foucault fails to theorize agency adequately but that he theorizes agency in a way his critics cannot or will not recognize as agency (see Muckelbauer). In making my argument about subjectivization, I want to be careful that I am not read as joining with those who critique Foucault on this score. My point is quite different. Rather than arguing that Foucault does not supply a theory of agency, I am saying that the theories of agency that emerge in psychoanalytic and Foucauldian discourse are different. These differences have consequences for rhetorical inquiry into agency. My purpose is not to supplant one theory with the other but to attend to what each does and does not make available for thought and to explore the possible ramifications for rhetorical practices.

In *Read My Desire: Lacan against the Historicists*, Joan Copjec argues that Foucault's works, and especially the works of others who are influenced by but less nuanced than Foucault, are problematic when they reduce society and the subject to immanent relations of power and knowledge (5). Foucault, she points out, theorizes power not as an external force that acts on society but as something internal and immanent to the social field. It is well-known that this constitutes one of Foucault's greatest advances in understanding how power functions. His analysis of the prison in *Discipline and Punish*, for example, concerns the flow of power and the ways it works in and through the bodies of prisoners to obtain proper behavior. His oft-cited example of the panopticon—a guard tower in the center of the prison that obscures the observing guards from view so that the prisoners cannot know whether they are being watched—derives its power less from the external manifestation of potential force than from the prisoner's internalization of an omnipresent threat. In this way (in conjunction with other institutionalized forms of power particular to the prison), the prisoner becomes a properly "disciplined" body.[1] The prisoner is, of course, able to resist in a variety of ways; agency emerges precisely at this conjuncture of forces and their possible expressions. Thus, it makes little sense to claim that this way of theorizing power precludes agency. Agency is simply a matter of acting within multifarious power flows and their complex entwinements. We see that the subject can be conflicted and contradictory without resorting to some extradiscursive, extrasocial realm or asserting that there must be an autonomous or solid agentive core from which resistance stems. Nevertheless, while we might not claim that such a theory precludes agency, we should take note that the kind of agency that emerges is ultimately produced within extant social, historical, and discursive forces.

For Lacan and Žižek, agency is not solely a matter of production or counterproduction (resistance) in whatever complex admixtures one wants to claim. In Foucauldian/poststructuralist accounts, the social and historical "absorb" the entirety of the subject; this is what Copjec refers to as "historicism." In contradistinction, the Lacanian version suggests that socio-historical contingency is not everything. There is an unsymbolizable "something" around which a subjective identity forms, and this elusive quality—elusive in the sense that it cannot be pinned down or made determinate through signification—is something that the social cannot absorb. We might say that this uncanny X marks the limits of disciplinary power. In other words, the subject should be understood to include elements that cannot be made determinate through discourses of power and language, with the attendant consequence that the function of representation is insufficient for a direct accounting of subjectivity.

My position is that this conception of subjectivity is important for obtaining more sophisticated understandings of the ways discourse affects and shapes individuals, groups, and the world. If one of our goals as rhetoricians and teachers is to grapple with forms of discursive power and their manifestations in all aspects of life, then it is useful to have a theory of the subject that can explain subjective actions and effects in a way that is not reducible solely to discursive factors. As I elaborated earlier, affective forces are powerfully integrated into our everyday lives, and their elusiveness with regard to signification, while presenting challenges to rhetorical theory, underscores the importance of attending to them by what means we have. Nevertheless, I see my project as one not of either/or but of supplementation, mutual questioning, alternate paths. My challenge is to suggest what a psychoanalytic perspective can offer over and above the common cultural studies approaches that have achieved prominence in the field.

While the question of agency is paramount for designing particular pedagogical approaches, also key is the issue of what models of subjectivity we will utilize to understand our students, our discipline, and ourselves. The three major figures on whom I focus—James Berlin, Linda Brodkey, and Susan Miller—rely primarily on poststructuralist narratives of subjectivity for theorizing strategies for individual, group, and larger social change. Brodkey makes explicit her preference for Foucault over Lacan, and Berlin, too, is leery of Lacan because he fears that psychoanalytic discourse lends itself to easy accommodation by expressivist rhetorics that neglect the social in favor of the internal psyche (see Alcorn). I will analyze Brodkey's presentation of Lacan in order to emphasize the advantages of theorizing a divided subject over the poststructuralist notion of a subject who occupies varying discursive and socio-political positions, arguing that Lacan's theory of a divided subject provides advantages for understanding what agency is and how it emerges. Miller analyzes problems facing composition as a discipline that parallel remarkably the problems described as facing human subjects. She offers strategies for composition's achievement of identity and recognition as a subject, but she abandons too quickly the path of achieving identity through what Žižek calls identification with the *sinthome* in favor of the dialectic of recognition by the institutional Other. Implicated in her chosen strategies is the dominance she assigns to the metaphor of "the carnival," which is linked to her use of poststructuralist theories of the subject.[2] I propose instead the metaphor of the "funhouse" in order to reinscribe metaphorically the complexities presented by mirroring, representation, and the Other, as described by Žižek and Lacan. The carnival, as a metaphor, is useful for understanding high-low distinctions, as Miller and her predecessors (Bakhtin, Stallybrass, White, Foucault, and others) successfully demonstrate, but it is considerably less so for understanding problems concerning how one is represented symbolically for the Other—and thus achieving recognition from the Other.

In "Postmodernism, Politics, and Histories of Rhetoric," Berlin presents a paradigmatic version of poststructuralist-derived subjectivity for rhetoric and composition. Berlin writes, "The unified, coherent, autonomous, self-present subject of the Enlightenment has been the centerpiece of liberal humanism," a perception that is challenged by "the postmodern conception of the subject as the product of social and material conditions, more particularly, as the effect of the signifying practices of a given historical moment" (171). For Berlin and other compositionists who helped introduce postmodern ideas to the field, the subject is conflicted and contradictory, composed of a multitude of competing discourses and signifying practices that derail pretensions to unity, self-presence, and coherence. As I argued earlier, this notion of the subject is substantially different from the neo-Aristotelian subject proposed by Kinneavy for the communications triangle. The model of the subject as an encoder who uses language corresponds to the Enlightenment subject that is challenged by postmodern theory. However, given that Kinneavy's intention was to ground his theory in language, the poststructuralist notion of the subject as a discursive effect can be considered an extension or refinement rather than a negation of subjectivity. It is also the case that much postmodern theory has moved the discussion far outside of the comfort zones of many scholars. For this reason, numerous scholars are now seeking a return to a modernist understanding of subjectivity or, if they are leery of a return, maintain skepticism regarding postmodernism's alleged advances.

In *Fragments of Rationality*, Faigley presents the problem of the postmodern subject succinctly, while also arguing against the reduction of the subject to discursive practices: "The tools of linguistic analysis can be useful in analyzing how subject positions are constructed in particular discourses. The notion of subjectivity itself, however, is far too complex to be 'read off' from texts. It is a far more complex notion than that of 'roles' because it is a conglomeration of temporary positions rather than a coherent identity; it allows for the interaction of a person's participation in other discourses and experiences in the world with the positions in particular discourses; and it resists deterministic explanations because a subject always exceeds a momentary subject position" (110). Faigley correctly points to the problem of theorizing the subject: it is far too complex to be determined solely on the basis of texts or roles. In fact, the basic gambit of his book, that many arguments in composition can be traced to disputes about subjectivity, is sound. At the same time, however, a distinct problem reemerges here: claims about the complexity of the subject are all well and good, but the crux of the matter for any theoretical intervention is how this complexity is to be explained. Faigley is unable to provide such an explanation, which has consequences for his argument. For example, in his final chapter, Faigley examines Iris Young's notion of the urban subject and Lyotard's notion of ethics in order to theorize a *responsible* postmodern subject. According to Faigley, Young conceives the subject in typical postmodern fashion, as a "play of differences that cannot be reduced to a whole," which would include the organizational uses to which notions of community are put (232). Faigley joins Young in advocating "an urban subjectivity open to unassimilated otherness," with the city modeling this possibility as an alternative to liberal humanism and the utopian ideal of community (232). Lyotard, argues Faigley, allows us to conceive "at a microlevel how urban subjects encounter boundaries in both crossing social divisions and in the personal experience of negotiating among many competing discourses" (239).

Faigley's readings of Lyotard and Young have in common a notion of a rhetorical subject amenable to positioning, as indicated by the concept of "negotiation." Subjects (rhetorically) negotiate different positions, boundary crossings, cultural roles, and so on. As I argued earlier, however, this conception ignores what we might call the "sticking points" of subjectivity, in particular affective forces like identification, desire, fantasy, and *jouissance*. This means, among other things, that the postmodern impasse is still implicit in what Faigley offers as a solution. It may be that Faigley at some level understands this limitation himself, since he closes his argument—and his book—with a call to respect difference and to acknowledge the limits of human understanding. His final lines state: "Ethics is also the obligation of rhetoric. It is accepting the responsibility for judgment. It is pausing to reflect on the limits of understanding. It is respect for diversity and unassimilated otherness. It is finding the spaces to listen" (239). Faigley's exhortations here are engaging and inspiring, but at the same time a certain triteness resonates in his "we're all in this together" pluralism. In the age of media amplification (the age of the boom box, we might say), the problem is not just that it is sometimes difficult to find the spaces to listen; it is that oftentimes it is no longer in our interests to do so. Or, as Žižek states, "Love thy neighbor? No, thanks!" (*Plague* 45). Žižek may be glib, but he points to a genuine problem most of us are at pains to avoid: there is only so much of the Other we can stand (*Plague* 67–68). Thus, while I might want to uphold the call for respect and understanding, I know that I cannot aspire to live up to its demands as an absolute in my everyday life. In fact, people would want to challenge such an ethic on innumerable occasions; instances of competition and struggle immediately come to mind as examples. We might then wonder whether our theoretical scholarship and everyday pedagogies should be placed under such an impossible ideal.

What Berlin, Brodkey, Faigley, Miller, and other scholars who rely on poststructuralist theories derived from Foucault and Derrida seem to have in common, then, is an understanding of the subject that is predicated on the notion of occupying and negotiating different socio-historical positions and the belief that movements among these positions can be induced by various rhetorical means, including exhortations of goodwill, respect for difference, toleration, and other tropes of cultural studies. Berlin makes this explicit when he draws on Paul Smith's *Discerning the Subject* to reclaim the possibility of agency (or, more correctly, a specific kind of agency). Smith and Berlin suggest that as each agent negotiates among different subject positions, the content and development of those positions also change, so that every individual can retain a capacity for action and uniqueness. Berlin grants that this does not mean that anything is possible, but he adds that it does mean that something is possible, as far as that something is perceived as happening within specific material and discursive constraints ("Postmodernism" 174). Brodkey, too, invokes this understanding of the subject as inhabiting differing positions in socio-historical space when she advocates the usefulness of the concept of "articulation" for rhetorical theory; agency as resistance, she claims, particularly benefits from this conception (*Writing* 23). Faigley admits ambivalence about the possibilities for agency in postmodern theory, claiming that it has not produced a "broad theory of agency that would lead directly . . . to political action" (*Fragments* 39). As I have argued, he nevertheless relies on a conception of the subject as occupying differing positions in constructing the primary thesis of his book: many of the conflicts in composition are centered on disagreements over what subjectivities students are to occupy (17). Faigley is self-reflexive enough to acknowledge the disparities among notions of subjectivity, but he falls back into a default notion of subjectivity as positioning, most likely because he lacks a conception of the subject that would allow him to escape the impasse he charts.

I suggest that the first place to rebegin theorizing the subject is precisely here, at the impasse between the subject qua positionality and the attempt to retain a conception of agency that does not fall back into humanist notions of an autonomous self. Rather than conceiving this problem as a barrier to be surmounted, we might conceive it phenomenologically as a primary condition of possibility for the subject. In *Tarrying with the Negative*, Žižek argues that the discursive subject of postmodern theory—the dispersed, plural, constructed subject—is not radically subversive but merely the kind of subjectivity that corresponds to late capitalism (216). A subject able to reposition itself as required is well suited to contemporary life. A fixed subject is undesirable insofar as it becomes "an obstacle to the unbridled commodification of everyday life" (216). We see here already in germinal form the problem so often confronted in the practical classroom application of cultural studies pedagogies: adaptable students easily accommodate themselves to what the curriculum requires, but there is little evidence that much of what is taught sticks—except perhaps the very lesson in flexibility. From critiquing objectionable advertisements to analyzing sexist television programs, the mutable student-subject can easily accomplish the required tasks. The real problem is inevitably the "fixed" subject. The stereotypical "biased" student who refuses to adapt or actively resists changing positions or shifting boundaries becomes the primary problem requiring redress. In some sense, this is precisely the reason for the resurgence of the problem concerning subjectivity.

The ostensible solution to this problem is to find the "right" way to theorize the subject, which brings us back to the postmodern impasse described by Faigley and others. Perhaps a better way to proceed is to stop seeing this inability to pin down the truth of subjectivity and lay bare its contingent, sociohistorical givenness within flows of power as a problem in the first place. What if our theoretical insufficiency regarding the essential core of subjectivity were reconceived as insight rather than blockage? This is where Žižek, taking cues from Hegel and Lacan, begins. Subjectivity emerges at our theoretical, symbolic limits, as the positive manifestation of the limit of the symbolic order to adequately represent the subject or, differently put, as a nonsubstantial empty point of self-consciousness whose contours evade all symbolization. However, this "point" is far from being the fixed, autonomous subject attributed to modernism. In line with the psychoanalytic tradition, Žižek posits a radically decentered subject, one that is divided across the symbolic order, the intersubjective realm, and its representation of itself to itself (i.e., in the way we are not self-present to ourselves).

This theory of the subject is integrated into a way of understanding and reading discourse called "speculative reading," and Žižek's favorite example of it comes from Hegel's *Phenomenology of Spirit*, on the passage from physiognomy to phrenology. Here Hegel cryptically states that "spirit is a bone." On first reading, this seems to be a non sequitur, like saying X is Y or an apple is an orange. But this is the kind of direct apprehension that speculative reading means to overcome. Žižek explains that Hegel is demonstrating how materiality can be invested with the ephemeral quality of sublimity. The Kantian sublime describes "the paradox of an object which, in the very field of representation, provides a view, in a negative way, of the dimension of what is unrepresentable" (Žižek, *Tarrying* 203). For Kant, the sublime was the experience of a "beyond" of representation indicated by the failure of the object to reach the Thing-in-itself. Hegel objects to this view of the sublime, claiming that Kant remained a prisoner of the field of representation. Žižek writes:

Precisely when we determine the Thing as a transcendent surplus beyond what can be represented, we determine it on the basis of the field of representation, starting from it, within its horizon, as its negative limit: the (Jewish) notion of God as radical Otherness, as unrepresentable, still remains the extreme point of the logic of representation. . . . Hegel's position is, in contrast, that there is *nothing* beyond phenomenality, beyond the field of representation. The experience of radical negativity, of the radical inadequacy of all phenomena to the Idea, the experience of the radical fissure between the two—this experience is already *Idea itself as "pure," radical negativity.* (205)

The proposition "spirit is a bone" achieves its meaning similarly, through the failure of the first, immediate reading. Žižek states that in Kant, "the feeling of the Sublime is evoked by some boundless, terrifying imposing phenomena (raging nature, and so on), while in Hegel we are dealing with some miserable 'little piece of the Real'" (*Sublime* 207). The Kantian sublime is evoked in terrifying and grandiose landscapes, tumultuous storms, and vertiginous mountains. The Hegelian sublime is of a different order. Sure, "spirit" is sublime, transcendent, unrepresentable, yet it is inevitably embodied in some material leftover. It cannot remain in the dimension of purely posited existence. Thus, "spirit is a bone" must be understood doubly: the failure of the first meaning—that spirit cannot possibly be a bone, that it must be much more than that—gives rise to the second meaning—that no proper signifier or object would be adequate for spirit's representation. The bone is a positive object whose presence fills out the impossibility of the representation of spirit. The sublimity of spirit, then, is already evoked in base materiality. The frailty of Mother Teresa, for instance, can also symbolically express the holy. Countless other examples could be brought forward—the sublime, after all, surrounds us. Žižek concludes that the proposition "spirit is a bone" is "correlative to the subject in so far as—in Lacanian theory—the subject is *nothing but* the impossibility of its own signifying representation—the empty place opened up in the big Other by the failure of this representation" (*Sublime* 208).

The subject may arise out of the impasse between empirical phenomena and the failure of the signifier to achieve adequate representation, but this does not explain how the subject achieves identity. In *Tarrying with the Negative*, Žižek again utilizes Hegel to explain the dialectical process in which a subject's identity emerges. Identity is not a simple one-to-one correspondence, where bird is a bird, or green is green; rather, it is "an essence which 'stays the same' beyond the ever-changing flow of appearances" (130). When we try to identify something, it becomes apparent that we typically identify it by means of its differential features (the characteristics that make it distinct from other things). Even when we try to identify something in its essentiality, we do so by separating it from other things; however, none of these differences is finally determinate. A person is a mother only in relation to a father or daughter, yet in another relation she is herself a daughter. What is crucial here is that within this notion of identity *contradiction already exists*. Žižek explains that "'contradiction' designates the antagonistic relationship between what I am 'for the others'—my symbolic determination—and what am 'in myself,' abstractedly from my relations with others" (*Tarrying* 131). We return again to the impasse of the failure of the signifier to achieve an adequate representation of its signified. Though "mother" may designate a particular person, she also exceeds that symbolic mandate. Žižek states, "Outside of my relations to the others I am nothing, I am only the cluster of these relations . . . but this very 'nothing' is the nothing of pure self-relating: I am only what I am for the others, yet simultaneously I am the one who self-determines myself, i.e., who determines which network of relations to others will determine me" (131–32). Thus, the subject is what maintains its identity through all the differing modes of representation in the symbolic. But it also remains a void because no signifier can give it final, determinate expression. Thus, in contradistinction to much postmodern theory, identity is not just positionality. While the subject retroactively constructs itself by threading itself through the symbolic and its past by means of its involvements with others and society, it remains fissured by its symbolic contradictions. No position is equal to its sense of what "it" is because this sense of "it-ness" appears as a sublime object, even if there is no "object" there to shine forth sublimely.

I should add that this is far less abstract than it may sound. It is a commonplace of parents that they can identify character traits in their children that continue to show up long into adult life—my parents, at least, never tired of telling me of things I did as a child that somehow bespoke attitudes and behaviors of my adult life. We recognize such traits in our friends as well. What is uncanny is that, while we may be able to describe such traits, in the end, these descriptions are only partial, temporary, or contingent. Some new wrinkle in that trait will emerge later, requiring redescription. We coin odd locutions to account for this, like "look at Friedrich being Friedrich." The thing to note is how the tautology functions akin to Hegel's proposition that spirit is a bone, evoking the sublime, unifying trait of personality in some mundane yet nevertheless remarkable action.

We have seen that the influx of postmodern theory into rhetoric and composition has wrought extensive transformations in the way the subject is conceived. This reception is perhaps best exemplified by Berlin; the astonishing transformation between his 1987 book, *Rhetoric and Reality*, and his last, *Rhetorics, Poetics, and Cultures*, is indicative of his vast amount of theoretical woodshedding. Nevertheless, certain gaps are present between what Berlin learned in his research and his rather less advanced pedagogical practice. The key to understanding this problem lies in examining how Berlin deploys postmodern theory to explain subjectivity. It will be useful to consider a lengthy passage for understanding the nuances of Berlin's melding of social-epistemic rhetoric with the challenges postmodern theory brings to bear on any unified and coherent notion of the subject. Berlin writes:

The speaking, acting subject is no longer considered unified, rational, autonomous, or self-present. Instead, each person is regarded as the construction of the various signifying practices, the uses of language and cultural codes, of a given historical moment. In other words, the subject is not the source and origin of these practices but is finally their product. This means that each of us is formed by the various discourses and sign systems that surround us. These include not only everyday uses of language (discursive formations) in the home, school, the media, and other institutions, but the material conditions (non-discursive formations) that are arranged in the manner of languages— that is, semiotically—including such things as the clothes we wear, the way we carry our bodies, and the way our school and home environments are arranged. These signifying practices are languages that tell us who we are and how we should behave in terms of such categories as gender, race, class, age, ethnicity, and the like. The result is that each of us is heterogeneously made up of various competing discourses, conflicted and contradictory scripts, that make our consciousness anything but unified, coherent, and autonomous. . . . To state the case in its most extreme form, each of us is finally conflicted, incoherent, amorphous, protean, and irrational in our very constitution. (*Rhetorics* 62–63)

From this passage it is clear that in theory Berlin accepts many of the arguments that postmodernists have made against the rational, autonomous, and unified modernist subject. Furthermore, Berlin implicitly makes arguments for the primacy of rhetoric in conceptions of the subject when he grounds subjectivity in language, making the subject an effect produced through a wide confluence of signifying practices. These "discourses and sign systems that surround us" are a varied lot, including discursive and nondiscursive formations. The common element uniting these disparate practices is that they can all be understood to operate as a language. As we shall see, Berlin's semiotic understanding of signifying practices has specific consequences for his pedagogy. He posits a subject malleable enough to generate critical distance, without an attendant consideration of the sticking points along the way that show up as student resistance.

Berlin's emphasis on the linguistic nature of signifying practices also includes the idea that the sheer number of competing codes introduces a fundamental discord into subjectivity. Codes and discourses are numerous, contradictory, conflicted, and, significantly, caught up with nonrational and affective influences. What remains murky is how we can theorize the linguistic nature of what is nonrational and affective. What we might mean by the terms *rational* and *nonrational* remains particularly unclear. The rational can be defined as that which follows the precepts of reason and logic, but the term is often used to indicate simply what can be articulated. The idea of "making rational" harkens back to the Enlightenment project itself (and to a particularly significant and pervasive ideological gesture): to bring something to light by means of logical discourse. The nonrational, as a concept, would then refer to what resists or falls out of the attempt at logical discourse; accordingly, it is often characterized as the darkness for which the light of reason will serve as a corrective. For psychoanalytic theory, phenomena like chance (Aristotle's *tuche*), the Real, *jouissance,* and the unconscious are examples of what remains beyond the bounds of the rational in the sense that they cannot be spoken or assigned a traditional logic. Berlin's rhetorical theory acknowledges the existence of these other elements, but it does not really use them and so finally remains concerned with what is significant, defined as what signifies in a semiotic system. In this way, too, Berlin's work remains tied to the modernist strategy of bringing the light of reason to (what is constructed as) the darkness of nonrationality, and the significant can be seen to parallel that which can be made rational and conscious. Tellingly, none of Berlin's work on ideology focuses on the ideological basis for this valuation. In addition, the emphasis on determination aligns itself with the logic of positionality. So while the subject is unstable, conflicted, and contingent, rhetorical positions can be determined or mapped out, at least with sufficient force to carry out desired political or pedagogical goals.

From another perspective, Berlin's understanding of the significant as the signifiable can be seen in his assessment of the work of Victor Vitanza, who has lauded the power and presence of nonrational, unconscious, and otherwise indeterminate or excluded elements in all aspects of human interaction.[3] While Berlin might acknowledge this on one level, on another he backtracks. He states that Vitanza's "incisive and witty explorations" show us "the formidable challenges of constructing a postmodern rhetoric" but then goes on to admit, "my proposals will still seem rationalistic and excessively systematic to [Vitanza]" (*Rhetorics* 69). Berlin indicates that to some degree Vitanza's work lacks value; it is only witty exploration. We can compare this assessment with those of other theorists Berlin utilizes. Paul Smith is "effective" in address- ing his chosen issues (69), Cornel West provides "telling criticism" (72), and Teresa Ebert "offers a scheme" that is "useful" (75). These theorists cited by Berlin thus provide effective, critical, and useful discourses for a social-epis- temic rhetoric. Together these examples sketch a road map for what is signifi- cant, in the double sense of what matters and what signifies. Berlin's claim to provide a space for indeterminacy is belied by his drive to discern the most useful semiotic codes for specific political goals. What is significant, then, is goal oriented and overtly political: critique, usefulness, and effectiveness. In comparison to the determinate, which is significant, the indeterminate is ulti- mately insignificant and useless.

CRITIQUES OF BERLIN: ALCORN AND MCCOMISKEY

Where does this leave Berlin's conception of the subject? Although he de- scribes the subject as being in theory "conflicted, incoherent, amorphous, protean, and irrational," in practice these qualities of irrationality and inde- terminateness vanish. The question becomes: is this notion of the subject sufficient to achieve the goals Berlin and other social-epistemic rhetoricians desire? If what is wanted is "a commitment to democratic practices" and the rhetorical competence to present one's position effectively ("Composition" 116), can a theory of the subject that privileges the determinate and rational account for the ways these goals are resisted and subverted in practice? In his excellent 1995 essay "Changing the Subject of Postmodern Theory," Mar- shall Alcorn Jr. argues that the answer to these questions is no. As he puts it, "Postmodern theory is still in a state of evolution, and its current account of the subject is, I think, insufficiently complex for understanding relationships among language, subjectivity, and ideology" (331–32).

Alcorn's project is to introduce Lacanian theory into discussions about the discursive construction of the subject. He examines the contradictions in Ber- lin's account of the subject and suggests what benefits might accrue from the adoption of a Lacanian model of subjectivity. Berlin, Alcorn charges, describes a "*constructed* subject in theory, but a *free* subject in classroom practice" (334). Many poststructuralist theories—the accounts of Derrida, Foucault, and Al- thusser—emphasize the passive nature of the subject. As an effect of discourse and ideology, the subject is quite literally subjected; in this model, while re- sistance to ideology can be accounted for, accounts about the capacity for ideological change remain slippery (336). Alcorn notes that Smith tackles this problem in *Discerning the Subject*, a book Berlin relies on, too. Smith utilizes Lacanian theory, as does Alcorn, to provide a more complex notion of the subject that incorporates the mediatory function of the unconscious in human affairs and depends on conflict in terms of external *and* internal discursive and socio-political positions. Alcorn states that Smith easily explains "the subject's potential for fluid transformation" (337). Unexplained, though, is the subject's resistance to transformation. From Alcorn's perspective, Smith and Berlin share the common problem of moving too quickly from a notion of the subject as a construct to a notion of the subject that retains its agency. In what sense is the subject both a passive construct and an active agent, and how are we to understand the passage from one to the other?

Alcorn suggests that one way to approach this question is to consider the phenomenon of student resistance. In any given class, certain ideas can generate resistance if not hostility from students. This predicament is captured in the commonplace adage "better dead than red," in which a political subject will choose biological over ideological death. Students often prefer biological death—which, in an educational context, is more likely "academic death" in the form of a bad grade—to ideological death. That is to say, there remains in subjects "something" that "operates to preserve and maintain a characteristic identity" (337–38). Although subjects are subjected to ideological discourse, they are not and cannot be theorized as being synonymous with it. Thus, even though Berlin acknowledges how the constructed subject is conflicted, he cannot acknowledge how these conflicts, while significant, nevertheless only describe a fraction of human subjectivity. Berlin claims that resistance is always possible because "contradictions between signified and signifier . . . continually provoke opposition to hegemonic ideologies" (*Rhetorics* 74). The difference between Alcorn/Lacan's and Berlin/Smith's conceptions of the subject hinges on this point: is ideological contradiction alone sufficient to account for agency and resistance?

It is at this juncture that I want to introduce another voice into the discussion concerning subjectivity in cultural studies composition pedagogies. In "Composing Postmodern Subjectivities in the Aporia between Identity and Difference," Bruce McComiskey charges, "Berlin's pedagogy ultimately maintains a modernist conception of the writing Subject as a product of identity/difference oppositions" (354). In other words, the notion of contradiction utilized by Berlin is primarily dependent on a modernist, structuralist binary logic. The result of this insistence on identity/difference—either democratic or capitalist, for example—is that students are led to discover binary oppositions without being able to move beyond simple agreement or disagreement, accommodation or resistance. In other words, the reading strategy that produces the discovery of the binary oppositions also works to disallow responses other than a similar binary opposition. Although McComiskey does not make the point explicitly, the upshot of his argument is that the common point between Berlin's theory of the subject and his pedagogy is an insufficient conception of conflict. McComiskey accepts that agency can arise from ideological contradiction, but he is critical of the pedagogical possibilities of contradiction when it depends on binary logic.

McComiskey's argument is compelling, but I am wary of his inability to move beyond the theory of discourse employed by Berlin. In the end, he remains just as enmeshed in the idea that agency arises from multiple, conflicting subject positions. In contradistinction, Alcorn argues that if the postmodern subject is in fact nothing but conflicting strands of embodied discourse, then any time it attempts to step outside of that conflict, "the subject reveals itself to be, in fact, not the conflict it claimed to be," and hence, "it reveals itself as something other than a mere passive effect of discourse" (340). Similarly, if a particular strand of discourse produces change in a subject, it is unclear what occurs that allows one discourse structure to transform another (341). In short, the notion of contradiction that underscores subjectivity should also take into consideration those forms of contradiction that elude easy translation into discourse. The challenge here is to find a way, in Lyotard's words, to "be witnesses to the unpresentable" (*Postmodern* 82). In other words, we should make space for the indeterminate aspects of subjectivity in our theories of subjectivity but do so in a way that declines to reduce them to the determinate.

These theoretical considerations have a bearing on pedagogical practice. For example, Berlin describes a typical classroom scene in which students are asked to identify and analyze terms functioning as key signifiers: "Students place these terms within the narrative structural forms suggested by the text, the culturally coded stories about patterns of behavior appropriate for people within certain situations. These codes deal with such social designations as race, class, gender, sexual orientation, age, ethnicity, and the like. Students analyze, discuss, and write about the position of the key terms within these socially constructed narrative codes" (*Rhetorics* 118). As Berlin leads his students to identify the ideologies operating through these terms and the codes in which they are embedded, they in turn disagree about how much stock to place in these terms, narratives, and interpretations. Nevertheless, these acts of critique and analysis contribute toward students becoming "reflective agents actively involved in shaping their own consciousness as well as the democratic society of which they are a part" (124). In this classroom scenario, all codes are questioned (131). Berlin asserts that students quickly internalize this pedagogy, noting that since they engage in peer critiques of each other's drafts, "unreflective generalizations about the inevitability of class, race, gender, or age behavior never go unchallenged" (129).

Certain assumptions are operative here. First, Berlin assumes that ideological conflict is primarily if not solely transmitted through cultural codes and hierarchically arranged binaries (as seen in the above discussion of McComiskey). Furthermore, these conflicts are understood as easily apprehended through demonstration and discussion or, in other words, through commonplace pedagogical techniques that foreground easily determinable factors. The conflicts that arise among students are only manifestations of a burgeoning critical sensibility predicated on the rational apprehension of determinate, conscious forces, not, for example, the emergence of desire and unconscious identifications. Indeed, Berlin is so sure of their abilities that he asserts that unreflective generalizations never go unchallenged in his classroom. Even granting Berlin some pedagogical license here, it seems that he sincerely believes that his students are incapable of imitating the critical procedures he demands (for a grade) by cynically pretending to be reflective without an attendant internalization of this form of knowledge production. He believes instead that he has, through his pedagogy, persuaded them to accept their once and future roles as critical agents.

Such a pedagogy may indeed sound reasonable on the surface. Berlin is eminently correct to suggest that pointing out conflicts in what appears to be a seamless whole can introduce cognitive dissonance and thereby also the possibility of change. But we should be wary of assigning too much weight to this possibility. Perhaps a concrete scenario, arrived at through a paraphrase, can reorient our perceptions. In "The Subject of Discourse," John Clifford sharply critiques the *St. Martin's Guide* because it makes recommendations for persuasion that are devoid of any of the real contextual factors that make up an actual argumentative situation. Clifford states, "I can just imagine my students using cogent reasons and cold facts to persuade Jesse Helms to support abortion rights or funding for AIDS patients, or perhaps students could use logic and statistics to persuade their professors to give up tenure" (44). Let us rephrase Clifford's statement to reflect Berlin's pedagogy: "I can just imagine Oral Roberts analyzing cultural codes on abortion rights or reversing the hierarchical binary between heterosexual and homosexual valuations and, after experiencing cognitive dissonance, coming around to a pluralist, liberal point of view, or perhaps college professors could self-reflexively examine the ways in which tenure contributes to the exploitation of graduate teachers and adjuncts and voluntarily agree to give it up."

Staged in this manner, Berlin's pedagogy may seem less compelling because we immediately open ourselves to nondiscursive, affective realms of human behavior—precisely those aspects of the subject that preclude determinateness. In trying to understand where Berlin is insufficient, Alcorn finds that he "describes ideological conflict as if it were a linguistic code a subject could logically read or write . . . and wants to be rational and appeal to the subject's ability to recognize conflictual codings and be free from bad conflict" (342). Alcorn further asserts contra Berlin that we must do more than acknowledge how descriptions of discourse and the subject must transcend the strictly rational. Rather, we must "discover, recognize, and take responsibility for the unconscious libidinal codes of desire and repression that underwrite [our] own subjectivity" (343). For Alcorn, personal growth and pedagogy are linked by the idea that coming to terms with what we do not know about what motivates us must be a primary function. It is precisely this orientation toward self-conscious awareness, personal and cultural, that links the projects of Alcorn and Berlin. In fact, we see here that Alcorn may amend and correct Berlin's theory of subjectivity, but he does so while remaining in the sway of a basic cultural studies pedagogical orientation, one that transposes the greatest obligation and responsibility of the student to the social. Where the approaches differ is in how they theorize a subject that can achieve such awareness. Alcorn urges us far more than Berlin to accept greater responsibility for what is harder to define or codify, for those aspects of our existence that resist being coded or made conscious and rational.

In a comment on Alcorn's essay, Berlin writes that he largely agrees with Alcorn's charge that he needs a more Lacanian description of the subject and has begun reading accordingly (Alcorn, "Changing" 344). Although this revision in thought arrived too late for Berlin to pursue it further, it can be inferred that the accommodation of Lacan could only have occurred within the parameters of the social-epistemic rhetoric he favored. Indeterminacy—of meaning-making, of truth, of subjectivity—has, from Berlin's perspective, the unfortunate effect of impeding education's goal: "to provide intelligent, articulate, and responsible citizens who understand their obligation and their right to insist that economic, social, and political power be exerted in the best interests of the community" (*Rhetorics* 52). Progress can only be achieved through the determinate or what can be made determinate, including the subject in its formation and its interactions with others and the world. Thus, Berlin's theory of the subject is ultimately a quasi-postmodernist one fundamentally at odds with the Lacanian subject, which, I am claiming, is ultimately less determinate and more flexible, especially for theorizing agency and resistance.

The understanding of subjectivity that Žižek brings to Lacan is strikingly different from most appropriations of Lacan made by scholars in rhetoric and composition. Linda Brodkey is a useful example in this regard. Her stated preference for Foucault, and the limitations of her reading of Lacan, shed light on the differences between poststructuralist and psychoanalytic theories of subjectivity. At the same time, her work can increase our insight into why one approach has been preferred over the other. I do not argue that in choosing the Lacanian path, we must necessarily exclude the Foucauldian path. Instead, I seek to show what could be gained from a more productive engagement with neo-Lacanian theory. Thus, given that Brodkey's reduction of Lacanian theory to the mirror stage is what allows Foucault to shine all the more brightly in her project, my goal is not so much to attack her Foucauldian-derived discourse theories as to broaden and complicate her reading of Lacan. Indeed, I like to think of Lacan as Brodkey's repressed, as evidenced by the omission of his name from the index to *Writing Permitted in Designated Areas Only*, even though Brodkey discusses his work.

Brodkey admits that her reading of Lacan is simplified (*Writing* 12). What that means for her readers is that Lacan has been reduced almost exclusively to the early Lacan of the mirror stage (see *Ecrits*). Brodkey explains Lacan's theory that the child accedes to the symbolic by way of the mirror; this process traumatizes the child into understanding that it is now completely separate from the mother. The symbolic becomes the means to rectify this fundamental fissure and reacquire the former oneness it once experienced. Brodkey, after her explanation, goes on to assert that "the plot is familiar." She explains: "It is a thoroughly modern romance, a quest—of the self for the self—in which the grail is language qua discourse. Discourse, in this version, replaces the sense of being one with self, other, and the world with a discursive practice that constantly maintains the illusion of a self unified as 'I.' . . . The discursive unity is only an illusion but a necessary (healthy) one, according to Lacan, if we are to survive the trauma of split or divided subjectivity" (*Writing* 12–13). Brodkey correctly identifies discourse as the thing that will allow the Lacanian subject to maintain a sense of unity in the face of the traumatic and Real condition of being constitutively fissured. What Brodkey neglects to mention is that even at this basic level in Lacan things are more complex than they appear. Certainly she is right that a palliative identity is constructed in the symbolic, but it is equally true that the subject is also alienated in those signifiers. In other words, subjectivity in Lacan cannot be theorized apart from this dialectic in which the subject is continually striving to achieve through the symbolic a unique and full expression, in spite of the traumatic Real impossibility of ever succeeding. As discussed above, it is for this antirepresentational reason—that no signifiers ever suffice—that the subject is properly "represented" only as a negative magnitude or the insufficiency of signifiers to fulfill their symbolic promise.

What Brodkey elides in her description of the mirror stage is the constitutive role of misrecognition (*meconnaissance*) for the achievement of subjective identity. Žižek explains, "we are autonomous subjects only to the extent that we misrecognize ourselves that way" (*Tarrying* 218). As Žižek amends Lacan via Hegel, the subject is always "positing its own presuppositions" (*For* 189–90). The subject is an effect of retroactive performativity in which an action, a decision, or a valuation comes after the fact (*Nachträglichkeit*)—after it has been enacted or actualized. The effect of this retroactive action is to create the appearance that the subject might always be identified this way. Identity, then, should be thought of in terms of temporality, an always ongoing and retroactive process. Stability-in-identity is little more than a perspective illusion brought about by means of retroactive movement. Brodkey omits this aspect of Lacanian subjectivity, asserting instead that in Lacan "discourse is thought to unify the self divided during infancy" (*Writing* 19). What should be clear is that the "unity" provided by discourse is in fact traumatically unstable, and this trauma, of course, feeds the desire of the subject to continue trying to find expression in the symbolic.

Brodkey's reading of Lacan sets up her presentation of Foucault, whom she sees as offering a superior narrative. As she explains: "In a Foucauldian narrative, by contrast, discourse concerns not the internal relations of psychoanalysis, but external relations between self and other and self and the world that are arguably alienating. . . . I think it is important to distinguish the multiply determined human subject in Foucault's work from the singly determined human subject in Lacan's" (19). I will mention in passing that the delineation between Lacan and Foucault is even murkier than this discussion intimates because of Foucault's own struggles with psychoanalytic narratives, which Derrida characterized as an "interminable and inexhaustible *fort-da*" toward Freud.[4] Perhaps it would simply be better not to divide Foucault and Lacan on the basis of multiply versus singly determined models of human subjectivity. The Lacanian subject, being fundamentally fissured with no possibility of unity—through discourse or otherwise—is *multiply indeterminate*. My suggestion is that Brodkey, like Berlin, prefers Foucauldian narratives centered on the subjectivizing and disciplining capacities of power/knowledge discourses because they can be made *determinate* and hence easily converted for use in the political arena. This loss of indeterminacy brings us back around to a theory of agency or resistance explained in terms of positionings and negotiations within power structures.

GOING BEYOND THE MIRROR

The basic premise of Lacanian ontology, states Žižek, is that "if our experience of reality is to maintain its consistency, the positive field of reality has to be 'sutured' with a supplement which the subject (mis)perceives as a positive entity, but is effectively a 'negative magnitude'" (*Plague* 81). As we have seen, this premise is applicable to human subjectivity as well. The subject is continuously engaged in a dialectic with the symbolic in which it appropriates a signifier that is ultimately alienating (such signifiers make us determinate for ourselves and for others in ways that suppress additional aspects of who we are) and insufficient (they fail to express us fully or wholly). In this sense, the subject is a void—but a void produced by the symbolic. Furthermore, this process necessitates that the discursive fields within which we conduct our affairs maintain a minimum of consistency. We are familiar with the poststructuralist understanding of discourse as opening up to free play and the endless semiosis of the sign, but Žižek wants to underscore how discursive consistency is necessary for constituting the subject's basic sense of reality. This minimum of consistency, however, is phantasmatic; it is posited by a subject. The "supplement" that Žižek discusses is the element that stands in for the impossibility of the field's consistency; what makes it "supplemental" is that it is excluded, or dropped, from the discursive field. In other words, discursive reality is neither whole nor consistent, but we make it so in our phantasmatic activity. This activity involves supplementing the symbolic field with a signifier that we take for an actual entity. As we shall see, this process can have pernicious effects when others—like a racial or ethnic group—take on the role of signifying the lack of social wholeness. Suddenly, they become "responsible" for a social problem that is entirely phantasmatic in the first place.

Just as the subject is a void that maintains the appearance of singular identity, so, too, is a discursive field something uncanny or unbalanced that gives the appearance of consistency. The "supplemental" element that maintains the field's consistency is connected to the void of the subject by the fact that both are negative magnitudes taken for positive elements. Thus, what sets the metonymic process of desire in motion is an element that stands for nothing, that shares a place in the "metonymy of lack" (Žižek, *Plague* 81). We can now see that, for Žižek, elements that function as negative magnitudes are "supplemental" in two senses: they function as support for the consistency of a subject or discursive field, and they fill out or stand in for what is not there. This relation between negative magnitudes hooks a subject into a discourse. The appearance of consistency in a symbolic field indicates the way the desire of the subject has already attached itself to an object within that field. Symbolic consistency and subjective identity, therefore, are achieved by means of affective processes—they are not a priori pregivens.

Lacan designates the inseparability of these two realms—the symbolic order and other existing subjects—with the phrase "the big Other." As Žižek explains it, the big Other is not only the impersonal symbolic order but also the radical alterity of the other person beyond our mirroring (*For* 199). Again, Brodkey claims that one of the reasons she prefers Foucault to Lacan is that Foucault moves beyond Lacan's emphasis on internal relations toward external relations between self and Other and self and world (*Writing* 19). It should be clear, however, that this is only a partial understanding of the Lacanian project. Although Brodkey accurately notes that a constitutive aspect of the subject is the internal disjunction between consciousness and the unconscious, it is unfortunate that she dismisses how externality, in the form of the symbolic and other subjects, is equally crucial to the formation of the subject. Since all attempts to understand other subjects necessarily involve our own misperceptions of who they are (because we cannot think from the impossible place of our Others and only have recourse to the slipperiness of communication and interpretation), understanding is always in part a function of who we are. Understanding occurs within our own phantasmatic frame and desires, impeding any "pure" access to the Other. Rhetorically, this moves us far beyond identification as a key modality for intersubjective relations, suggesting that unconscious elements of appropriation or imposition are at work in our symbolic interactions.

This opens us to the question of how desire functions intersubjectively, not only in one subject's internal psyche. Mark Bracher provides a useful breakdown of the modes of desire in *Lacan, Discourse, and Social Change*. There is passive narcissistic desire, whereby we aspire to be the object of the Other's love; active narcissistic desire, a form of identification or love/devotion in which we want to become the Other; active anaclitic desire, in which we want to possess the Other, or this possession becomes integral for our enjoyment (*jouissance*); and passive anaclitic desire, in which we want to be desired or possessed by the Other (as an object of the Other's enjoyment) (22–31). These modalities demonstrate that the flow of desire among subjects is both complex and highly relational, to the extent that it would be impossible to speak of the Lacanian subject as being in any way singly determined. So not only is the Lacanian subject decentered in the internal psyche (i.e., the conscious/unconscious split) and the external world (i.e., the radical alterity of the

Other or alienation in the signifier), but the multiple and conflicting desires that arise from its intersubjective relations speak to the subject's radical dispersion through desire.

So far I have been demonstrating that Lacan's work moves far afield from identification (mirroring) to include desire, fantasy, and *jouissance*. For Lacan, desire, like the subject itself, is always multiple, but the retroactive performativity of the subject is such that desire, like identity, is often misperceived as being singular. Quite often this takes place through the work of what Lacan calls Master Signifiers, or terms and concepts that subjects continually find appealing. As Žižek explains, "The interplay of imaginary and symbolic identification under the domination of symbolic identification constitutes the mechanism by means of which the subject is integrated into a given socio-symbolic field—the way he/she assumes certain 'mandates'" (*Sublime* 110). The problem here is that, far from explaining everything, this process is incomplete because it leaves a leftover, a gap, that is encapsulated in the question "Che vuoi?" After one assumes a mandate, after one accepts the message of the symbolic (or the Other), even after the process of identification and interpellation has occurred, the question still remains, "Well, what do you want me to do with it?" As Žižek explains it, there is a difference here between (symbolic) demand and what that demand may be aiming at (what is desired) (*Sublime* 111). Another way of explaining this is that although the subject may find a certain identity or symbolic mandate, *neither the symbolic nor the Other can finally answer the question of why that particular identity or mandate is for the subject.* There is no one to tell us why we are what the big Other is saying we are (*Sublime* 113). Desire erupts from the process of identification because the subject is nonjustified by the big Other.

FROM DESIRE TO FANTASY

Since the subject is nonjustified by the big Other, a gap appears in the smooth edifice of the socio-symbolic order. We cannot with any certainty determine what the desire of the Other is or answer the question of what the Other wants. Students constantly ask this question of their teachers in the hope that figuring out what the teacher wants will get them a good grade on the assignment.[5] As children, when we failed to please our parents, we were often traumatized in figuring out what went wrong and what they *really* wanted. Freud never figured out what women wanted. And so it goes. The desire of the Other plays a primary role in shaping who we are (as Lacan formulates it, desire is the desire of the Other), yet in the end we can never be sure about what that desire is. We are interminably ensnared in this unanswerable question. Even with those whom we know the best or love the most, there is never surety. We wonder: Is that what they *really* meant? Does the other *really* love/like/respect me? They can tell us so a hundred times, but still we wonder.

This sense of wonder, as it works unconsciously, is integral and productive for human subjectivity because it drives the emergence of fantasy. Fantasy fills out the impossibility of knowing the answer to "Che vuoi?" This suggests that fantasy is compensatory; it is an everyday coping mechanism and hence also creative or inventive. As Žižek describes it: "Fantasy functions as a construction, as an imaginary scenario filling out the void, the opening of the *desire of the Other*, by giving us a definite answer to the question 'What does the Other want?', it enables us to evade the unbearable deadlock in which the Other wants something from us, but we are at the same time incapable of translating this desire of the Other into a positive interpellation, into a mandate with which to identify" (*Sublime* 114–15). Žižek tells us that the process of identification with the Other is blocked when one is confronted with the question "Che vuoi?" To navigate this deadlock or blockage, fantasy arises as the answer to the question of what the Other wants/desires/thinks of us, thus filling out the (symbolic) void in the Other. But it is crucial to understand that even as fantasy provides a defense against our nonknowledge concerning the desire of the Other, it also begins to provide the coordinates, or framework, for orienting and guiding our desire. Fantasy functions for the subject by covering over the abyss opened up by the Other, whose question we can never ascertain. But rather than providing for the satisfaction of desire, which is the everyday, common meaning of fantasy, fantasy frames the objects of our desire (*Sublime* 118).

At this point, we can reemphasize some of the differences between the Lacanian and the Foucauldian versions of subjectivity. Foucault describes a subject of multiple positions, whereas Lacan describes a divided subject.[6] Often overlooked is how the notion of the divided subject provides a different account of agency. In this regard, we should reconsider Faigley's characterization of the advent of poststructuralist thought as a "terrorist bomb" robbing us (theoretically, at least) of the essential core of subjectivity necessary for agency as something that transcends the social production of the subject. What is wanted, of course, is a theory of agency that allows for the continued belief that the given social totality can be transcended and thereby remade. Consider this statement by Brodkey: "The narrative plot produced from Foucault's considerably more complex argument on discourse and discursive practice interests me because I am not only fascinated by the possibilities of socially constructed political reality, but also committed to the possibility of teachers and students resisting representations that demean them and their labor" (*Writing* 20). We see that Brodkey's interest in Foucault stems largely from her desire for political commitment. The phrase "socially constructed political reality," however, should—after the above discussion of the Lacanian subject—give us pause. Brodkey's reliance on Foucault legitimates the idea that there is a social totality we can apprehend and that this totality corresponds to our understanding sufficiently enough to warrant confidence that our interventions will be effective. By emphasizing different subject positions, Brodkey proffers political action as sets of multiple codes and their endless permutations of articulation and rearticulation. While this is of substantial use, as Brodkey, Berlin, and others have demonstrated, it is less productive for investigating why subjects cling to their particular narratives and beliefs so tenaciously or what elements make the processes of articulation and rearticulation—in short, real political change—so difficult. In this narrative, agency is thus also socially produced, decided in advance through the extant narratives circulating throughout the social. Resistance becomes a matter of reengineering social codes, practices, and institutions. In this regard, we can see that for all their differences, Berlin and Brodkey are working out of similar presuppositions concerning discourse and its operations in and through the subject.

Foucault, for Brodkey, evokes hope. But the kind of agency that Brodkey derives from his work does not suggest how it is that the subject can ever exceed what is socially given or transcend the immanent plane of any given historical moment. Such a subject is reduced to the extant, thereby limiting its potential for transformation to existing social permutations. All possibility is in a sense predetermined, albeit within a highly complex and slippery social matrix. But as I have argued, the Lacanian divided subject offers other theoretical nuances than the multiple subject described by Brodkey, if only because it accounts for aspects of subject formation that disrupt the easy correspondences of discursive identification and socio-political production and resistance. Power produces, but this process is not just a "mirroring" that we internalize to greater or lesser degrees. Rather, it is the excess, the leftovers that cannot be accounted for in the mirror, that brings us back around to a sense of agency. In other words, the possibility for agency ultimately stems from what cannot be accounted for within the immanent social totality; it comes from what is Other to the socially given. Agency does not arise directly as a response to power solely within power's scope; rather, agency also exists as what eludes the grasp of power. Agency in this sense marks the limit of power's range, even though subjective actions always occur within networks of power. As Joan Copjec states in *Read My Desire*, we can have a viable theory of agency only if we also have a notion "of a surplus existence that cannot be caught up in the positivity of the social" (4).

Agency also derives from the impossible question of the Other, the "Che vuoi?" that disrupts the possibility of identification or breaks the mirror. Once again: the subject as described by Lacan cannot be reduced solely to the processes of subjectivization or identification. Since the question of the Other is unanswerable, there must be something in the subject (a something, however, that elides signification) that allows it to posit itself, to bring itself into being as that which, while socially produced, is never equivalent to the social mandate. Bruce Fink provides an apt description of this process, in which the subject's goal is "to subjectify the cause of his or her existence—the Other's desire that brought him or her into this world—and to become the subject of his or her own fate. Not 'it happened to me,' but 'I saw,' 'I heard,' 'I acted.' . . . Hence the gist of Lacan's multiple translations of Freud's 'Wo Es war, soll Ich werden': where the Other pulls the strings (acting as my cause), I must come into being as my own cause" (*Lacanian* xiii). "Coming into being as my own cause" is nothing less than the return of agency, brought about precisely by the finitude and incompleteness of the Other. Not only do we not have "it" (harmony, identity), not only are we divided (constitutively split), but the same is true for the Other! Political possibility springs from our subjective limitations (or, to put it differently, our singular finitude)—from the impossibility of being who we (think we) are, in conjunction with the gaps and fissures that characterize the Other. Our interventions in the social arise because ultimately the Other does not have "it" either. We should then recognize that such radically intersubjective, indeterminate, and uncertain space is precisely the space of rhetoric.

OF CARNIVALS AND FUNHOUSES

Alienation means you want in, and I don't want in.
     —Henry Rollins to Gina Arnold, *Route 666: On the Road to Nirvana*

Poststructuralist-derived theories of political possibility and intervention ultimately maintain a faith in the power of representation, so I will next consider how Lacanian notions of misrecognition and fantasy complicate representation. I want to orient this discussion on an examination of Susan Miller's *Textual Carnivals: The Politics of Composition*, specifically one metaphor, the carnival, in order to propose a countermetaphor, the funhouse. Funhouses, it should be noted, are frequently found in carnivals, or, better, contained within carnivals, but unlike the carnival proper, funhouses have mirrors that distort perception. The addition of a metaphor that accounts for faulty, distorted representation functions as a supplement to the original notion of carnival as developed in Bakhtin, Stallybrass and White, and others to examine a site that displays to a high degree conflicts between high and low culture. I intend to show how the funhouse metaphor in some sense captures the way Žižek explains the intricacies of Lacanian intersubjectivity. I will attempt to tease out the implications of these concepts as I go along, but I want first to emphasize the importance of these metaphors. In a sense, they are just metaphors. Why, then, are they important?

Language is not only the medium through which the subject achieves identity (through signifiers, or, more properly, what Lacan calls Master Signifiers—brother, sister, student, teacher, Christian, bourgeois, lover, and so forth, ad infinitum) but also the medium through which we represent ourselves to society. Of course, there is considerable conflict in all this. The Master Signifiers that interpellate us are often in conflict. In other words, we seek identity in many signifiers, and these signifiers form chains with other signifiers, but without any achievement of harmony or unitary stability. My roles as teacher, scholar, husband, and citizen may be traced back to me, but they do not form any stable unity, being conflicted to varying degrees. Yet it is also the case that the ways we represent ourselves and the ways others represent us are seldom the same. We see here again a demonstration that the subject is not simply a confluence of multiple and competing subject positions but is fundamentally fissured, with no possibility of achieving a harmonious wholeness. But it is also true that, as Bracher explains, whatever sense of being or identity we do forge from these irreducible conflicts "is determined to a large degree by what happens to those signifiers that represent us—our master signifiers—particularly the alliances they form with and the wars they wage on other signifiers" (*Lacan* 25). Indeed, Miller says much the same thing when she considers the results of her proposals for the future of composition, concluding, "The field would thus be guided by metaphors that begin in the results of writing" (*Textual* 195). The dominant metaphors and signifiers we use are integral to the ways we understand ourselves and represent ourselves to our Others. Thus, in a very real sense, our subjectivity is dispersed through language, and this dispersal amounts to yet another permutation of the fissuring psychoanalysis claims for the subject.

The metaphor of the carnival serves Miller by providing an apt characterization of the composition classroom. As she understands it, the carnival is a metaphorical representation "used to understand relations between high and low discourses"; in this way, "both actual and imagined carnivals offer . . . historically enclosed, ad hoc, and transient sites for examining 'the low'" (*Textual* 1). Miller adds the modifier *textual* to the carnival to underscore how it functions as a "foundation for established discourse," as well as a "debased intrusion of the unregulated 'real' into that discourse" (1).[7]

With the carnival established as a framework for situating composition within institutional, historical, and socio-political narratives, the detailing of which comprises most of the book, Miller proceeds to consider strategies for improving composition's standing. She identifies two widespread, prevailing strategies, calling them "integrationist" and "separatist." Neither one, she claims, has done much to correct the lowly perception of composition, except insofar as they have made it "a force to be reckoned with" (*Textual* 183). Miller argues that neither strategy "openly examines the system of privilege or separation that creates both alienation and the desires to overcome it" and states that "the hegemonic strategy in question here makes 'low' status intrinsic to student writing and by extension demeans those who are deeply involved in its academic treatment" (183). The carnival status of the writing classroom presents unique problems for elevating the status of composition. Student subjectivities, which, Miller points out, are already constructed as having a childlike innocence that requires civilizing (196), are preconceived in terms of the intrusion of the "low" into the "high" of academic subjectivities. Miller's proposed solution is intriguing. What the field might do to enjoy a new identity is acknowledge "how it is a culturally designated place for political action" and thereby "transform its marginalized culture into a site where cultural superstructures and their privileging results are visibly put into question" (186).

Miller's strategy is to turn the carnivalesque aspects of composition used to denigrate it into arguments for its elevation. Thus, a change in the status of composition "depends on openly consolidating the field's internal, existing resistances to the cultural superstructure that first defined it" (*Textual* 186). Two items of interest emerge here. First, Miller insists on discussing the field of rhetoric and composition as if it were, quite literally, a subject. That is to say, she wants composition to have a subjective identity in the same way that a person is said to have one. This is the way we must read her insistence on obtaining recognition from the larger institutional and cultural Other. At stake is precisely the transformation of a marginalized subject (in the double sense of subject matter and subject qua subjective identity) into a respected subject. Hence, Miller's reliance on feminist theorists such as Toril Moi and Julia Kristeva can be seen to legitimate connections between the denigration of composition and the devalued status of female subjects. Furthermore, this underscores how she theorizes composition as a subject in its own right (186, 188).

The second thing that interests me is that Miller's strategy—a strategy she will abandon as she brings the chapter to a close—is remarkably similar to what Žižek calls "identifying with the *sinthome*," the final moment in therapy that brings an analysis to its close. Here is how Žižek explains the process: "The analysis achieves its end when the patient is able to recognize, in the

Real of his symptom, the only support of his being. That is how we must read Freud's *Wo Es war, soll Ich werden:* you, the subject, must identify yourself with the place where your symptom already was; in its 'pathological' particularity you must recognize the element which gives consistency to your being" (*Sublime* 75). Miller discusses composition in terms of its achieving an identity—in other words, as if it were a subject—in relation to its Others. Furthermore, she brilliantly leaps onto the strategy of elevating the standing of that identity by finding in its "pathological particularity" its very reason to be. In other words, Miller finds reasons to affirm composition where the institutional Other finds reasons to denigrate it, but she does so precisely by means of an identification with the characterization of composition as carnivalesque, without the attendant devaluation that comes with this.

What must be emphasized is that Miller's strategy also makes clear the limitations of the carnival metaphor. Although the carnival metaphorically provides for conceptualizing the mixing of categories, such conceptualizations are very much in line with the poststructuralist narrative of subjectivity as multiple and conflicted subject positions. What is thereby discounted is the notion of a *divided* subject. A funhouse, however, by virtue of the fact that it contains mirrors that distort, reinforces the idea that our reflections of ourselves invariably come back to us from our Others in distorted forms: we are as constitutively divided from these images as we are from our Others. The strength of Miller's proposed strategy is that her invocation of the image of composition, derived from the Other as the devalued site of low "student" discourse, becomes the means to achieve identity by circumventing the demand for recognition from that Other. However, given that academic discourse is defined by its exclusion of the low, we should realize that *such a recognition will never be forthcoming.* Because of this, identification with the *sinthome* is ultimately the most effective strategy that composition can undertake—finding in the refusal to be recognized the very argument to consolidate status in composition's own terms.

Unfortunately, Miller backs away from the full implications of attempting to move beyond the demand for recognition.[8] This happens in part because of her reliance on the carnival metaphor but also because of her adherence to a belief in the power of rationality and perception, a belief in the ability to see things clearly and describe them accurately; the title of her final chapter is, after all, "On Seeing Things for What They Are" (*Textual* 177). In other words, we see here the glimmerings of a return of the liberal, autonomous, and objective humanist subject, precisely where it has supposedly been superceded. Furthermore, with the return of this modernist subject, we also see a movement back into the dialectics of recognition, whereby the subject requires validation from the Other in order to feel secure about working from a low or devalued status.

Again, I emphasize that the metaphor of the funhouse is useful to the extent that it frustrates this kind of thinking and underscores problems with rhetorics of identification. There is a strong parallel between how funhouse mirrors reflect back multiple and distorted images of who we are and what our environs look like, and how other subjects and discursive narratives present multiple and distorted images of us and our world. Indeed, Miller calls her own work "blatantly a fiction" and weaves throughout her book the theme that theory and history are "good stories" (*Textual* 1). The benefit of the funhouse metaphor as a stretching of or supplement to the carnival is that it allows Miller's own themes to be understood in terms of an unbridgeable division, rather than as simply one more possible position among several. In other words, our partiality stems not only from the matrix of possible relations but from an irreducible fissure in the very structure of our world and our relations with Others. The possibility of "seeing things for what they are" is deflected in that it is necessarily heir to all the distortions and misrecognitions that inevitably arise from this divided perspective. Similarly, the assignment of a low or devalued status by other university disciplines is also deflected insofar as such a perspective is itself a misrecognition, produced out of the very same irreducible division—the fact that ultimately, they do not have "it," the special something granting harmony and fullness—that characterizes composition. Literature's job market tribulations exemplify this point.

After proposing a strategy for composition that approaches identification with the *sinthome*, Miller abandons it in favor of strategies that return composition to a battle for proper institutional recognition. Most troubling for me is her assertion that for composition's status to improve, it must "promote an academic language and show signs of status that other theorists and scholars can recognize" (*Textual* 193). Although she remains aware of the dangers of "imitating the symbolic identities of those who spawn us," she still maintains that such recognition is possible so long as composition "openly criticize[s] the workings of identity formation" (194). By reconceiving "the project that composition represents in political terms and [defining] immediate goals that groups of variously qualified people can meet" (194), Miller believes, composition can avoid the hegemonic pressure resulting from the need to obtain recognition from the Other. This accordingly requires a "full consciousness of its [composition's] politics" (195).

Unlike her previous strategy, what Miller advocates here will have the effect of maintaining the structures of unequal power and status that she argues against. If composition promotes an academic language that will achieve the recognition of the institution, student writing, which is defined a priori as what is not yet academic writing and in need of disciplining and/or remediation, will remain as the "low," without consequence except insofar as it is a step on the way to the achievement of "good" (institutionally recognized) writing. The status of composition will ultimately remain similar to what it is now because the hegemonic discourse that stems from the Other and marginalizes student writing remains unchallenged. Her appeals to rationality and clarity demonstrate the extent to which Miller finds herself trapped between these two choices: accommodation (to gain recognition from the institutional Other) or resistance (with the attendant price of low status). In part, this dilemma stems from the metaphor of the carnival. Seeing only various subject positions for composition and locked into a high-low binary, Miller misses how she herself has already traced a path from the carnival to the funhouse.

4

Politica Phantasmagoria
Ideology in Cultural Studies Rhetorics

The unbearable is not the difference. The unbearable is the fact that in a sense *there is no difference*: there are no exotic, bloodthirsty "Balkanians" in Sarajevo, just normal citizens like us. The moment we take full note of this fact, the frontier that separates "us" from "them" is exposed in all its arbitrariness, and we are forced to renounce the safe distance of external observers: as in a Moebius band, the part and the whole coincide, so that it is no longer possible to draw a clear and unambiguous line of separation between us who live in a "true" peace and the residents of Sarajevo who pretend as far as possible that they are living in peace—we are forced to admit that in a sense we also imitate peace, live in the fiction of peace.

—Slavoj Žižek, *The Metastases of Enjoyment*

But the cold lesson of masocritical science is that nothing is more aggressive than the desire to serve the other.

—Paul Mann, *Masocriticism*

E ARLIER I DESCRIBED a neo-Lacanian theory of discourse, arguing that it offers challenges to the communications triangle and the discursive models that work out of it, concluding with a brief explanation of the ways in which different discourse theories comprehend concepts, with "democracy" as an example. Neo-Aristotelian discourse theory sees a concept as something relatively stable to which positive features accrue, whereas poststructuralist theories, which emphasize the constitutive role of language, understand a concept as something unstable, prone at any time to unravel in endless semiosis. A neo-Lacanian theory of discourse, while it shares with poststructuralist theory an investment in language as constitutive and an understanding of concepts as unstable, holds a radically different perspective: concepts are unstable because they were never unified with positive features to begin with. It is not simply that concepts are caught in the play of differences, such that they mean more and differently than they intend; rather, concepts are fissured from within, so that, from the perspective of the symbolic, they can appear voidlike. Note that this is a function of the symbolic; in the Real, nothing is actually lacking. Ultimately, this means that conceptual stability stems from a dialectic of misrecognition. Although nomination gives the appearance of positive qualities to a concept, this actually covers over how it is split and conflicted. This is why the same term can mean so many things to so many different people, or why some terms elude stable or satisfying definitions, even as they provoke continual attempts to create such definitions (love, freedom, human, etc.). Thus, while nomination provides stability, the social conflicts surrounding a given concept—such as "democracy" or, for that matter, "good writing"—are an index of how empty the terms are in themselves. The play of power and forces in the social realm fills out this "void" in the signifier. So just as democracy means many things to many people, so too does good writing. For example, to use James Berlin's taxonomy of the field of composition, an expressivist would bring criteria such as authentic voice to an understanding of good writing, substantially different from the emphasis on citizenry a social-epistemic rhetorician might bring.

The conclusion to be reached here is not the poststructuralist one emphasizing a battle over the existent albeit conflictual characteristics of "good writing," which would indicate that such a thing really exists "out there" in the world, nor the postmodernist position that "good writing" is subject to social, historical, and hegemonizing forces. Rather, "good writing" does not exist in itself. Conceptual stability is achieved retroactively, and insofar as this occurs through hegemonic formations, we should see that these stabilities can achieve striking sedimentation. One cannot willy-nilly enact at the social or academic level a new conception of good writing. One must establish networks of support with others, and this would include engaging with contemporary knowledge, institutional procedures, community standards, and affective investments. And as we have seen, our affective attachments to concepts are strong. These attachments are given a kind of objective life in the social field that can reinforce conceptual sedimentation. Thus, not only might a teacher posit standards that define good writing, but a sense of self and world might become entangled with these standards.

In fact, a classic text like Strunk and White's *Elements of Style* suggests that a teacher can even derive considerable *jouissance* from his or her "neutral" or "practical" sense of good writing. Derek Pell's parody of Strunk and

White, also called "The Elements of Style," but as redone by the Marquis de Sade, lays bare this sadistic/masochistic economy with "painstaking" detail, complete with pictures. For example, next to a seventeenth-century painting of a man whipping a woman, Pell presents Strunk and White's rule for split infinitives: "There is precedent from the fourteenth century down for interposing an adverb between *to* and the infinitive it governs, but the construction should be avoided unless the writer wishes to place unusual stress on the adverb" (235). Pell then supplies two examples, "to diligently *Whip*" and "to *Whip* diligently" (235). The parallels among the commanding tone of the passage, the picture, the emphasis on stress and its application, and the desire for mastery suggest that Pell is not simply being funny or nasty. *Jouissance* emerges in the ways one deals with one's prose, perhaps especially when it is at its most disciplined. A further irony is that de Sade is noted as being an exemplary prose stylist. Pell's Strunk and White parody indicates that all notions of "good writing" are sites of libidinal investment and sources of enjoyment, which reinforces the point that "good writing" never simply speaks for itself.

I want to underscore the fact that conceptual meaning in neo-Lacanian theory emerges within but is not equivalent to the play of socio-historical forces, whereas for postmodernism the play of socio-historical forces shifts already existing albeit conflicted and mutable conceptual meanings. A similar logic is at work in theories of subjectivity. I argued earlier that the subject, like discursive concepts, is constitutively fissured. Additionally, it can be usefully conceived as a void produced by the failure of the symbolic to express it, which helps us to move beyond notions of subjective identity tied to the mirror of representation. One's identity and comportment as a "disciplined body" are not simply negotiated or conflicted mirrorings of what social power requires. A subject supposes a phantasmatic beyond to a given social or symbolic edifice, and the investments in this beyond—as object, feeling, or practice—can be profound.

This last point brings us into the purview of the current chapter, for the forces of ideology take part in and help organize these phantasmatic suppositions beyond our immediate symbolic appearances. Ideology, then, remains an important concept in attempting to grapple with issues of why people remain subject to if not participants in troublesome or objectionable forms of social power. This further suggests that it will not do to dismiss ideology critique out of hand. At the same time, the problems with ideology critique are many and complex, and they call for a careful working-through of their complexities. One of the primary goals here is to demonstrate that much ideology critique rests on a rationalist view of knowledge and belief, and I argue that this is a key reason for its insufficiency. Put more succinctly, ideology critique in cultural studies (and critical pedagogy, for that matter) has been less successful than its proponents might have hoped, producing more resistance and cynicism than critically engaged citizenship. Thus, it may be helpful to rethink what we might mean by the concept of ideology and consider anew how ideology functions.[1] This means in particular the abandonment of narratives of false consciousness, whether they come in the original Marxist clothing of the camera obscura or in the more nuanced apparel of postmodern cultural studies' social hegemony.

Instead, taking cues from Žižek, we might see ourselves as being active, consciously and unconsciously, rationally and affectively, in our ideological enmeshments. Subjectivization is only one facet of ideological work. Another facet is that the taking on of an ideological narrative is a productive act. Of course, this insight goes back further than Žižek, to Althusser and the ideological hail. When the policeman says, "Hey, you!" and you look up, you have recognized yourself in the hail and therefore have some complicity in the matter. Althusser labels this process "interpellation."[2] Žižek rethinks interpellation through a neo-Lacanian theory of subjectivity that makes sense of and broadens our understanding of the work of interpellation within ideology. The things that make ideology so sticky and difficult to extricate ourselves from, on the one hand, and so satisfying and seductive, on the other, are fantasy and *jouissance*. What we see is that ideology is not something that we can simply switch, dislodge, or banish by means of critique. First, we seldom have any direct, rational access to it; and second, an ideology matters to us in part because there is some aspect of it we have come to enjoy. Thus, if a critique does work to dissolve an ideological investment, this is because that critique engages other affective elements at work in the ideological investment, suggesting that what is rhetorically effective is not first and foremost the critique itself.

Ultimately, ideology is not a social illusion propagated by those in power, nor is it a cultural resolution to fundamental social contradictions, nor still is it the hegemonic cultural codes that discipline and hail us into particular subjective positions. Instead, ideology is the complex dialectical interplay between our conscious and unconscious selves as they emerge in specific social practices and material environments. Social reality, as it is experienced by an individual, is not simply screened by ideology; rather, ideology takes part in the social and the psychical, so that both become bound up within an ideological field. For Žižek, ideology is linked to subjectivity, and therefore also aligned with fantasy, because it helps to sustain our sense of reality. In order to understand this, it will be useful to clarify what is unique about this position by revisiting some grounding theories of ideology.

Karl Marx's original definition of ideology has been understood as false consciousness, along the lines of "They do not know it, but they are doing it."[3] Ideology in this sense is mystification. The key to seeing the world for what it is, with all its exploitation and injustice, is a critical education that demystifies social conflict (especially class conflict). This basic Marxian idea has continually evolved over the years. For instance, the Frankfurt School moved beyond the idea that ideology is predominantly concerned with class conflict and the interests of the ruling class. As they saw it, ideology is written into and reproduced through the very fabric of culture. This insight, especially as developed in Horkheimer and Adorno's 1940s work on the culture industry in *Dialectic of Enlightenment*, has proven to be highly influential in contemporary ideology theory. For instance, Henry Giroux's theory of ideology, which has been heavily cited in rhetoric and composition, takes its cues from the Frankfurt School and Althusser. In Giroux's view, ideology is not only both oppressive and productive but also is composed of conscious and unconscious elements at work in all cultural arenas. However, according to Giroux, an element of mystification is still at work that is crucial to understanding how ideology functions to oppress and delimit subjects, despite the fact that ideology can also function to create agency (*Pedagogy* 76–77). For this reason, claims Giroux, the critique of ideology "must be informed by a spirit of relentless negativity" (*Pedagogy* 86). It is here, in the tying of a project of emancipation to "truth claims" that are the product of this relentless critique, that Marx's original notion of ideology as false consciousness still manifests its trace (*Pedagogy* 76).

In *Critique of Cynical Reason*, an unlikely best seller when published in Germany in 1983, Peter Sloterdijk makes the argument that false consciousness no longer suffices as a critical concept in the postmodern age. We have become cynical; our experience now is "enlightened false consciousness" (5). Sloterdijk explains that the "essential point in modern cynicism [is] the ability of its bearers to work—in spite of anything that might happen, and especially, after anything that might happen" (5). Enlightened false consciousness, then, finds itself both well-off and unhappy, yet also unaffected on any significant level by the knowledge obtained through ideology critique. People's cynical accommodation of social disadvantage and injustice frustrates the attempt to motivate people to challenge ideological discourses and practices. Even though they have become aware—enlightened—they have already lost the essential faith that things can really be changed for the better and likely harbor doubts that anyone can really know what to do that would make things better. People *know* already that they are implicated in ideology, even if they do not really *believe in* that ideology. The state of enlightened false conscious-ness means that ideology critique only reinforces what people already know or intuit. Sloterdijk's argument is that given these circumstances, critical dis-course tends to generate cynicism. For this reason, Žižek understands Sloter-dijk's point across a rewrite of Marx's formula for ideology: "They know very well what they are doing, but still, they are doing it" (*Sublime* 29). However, Žižek further amends Sloterdijk's formula: ideology is the condition in which "they know that, in their activity, they are following an illusion, but still, they are doing it" (*Sublime* 33). It is not so much that people are engaged in a per-formative contradiction between belief and activity, but that *this performative contradiction is ideology*.

Another way of explaining Žižek's point is that the fundamental ideologi-cal illusion lies not on the side of knowing but on the side of doing.[4] Poststruc-turalist accounts of ideology can easily diagnose injustice in the social realm, but they suggest that our accommodation of these injustices takes place inter-nally—it is primarily a matter of belief. Giroux, for example, makes explicit in one of his early essays that ideology must not be conceived as having too great an external, material component because such a conception confuses struggles over meaning and representation with struggles over the concrete (*Pedagogy* 74). However, Giroux's criticism of Althusser misses how belief it-self is split between the internal psyche and external, material practice. Teresa Ebert, in "For a Red Pedagogy: Feminism, Desire, and Need," makes a simi-lar move when she argues against libidinal pedagogies by means of concrete scenarios of poverty and oppression. For example, in one paragraph she points out "the Indian women who sell their kidneys to feed their children" and the "hundreds and thousands of women, young girls, and boys" who are "being sold, kidnapped, and coerced into prostitution in the international sex trade" (805). For Ebert, these social facts speak for themselves. This allows her to ar-gue that anything less than a direct, material, Marxist-inspired engagement with such issues is direct complicity. Ebert thereby returns us to a notion of ideology predicated on false consciousness, where critique becomes the means to change one's (false) internal beliefs about the world to discern anew the (real) oppression and injustice that is going on, and these new insights will accordingly move the individual to take action.

Further complexities emerge when we note that Ebert's critique of libidi-nal pedagogy hinges on a very particular reading of "desire" that separates "desires" from "needs." She attributes to Lacan, Deleuze, Guattari, Lyotard, and others (whom she generally conflates) the position of equating desire for an object of consumption with the need for food, shelter, and so on. Ebert's argument flows directly from her conception of ideology. Her appeal to the factual knowledge of injustice mirrors her appeal to basic need. In both arguments, proof is presented on a bedrock of irrefutable fact, so that it becomes a matter of breaking through the ideological defenses and illusions that allow us to keep disturbing truths at bay. But if we look more closely, matters are not so simple. Needs and desires overlay, influence, and commingle with each other. We need food, water, and shelter at the most basic levels, true enough, but desire is part of such needs. This does not deny basic needs or wish them away; it simply acknowledges that desire suffuses all human needs. The homeless, for instance, decorate and take pride in their makeshift shelters. Ultimately, denial of the confluence of needs and desires makes little sense and presents an impoverished understanding of human beings.[5] Ebert offers an argumentative position that is absolute, one that will brook no further disagreement. And yet, what are we to make of her absolute needs and fundamental facts that admit to no other interpretation or experience beyond the ones she outlines for us? We can gain insight, perhaps, by considering the reactions of students. What knowledge will come to matter more for them: the facts of social injustice ongoing in the world or the equally real facts of their needs to find patronage, work, and love, all while competing with others?

From Sloterdijk's perspective, then, it matters little whether Ebert's diagnosis of social ills is right or wrong. Above and beyond the return to ideology as false consciousness and the impoverished view of subjectivity that accompanies it, we see the core of the problem: the assumption that students will actually maintain their commitment to change the world once they know some of the precise details concerning how "evil" it is and how it got that way. Sloterdijk argues that this kind of critique ultimately generates cynicism — Ebert may induce some guilt, but sooner or later benefactors will appear, the job market will call, love will emerge, and Ebert's annoying truths will be dealt with in ways that allow students to pursue their own lives as best they can.[6] The claim to a bedrock, irrefutable need or social fact cannot deny that needs are caught up with desires and can be satisfied in many ways or that social facts are mollified by other social facts. The social fact of injustice or exploitation may conflict with a student's life goals, but that does not in any way allay, dissolve, or devalue those life goals. Ebert's arguments lack the nuance to grapple with this problem; from her perspective, accommodation to life's urgencies is already complicit with social injustice.

For reasons such as these, Žižek claims that ideology is no longer just a matter of false consciousness, cynical and knowing or otherwise, but a matter of actual practice: "I know very well what I am doing, but still I am doing it." All the critique in the world cannot assuage the fact that people do what is necessary for success, to the extent they are able to find it, within the bounds of the hegemonic ideologies in circulation. We see that if an ideological scene must include both internal and external components, then no amount of internal change in the student can legitimate the claims that such knowledge will ground material, political progress. In contradistinction, Giroux, Ebert, and others share the belief that students can be taught to be self-reflexively critical enough of their ideological embeddedness that this enlightened stance can drive social change. Berlin's goal remains grasping how "signifying practices are shaping consciousness in daily life" ("Composition" 101). We might note that the agency most supported is that of being self-reflexively critical. Ebert and Mas'ud Zavarzadeh go even further, demanding full recognition of the "'OBJECTIVE FACT of capitalist relations of production'" (Ebert 809). Once the truth of exploitation or social constructedness is seen, once the veil of ideological illusion is torn, action will follow. Barring resistance, knowledge will change belief, and a change of belief will lead to a change of practice. If we have learned anything from Žižek at this point, however, it is that the ideas of subjectivity and rhetoric underpinning these assumptions are inadequate.

INTERPELLATION, SOCIAL ANTAGONISM, AND PEDAGOGICAL FANTASY

Postmodern theories of ideology have been successful in challenging older theories of ideologies as monolithic constructs of ruling ideas and demonstrating how ideologies are multiple and conflicted. Further, they have helped expand our knowledge about the ways culture and power come together to influence, constrain, and shape a sense of self and its possibilities in the world. However, these conflicts are theorized as being contained within the social field itself, so that they are simultaneously internally conflicted (or incoherent) and in conflict with each other. Although such conflicts create complexities concerning how ideology functions, ideology is still held to resolve conflicts for individuals. As Berlin describes it, following the leads of Althusser and Göran Therborn, ideological discourses (such as TV programs and other narrative forms) offer an *"imaginary resolution of conflicts and the fulfillment of cultural expectations"* (*Rhetorics* 123; my emphasis). Žižek, in contrast, places ideological work within the order of the Real, not the imaginary. In this view, social conflicts are manifestations of fundamental antagonisms—ahistorical givens that cannot be ameliorated or dissolved—operating at the personal and social levels. The antagonisms take many forms, such as between the conscious and the unconscious, between how people see themselves and how others see them, between social groups, and other permutations. All are historically situated as regards their particular articulations but are ahistorically universal as regards their inevitable return in different permutations. Our attempts to canalize these antagonisms—what Žižek calls traumatic kernels of the Real—contribute to the emergence of fantasy and ideology.

Thus, Žižek not only offers a consideration of ideology in its external materialization but also reformulates the connections between these external manifestations and the always continual process of our internal accommodation of them. Ideology is a dialectical admixture of what is historical/ahistorical, internal/external, rational/irrational, and conscious/unconscious. As mentioned previously, we see here a connection to Althusser's theory of interpellation whereby a subject emerges as a response to an ideological hail. I mention this connection because we see Žižek developing Althusser's theories through Lacanian psychoanalysis, which presents a different ideological subject than what comes to us through cultural studies. In the cultural studies lineage, Althusser influences Therborn's theory of ideology, which combines the concept of interpellation with elements taken from the thought of Foucault and Antonio Gramsci; moving on to composition, Berlin in turn relies heavily on Therborn. Thus, Berlin's theory of ideology does something very different with Althusser than what Žižek's does. Berlin writes: "Ideology interpellates subjects—that is, addresses and shapes them—through discourses that offer directives about three important domains of experience: what exists, what is good, and what is possible. Significantly, it also promotes versions of power formations governing the agent in his or her relation to all of these designations" (*Rhetorics* 78). This understanding of interpellation sees ideological discourse as the imaginary resolution of conflicts. Through interpellation, a subject's worldview is brought into correspondence with an ideological narrative, which thereby covers over or makes difficult to see still-present, really existing conflicts. Another composition scholar, Judith Goleman, mines similar territory using Althusser, although she emphasizes representation over the imaginary. She points out that an ideological structure is never seamless or whole but that through the procedures of effective, local critique, we can "historicize and demystify" an ideological apparatus, coming to know its effects on us (20). While such knowledge may be partial, Goleman assures us that we are sufficiently poised to "read" the ideological effects and their mechanisms and thereby attain the position of a "critical subject" who can rewrite and therefore re-present cultural artifacts and practices (21).

Still murky in these theories is an explanation for how this correspondence between ideology and subjectivity is achieved. What is the motor driving the leap into ideological belief? We are given little beyond explanations derived from Foucault and Althusser about how power disciplines bodies. However, what if we consider that interpellation functions not only in the registers of the symbolic (representation) and the imaginary but in that of the Real? Or, to expand beyond interpellation alone, what if we grant a new level of material, symbolic, and affective efficacy to ideology? One consequence is that an ideological interpellation might not be thought of in terms of success (so that an interpellation that is only partial or goes awry produces bad subjects or produces conflicts in the subject that in turn allow for the subject's agency or resistance) but as failure. As Judith Butler explains, "interpellation works by failing, that is, it institutes its subject as an agent precisely to the extent that it fails to determine such a subject exhaustively in time" (*Psychic* 197). It is in the fact that an ideology is fissured and incomplete that a subject's agency and affective investments emerge, with the consequence that we can no longer relegate the workings of ideology to belief or received behavior patterns. An ideological interpellation always involves (1) fundamental, Real conflicts that (2) generate cultural narratives making sense of these conflicts that (3) hail a subject so that (4) the subject takes an active role in achieving coherent ideological integration. At this point, *jouissance* emerges as well. A subject's active role in this integrative assumption is also an occasion for enjoyment, whereby the subject derives satisfaction and a likeable sense of self. We here come full circle back around to my earlier discussion of the retroactive or belated character of subjectivity. In this case, however, we see that the retroactive work of ideology also produces enjoyment.

An image that helps me to visualize this ideological process is that of a "wormhole," which is a cosmological phenomenon where two different space-time dimensions exchange matter and energy. A wormhole is a tear in the fabric of space-time allowing for the interaction between otherwise separate and distinct dimensions. Interpellation, like a wormhole, is characterized by the always ongoing flow of libidinal energy and discursive material between the internal psychical and external material dimensions. The subject comes into being as a nonsymbolizable entity caught in the flow, (mis)recognizing itself retroactively within the ideological field: "That's me!" The (mis)recognition, however, is not so much on the side of mirroring or representation, whereby I come to think that the ideology really reflects me. Instead, it is on the side of agency: subjects produce themselves in the act of making the antagonisms inherent in any ideological field acceptable and coherent.[7]

Since antagonism is on the side of the Real, not the imaginary or representation, social reality and all our activity within it can be seen as an escape from this antagonism, which is ultimately but the particular, historical manifestation of fundamental, ahistorical contradictions that cannot be resolved. Belief, insofar as it participates in this escape, therefore operates both internally as personal adherence and externally as concrete practice, regardless of whether these two modalities are congruent. Furthermore, we see that belief is not a passive acceptance of ideas. Belief requires conscious and unconscious activity, which takes place internally and externally. As Žižek points out, the externalization of belief is not a new concept, and it has many different, extant forms: prayer wheels and canned laughter are two current examples; an older example is the chorus in ancient Greek tragedy (*Sublime* 33–35). Taking this idea still further, we can see that rituals like Catholic mass, business meetings, formal speeches, marriage vows, and so on, all share in this externalization of belief. In the case of practices like marriage vows, this externalization has a positive function. However, in terms of ideology, it can be more pernicious. In order to escape its implications, when we are faced with the call to explain or extricate ourselves from an ideological practice, whatever we in fact are telling ourselves ("Sure, I know that these running shoes may have been made in a sweatshop, but my child really wants them, so . . . "), critique suffices to assuage the guilt that may arise. In other words, critique's operations are palliative, not liberatory. This is, I think, the crux of Ebert's argument against libidinal pedagogies. Consider the following passage: "The only question left for [libidinal pedagogy], as I have already indicated, is the question of liberty—the freedom of desire. However this is a liberty acquired at the expense of the poverty of others. . . . What are elevated and given names such as 'knowledge' and 'ethics' are all various forms of reproducing and training the kind of labor force that is most useful for capital" (813). Despite my earlier criticisms of her work, we should see that Ebert has something compelling to say here. Libidinal pedagogies can function as a fantasy screen, allowing us to escape from the traumatic reality that our pedagogies do very little to change the actual injustices occurring throughout the world. Unfortunately, Ebert avoids the truth-dimension of her claim by excluding her own pedagogy from the reach of her argument.[8] Indeed, I would argue that Ebert's "Red pedagogy" functions even more obviously as a phantasmatic escape because she uses it to convince herself and likeminded others that students and citizens can really be persuaded to change their minds, individually and presumably collectively, to eliminate the world's "evils." The "OBJECTIVE FACT," such as it is, is that these evils cannot be adequately addressed by the means Ebert proffers. Neither the theories of subjectivity and rhetoric she deploys, nor the pedagogy she builds from them, give us complex enough understandings about how rhetoric motivates action, much less formulate workable solutions to the problems she pinpoints (although she may well believe in her Marxist solutions). The small, perhaps banal conclusion is that no pedagogy of critique will suffice to challenge the many forms of exploitation stemming from capitalism (which, it should be recalled, remains Ebert's primary target). The much larger point, which can be extended far beyond the *petite* Marxisms of Ebert, is that all pedagogies engage in this phantasmatic escape that they are "really" doing something, while in fact, *all pedagogies have elements that are complicit with exploitation and advantage.* Obviously, I am not limiting this claim to the targets of critical theory and cultural studies, for the same can be true, to greater and lesser degrees, of right- and left-wing pedagogies. And, I would argue further, none are more complicit than those that claim they are not, which puts us right back into the ring with cultural studies and critical pedagogies. The claim to make a difference, and the denials and elisions of complicity, demonstrate the role of (a leftist) ideology in instituting and structuring pedagogical fantasy.

The upshot of pedagogies like Ebert's is that one can ignore the contradictions as long as one acts committed enough—we might even label this the leftist ideology of "making a difference."[9] Furthermore, this commitment functions retroactively to transform one's experience of what it is to have an ethical academic life.[10] One posits the larger world of a political "outside" where one's teaching can make a difference, in contrast to the "inside" of everyday academic duty. This phantasmatic beyond to one's given circumstances is certainly seductive, but it also has the effect of injecting discontent into everyday teaching, which can lose its luster or even appear ethically suspect. Politically committed academics can see themselves as more ethical than others and, crucially, thereby derive surplus *jouissance* from their activity. This retroactive movement (*Nachträglichkeit*) can be seen to introduce a traumatic element into pedagogy. One who merely teaches is somehow in a secondary position, doing less good, politically motivated, ethical work and arguably deriving less *jouissance* as well. It's little wonder, then, that cultural studies pedagogies can be so seductive—and little wonder that such pedagogies tend to thrive in an era when the traditional understanding of the university and the mission of the liberal arts within it are jeopardized. Bill Readings argues in *The University in Ruins* that cultural studies emerged because globalization and other factors had washed away the university's previous nationalistic, literary focus; culture arises as a concern when it becomes a general, empty term (89–92). But we might add to Readings's argument the idea that cultural studies also arises as the liberal arts become jeopardized, when they lose the sense of mission and importance they formerly held. Political commitment becomes a substitute for what has waned. Cultural studies offers the hope of an ethical outside and therefore of an alternative way of having an academic life. Nevertheless, while this hope stems from fantasy, I would also argue that the anger and tonal pressure suffusing cultural studies scholars are simultaneously driven by but also screening a profound cynicism. It is as if the performance of commitment alone were ethical enough, sufficient to maintain fantasies of political efficacy and its inculcation in students, despite overwhelming evidence suggesting otherwise.

Still, we see here that this issue of performance is a serious one. What I want to turn to next is a more thorough exploration of the performative dimension in teaching, pointing to some of its pernicious features. For despite the ostensible "content" of many pedagogies, especially those that seek to inculcate critique in students, the performative truth—their *jouissance*-infused authoritarianism—calls that very content into question. Consider, for example, the picture James Berlin and Michael Vivion present of cultural studies as a general project of ideology critique motivated by the desire to produce empowered citizens. They claim that "both composing and interpreting texts become overt acts of discourse analysis and negotiation" (x), so that cultural studies becomes a process in which "English teachers are engaged in a cultural politics in which the power of students as citizens in the democratic public sphere is at stake. The aim is to make them subjects rather than objects of historical change. Both teachers and students then will engage in critique, in a critical examination of the economic, social, and political conditions within which the signifying practices of culture take place" (xii). Students are to become objects of historical change—to become empowered. Critical consciousness is the road that will get them there. The other side of this desire to empower students through critical consciousness is the move to redistribute the flow of authority and power in the classroom. What are the relations between these two pedagogical drives? How do they impact each other? These questions invite us to look carefully at the pedagogical relationship as a way to discern more clearly how course content emerges as student learning. The so-called decentered classroom is an ideal model for exploring this issue.

THERE IS NO PEDAGOGICAL RELATIONSHIP

The decentered classroom, in which the authority of the teacher is to some degree dispersed, is relevant to our discussion because cultural studies and critical pedagogies frequently emphasize the study and critique of power relations at the local level, including the college classroom. One of the driving ideas behind such decentering is that students are more apt to learn if they are active participants in the acquisition of knowledge separate from the authoritarian strictures of teacher and institution. This has not always worked as smoothly as hoped, of course, but it is worthwhile thinking about why not. One reason we might offer is that the claim to have achieved a "decentered" classroom follows a logic similar to that Ebert deploys with her belief that the inculcation of critical consciousness will lead to social change. In the case of realigning classroom power structures, we see a belief that the power of the teacher can be sidestepped in a way that empowers students. Such empowerment operates either by giving students the knowledge and ability to rectify cultural problems or by dissolving the authority of the teacher in order to spark students into being active, self-sufficient learners. What I have been arguing so far is that in both cases, pedagogy works to screen us from fundamental antagonisms or conflicting modalities that cannot be bridged. Pedagogy offers its quite real organization of energy, discourse, and activity as an escape from these antagonisms; in doing so, it operates in accordance with ideological fantasy. I want to tread carefully on this point, however. I do not claim that we should stop critiquing or stop re/thinking and re/designing pedagogy; rather, I am asking that we think carefully about how critique and pedagogy go together, as well as the ramifications that this match produces. Critical thought retains its usefulness, of course, but we should be wary of accepting the idea that the achievement of critical consciousness suffices to place one on the road to liberation.

What are these fundamental antagonisms that critical and cultural studies pedagogies serve as an escape from? As I argued earlier, cultural critique offers us the sense that we are actively intervening in the transformation of cultural wrongs by inculcating critical consciousness in students, despite the fact that students' material practices and accommodation to everyday life exigencies countermand such claims. This point is underscored when we consider critique's performative dimension. Do students really acquire critical consciousness—are they enlightened—or are they pleasing the teacher? Here we see the true import behind the decentered classroom: if teachers can inculcate critique and sidestep their own authority, then it is all the more plausible that students can really attain a critical sensibility on their own terms, not just to please the teacher and acquire a good grade.

The immediate question that follows is, does decentering accomplish what it claims? Many articles already make the point rather firmly that teachers never can escape their institutionally granted symbolic authority, no matter what strategies for decentering are brought into play. For instance, Ann Murphy's article "Transference and Resistance in the Basic Writing Classroom: Problematics and Praxis" points out that whatever our pedagogical orientation, "we are still (however reluctantly) governmental figures of authority and power to our students" (175). Similarly, Stephen M. North's essay "Rhetoric, Responsibility, and the 'Language of the Left'" explains that the language of the left is problematic because it calls on teachers to ignore the contradictions inherent in being employed by the system they are fighting. North in part responds to John Clifford, whose "Review: Discerning Theory and Politics" also points out this contradiction but argues instead for a certain modesty in claims to resist and raise consciousness (523). Looking back over the ground we have covered, three representative positions become clear: Ebert's radical embracement of resistance, North's rejection of it because of its conflicts with a teacher's state-mandated mission and authority, and Murphy's and Clifford's attempts to find a livable middle ground. Each proposed pedagogy, however, is linked to the others by a certain blindness that constitutes its core fantasy: North finds the good life as defined by the American economy and the guilt stemming from the embracement of leftist discourses reason to jettison leftist critiques, Ebert finds the call of Marxist Truth reason to ignore her institutional complicity (and maximize her *jouissance*), and Clifford justifies his position by means of a guilt-ridden apologetics for trying to intervene in the face of an institutional conflict of interest. What I would like to highlight is that each of these pedagogies is marked by an unwillingness to engage *pedagogically* the very conflicts produced by their pedagogies. That is, they engage the issue from a theoretical, metadiscursive level rather than from a level of actual classroom practice.

This claim may sound like a rebuke, but it is not. Rather, it points to a problem we all wrestle with as teachers. I would rather have us view these discourses as inventive attempts to escape a fundamental, structural antagonism between student and teacher, and between teacher and institution. In other words, we should recognize the element of fantasy at work in these respective pedagogies but also the subjective investment and agency that produce them. Still, these efforts are not enough to canalize or dissolve the conflicts they address. It is in this context that I want to state that "there is no pedagogical relationship." This statement is a reworking of Lacan's famous statement that "there is no sexual relationship." Lacan did not mean that sexual relations do not take place; he meant that these relations are structured by fantasy, so that what the relation means to each partner is fundamentally different. For Lacan, the ancient Greek myth in Plato's *Symposium* about males and females formerly existing as one complete being is precisely the fantasy; he demonstrates that this fantasy gives us hope of achieving a kind of union that is in the end denied us, although the hope has its benefits anyway. I am making a similar claim concerning pedagogy: the various antagonisms informing the pedagogical situation preclude the possibility of "teaching" ever becoming an organic, complementary practice in which the teacher imparts knowledge and skills and the student simply learns them, in a frictionless, perfectly understandable manner. While we might aspire to or even believe in such a pedagogical relationship, the lesson of Lacan is that this is a phantasmatic vision of what occurs. Instead, what the teacher "teaches" and what the student "learns" will always be different, even radically so. But it is precisely the role of pedagogies and theories of pedagogies to cover over this radical split and impute to the pedagogy a certain cause-and-effect relation: teaching directly causes the learning it intends. Learning, of course, does happen. But there will always be a radical undecidability about it that is filled out by the pedagogical fantasy, which in turn allows the teacher to act *as if* learning were occurring according to pedagogical plan: if I teach X, students will learn X. In fact, they undoubtedly will learn Y and Z as well, and the version of X they take away may have little or no correspondence with my intentions.

To further explore the emergence of a fundamental dichotomy in the teaching relationship, I turn now to an essay on decentered pedagogies by the psychoanalytic critic Gregory Jay. He is concerned with finding ways to make students good critics of ideology, on the one hand, but he is also concerned with decentering his own authority so that students become producers of knowledge in their own right, not just empty receptacles for the teacher's knowledge. As a counterbalance to Jay, I examine an early work of Gregory Ulmer, whose essay constitutes an advance over Jay's, but who still maintains investments in criticism that belie the claim of achieving student-centeredness. I should emphasize that I do not think this claim can be extended to Ulmer's later work, such as *Heuretics* and *Internet Invention*, where the will to critique is abandoned.

A LITTLE JOKE

In "The Subject of Pedagogy," Jay invokes a now-classic classroom scenario: the student—having been instructed in the lessons of the indeterminacy of meaning, multiple interpretations, and other common topoi of a postmodern, pluralist pedagogy—asks, "Why isn't *my* interpretation just as good as yours, or anyone else's, if there is no one right interpretation?" (793). The student who feels threatened by the implications of ideology critique quite naturally feels the ideological right to be entitled to the right ideology. Rather than defend this ideological orientation in the academic language to which the student is being subjected, the student instead utilizes the same rhetorical strategies of indeterminacy invoked by the teacher, returning them in an inverted and now scarcely recognizable form.[11] The leftist, multicultural call for a transcendental framework providing tolerance for difference becomes a relativist defense of the student's ideological perspective. Intriguingly, Jay provides a (somewhat) joking answer to his student's challenge: "It isn't *your* interpretation, but a reading effect produced by the operation of a transpersonal method oriented by a social position" (793).

Although Jay's answer is tongue-in-cheek—what student of first-year English would understand a word of it?—it nevertheless reveals a troublesome aspect of the postmodern, pluralist classroom: the use of force appearing through the very strategies that try to empower students in the classroom. Student resistance to opening interpretation to undecidability, we learn, can be overcome if we shift them from being receptive learners to being active producers of knowledge. Jay argues that "students will respond with immediate relief when they realize that the multiple meanings of a literary text are not the product of some inscrutable genius on the part of the author or the teacher, but can be arrived at through the practical application of specific interpretative frameworks" (793). What is unspoken but implied here is that students must accept an a priori pluralist outlook for this to happen. With this in mind, if we reread Jay's little joke, we can see a slight twist in the flow of power. Jay has come to occupy the position of "the subject presumed to know," a Master who has the proper diagnosis of the ideological situation.[12] Putting it more directly, Jay's classroom strategies help set up a transference between him and his students. In a kind of bait and switch, Jay presents his students as active learners while downplaying his role in getting them to accept beforehand the proper outlook that allows them to believe in the role he has carved out for them. Jay takes on the position of the subject presumed to know even as he denies fulfilling that role; it is as if he himself has come to believe that he has reformulated the classroom scenario from the traditional "teacher talks, students listen and believe" to "teacher and students talk, students produce and believe."

Jay explains that traditional pedagogy is objective: students come to learn from those who know how and why things are, and they also learn the proper means for acquiring such knowledge (789). From this perspective, which puts students in the position of empty vessels, Jay thinks he has succeeded in getting beyond the authoritarian structures of traditional pedagogy. However, we should keep in mind Shoshana Felman's insight that "teaching, like analysis, has to deal not so much with *lack* of knowledge as with *resistances* to knowledge" (30). Students can be unsettled when they learn something that generates cognitive dissonance with their ordinary values and perceptions. Jay shows that on one level he is aware of this, as for instance when he warns of the difference between students who learn to repeat liberal platitudes and those who genuinely open themselves to the concepts expressed (793). In this way, Jay raises the problem of the internalization of belief. Will students feign this new knowledge to achieve a grade, which can be read as a form of resistance, or will they be persuaded to assume the new subjective position this knowledge requires? How can we even tell the difference if the student feigns well? At issue here is the role that Jay will overtly or covertly play. Jay seeks a pedagogy of production rather than consumption, so the role he wants is one of coparticipant, or perhaps guide, which is very different from that of the Master, or the subject presumed to know. Thus, he is able to claim that a pedagogy of production is a "practice in the performance that makes knowledge," one that has the effect of reversing the transference and putting "the students into the position of the subject who is supposed to know" (798–99).[13] What remains covert here is the persuasive force required to shift students to this new pedagogical position.

Jay is subtle enough to recognize that the transference is not completely dissolved because in part the teacher's authority comes from the position itself (786). Some semblance of authority always remains; as Žižek might say, it is "in you more than you"—that is, it is a symbolic mandate that can never be shaken off, sidestepped, or transcended.[14] Thus, Jay is correct when he notes that "both teacher and student are subject to pedagogy" (786). He is also aware of Lacan's famous slogan that "desire is the desire of the other," pointing out that this relation is at work in classrooms. Jay, however, turns his argument from a discussion of how the desire of a teacher is taken up by students to a discussion of how resistances and defenses in the student are broken (789). By inducing the students to become active producers rather than passive receivers of knowledge, Jay suggests, the teacher has also shifted the locus of desire to the student. The implication is that because students have been induced to become producers of their own knowledge, their resistance will dissipate. In this way they will more readily come to accept what the teacher already knows about the indeterminacy of meaning.

At this point, the trick is complete. Students have come to accept postmodern indeterminacy and pluralism as if they themselves were producers of these insights; the transferential relation only worked to guide them, and therefore Jay can lay claim to working with the transference while evading the Master position of the subject presumed to know.[15]

DOING IS ALREADY BELIEVING

I have intimated that Jay has not adequately accounted for how the play of power flows in his classroom, despite his claims to have shifted the power locus from himself to his students. However, it is still less than clear what these power flows are. In order to further develop the intersubjective intricacies that Jay brings forth, we should examine the relations among production, belief, and ideology. We might begin this inquiry by considering Blaise Pascal's argument that "proofs only convince the mind; habit provides the strongest proofs and those that are most believed" (qtd. in Žižek, *Sublime* 36). As Žižek points out, Pascal's point is keenly illustrated in *Pensées*, which contains the infamous argument against atheism. Pascal presents a debate between a believer in God and an atheist. As the two converse, all the usual polemics for believing in God are trotted out, but the hypothetical atheist objects because his passions rebel. He simply cannot get himself to believe in such stupid religious tales, and the pressure he feels from others to accept them is equally intolerable. It is not difficult to see the link here between the atheist's resistance to believing in God and the student's resistance to the pluralist line on multiple, indeterminate interpretations; in both cases, resistance manifests itself precisely where force is perceived. Indeed, this is the classic Foucauldian formula of power producing counterpower. Pascal, however, has an answer for his resistant atheist. Žižek's paraphrase of this solution is priceless: "Leave rational argumentation and submit yourself simply to ideological ritual, stupefy yourself by repeating the meaningless gestures, act *as if* you already believe, and belief will come by itself" (39; cf. Pascal 51).

Pascal's advice reminds me of Funkadelic's 1974 album title, *Free Your Mind . . . And Your Ass Will Follow*. But notice the reversal. Pascal is actually saying the opposite: "Free your ass, and your mind will follow." But even this does not quite capture Pascal's nuance; it is habit or custom that becomes belief, simply by virtue of habituation. This strategy has the effect of dissipating any overt application of force in favor of acquiescence, but an odd sort of agentive acquiescence. Belief stems not from authority but through activity, and it matters not whether one believes initially. To return to Jay's classroom, I think we can see the same mechanism at work with the students who are convinced (I am assuming that not all of them are). We might say that in accordance with Pascal, the side effect of students becoming (habituated) producers rather than receptors of knowledge is belief in indeterminacy.

While Jay's classroom pedagogy betrays a kind of Pascalian subterfuge, Gregory Ulmer attempts to circumvent such power plays while still maintaining the goal of students becoming producers rather than receivers of knowledge. Ulmer also has the virtue of seeing resistance as an advantage for pedagogy rather than an obstacle. He points out in "Textshop for Psychoanalysis" that after they accomplish the task of constructing a surrealist object, modeled on classic surrealist and Dada texts, "students are able to explain the theories involved, but they don't believe it [*sic*]" (762). Their knowledge has changed, but their opinions and habits remain intact. The next step is to allow a forum in which students stage their objections, which has the added benefit of inducing students to articulate their cultural ideologies. Ulmer adds that in this way the airing of resistance "allows for the recognition of it as ideology, after which it can be dealt with in a constructively critical way" (763). The crucial and instructive difference between Ulmer and Jay is that Jay's pedagogical goal remains in the imperative: "Our job in the classroom," he states, "is to teach criticism" (799). More specifically, the will to criticism suffuses all the strategies Jay brings to his pedagogy. In contrast, Ulmer moves beyond the realm of the critical into that of invention. We could simplify the difference between them thusly: whereas Jay advocates production in order to teach the proper critical attitude, Ulmer advocates criticism in order to "produce a person capable of inventing something oneself" ("Textshop" 760).

Although I am arguing that Ulmer's pedagogy has a number of benefits, some have greeted it with suspicion. John Schilb argues that Ulmer neglects the extent to which the avant-garde art he utilizes has been co-opted by capital, thereby negating whatever critical and subversive force it may once have had (*Between* 112–13). Thus, the students who are now capable of invention are in advance circumscribed to work, think, and invent within the framework of capitalist ideology.[16] Zavarzadeh argues that Ulmer's brand of "pun(k)deconstruction" marks "a return to 'experience'" in which Ulmer neglects to consider the fact that "experience is not a given but is in fact a construct of the dominant ideology" (33, 38). Both of these critics, especially Zavarzadeh, are motivated by the desire for an overt political presence in the classroom that subverts their criticisms. A return to the kind of pedagogy they seem to advocate places us right back in the middle of all the problems inherent in top-down, "teacher knows, students will be receptive" pedagogies. Worse, such teachers subscribe to an investment in combating the evils of capitalism that configures the classroom as a war space, with the inculcation of cultural critique as the spoils. Thus, I would argue that the criticisms Schilb and Zavarzadeh levy at Ulmer actually function as praise, demonstrating the extent to which Ulmer has achieved a real advance.[17]

THE IDEOLOGY IS OUT THERE

What would happen if we jettisoned faith in critical consciousness as the road to liberation? What if we recognized ideology critique as primarily a cultural heuristic, a means of invention and production, and hence caught up with but not prior to rhetoric and rhetorical production? If our understanding of ideology is to greater or lesser degrees one of false consciousness, for which the inculcation of critical consciousness will serve as challenge (or cure), such questions will remain troublesome. That is, such a theory of ideology already inscribes its own challenging answer: false consciousness requires true consciousness—either the capital-T "objective" Truth demanded by Ebert and Zavarzadeh or the postmodern little-t truths of indeterminacy and pluralism touted by Jay.

Having an alternative, more sophisticated theory of ideology, then, is clearly a first step toward getting us to think about a broader array of pedagogical moves—and goals. This is further reason to explore Žižek's theory of ideology. As I discussed above, Žižek gives ideology a material dimension. Ideologies are not simply the agglomerations of beliefs, desires, and attitudes that organize and naturalize our world. Instead, we should think of ideology in accordance with the slogan from the X-Files: "The Truth Is Out There" (*Plague* 3). Ideology manifests itself on the side of doing—"I know very well what I am doing, and still I am doing it." Disbelief, cynicism, ironical distance, even opposition fail as strategies because accommodation is how the material dimension of ideology shows up. This was Pascal's insight, of course; habits inculcate belief better than proofs. Terry Eagleton captures this idea with the example of racism and a park bench: "It is no good my reminding myself that I am opposed to racism as I sit down on a park bench marked 'Whites Only'; by the [act] of sitting on it, I have supported and perpetuated racist ideology. The ideology, so to speak, is in the bench, not in my head" (*Ideology* 40). It is important to note the difference here between external materializations of ideology and social attitudes or beliefs. Cultural studies critics, for example, can easily diagnose injustices in the social realm, but their theory of ideology suggests that our accommodation of these injustices takes place internally, as a matter of belief or acceptance. Žižek points out, however, that belief, "far from being an 'intimate,' purely mental state, is always *materialized* in our effective social activity" (*Sublime* 36). In other words, a constitutive dialectic is at work that avoids the internal/external split operative in cultural studies; for Žižek, internal matters and external phenomena are continually intermixing.

To put it more succinctly, in cultural studies, ideology is the subject's internal relation to external social conditions, which requires an overt politicism that addresses student resistance directly and attempts to defeat it by making students cognizant of their particular ideologies. Considered in conjunction with classroom dynamics, however, we see that pedagogical practices get mixed up with lessons in cultural critique. Not only does ideology manifest itself in the classroom through the authority of the teacher, but it is inscribed in every aspect of the pedagogical situation itself, from the room layout, to evaluation, to the school structure, to the ways education is valued and utilized socially. The hope of cultural studies in making politics determinate in classroom pedagogies is that bringing students' ideological biases to light, whether through discussion or student activity, will induce students to change. What makes this hope a fantasy of political intervention is that no amount of internal change in the student can legitimate the claim that such knowledge will enact material political progress in the external world. That is to say, there is no necessary correlation between one's inner beliefs and one's actions in the material world. Fantasy works to supply, or fill in, the necessity for this correlation, but as I have argued, this also amounts to a misrecognition of how ideology itself functions.

In the essay "Knowledge as Bait," Laurie Finke attempts to articulate how this disjunction between belief and practice is played out in students' lives. As she points out, the "appeal to consciousness-raising cannot tell us why the student who can intelligently critique patriarchal institutions in a brilliant seminar paper can still suffer from date rape, domestic violence, an eating disorder, or a crisis of sexual identity" (9). Finke pinpoints the crux of the matter for those who hope to meld critique and realigned classroom power structures with personal and social transformation. Also implicitly raised is an ethical question: can we find a way to set aside classroom models that reinscribe the patterns of force we decry? Is it possible to abandon the (c)overt legislation and policing of student values through the mechanisms and rituals of pedagogical authority? Ultimately, I think the answer is no, but we need to be careful about how we read this "no." It is not a "no" that would then grant license to return to critique as usual. Rather, it is a "no" that seeks something affirmative. In other words, I am looking for an ethical stance that works through the inevitability of force, one that acknowledges that pedagogy is in part always characterized by an a priori accommodation of classroom power.

It may be objected that such an ethics is, nevertheless, still troublesome. My use of the word *accommodation*, after all, seems to parallel my claims about how ideology works through accommodation. Haven't I just said that although we may try to curtail our power in the classroom by deflecting it through strategies of decentering, those forces still reemerge through the will to critique? What, then, has been accomplished? Our accomplishment, I would argue, is that we have worked through two fantasy scenes (critical consciousness-raising and decentering classrooms as ways to empower students) and have come to identify with the impasse that empowerment cannot be leveraged through pedagogy. In other words, the critically minded, decentered classroom is not a limit threshold toward which we must continually strive; rather, it is the limit that already defines the pedagogical scene. More bluntly: pedagogy is the process that organizes itself around this impasse, a dichotomy that exists in the material social situation of the classroom. There exists a fundamental antagonism between teacher and student that cannot be avoided or dissipated. We might then see our pedagogies as attempts to avoid or sidestep that fundamental conflict, but that also makes them thoroughly ideological. As Žižek argues, "the function of ideology is not to offer us a point of escape from our reality, but to offer us social reality itself as an escape from some traumatic, real kernel" (*Sublime* 45). Pedagogy, then, always has an ideological component, but this component manifests itself on the side of the actual, in our concrete pedagogical experience, which is characterized by an attempt to bridge this gap between teacher and student.

This claim about pedagogy is one way to think through the implications of Lacan's formula that desire is the desire of the Other. To forget this insight into intersubjective affective flows is to place in jeopardy any pedagogy that claims to put students in the role of productive agents. A different pedagogical ethics would see students as productive agents already and acknowledge that the teaching of writing functions to both create and delimit them. Pedagogy does not so much instill productive agency as reshape, redirect, and redistribute what is already there. This further means that learning should be completely sundered from concepts like empowerment. As Vitanza has argued, this is little less than the perpetuation of a hoax on students ("Three" 157). Empowerment is not for the teacher to give, even if this were possible. The learning that occurs in the classroom, if it does occur, arises from the intersecting continuums of creation and delimitation, production and subjectivization. Learning is a way of being molded and disciplined, and the productive agency it can open up is nevertheless far from anything resembling empowerment. The flip side is that we cannot evade our own responsibility as teachers, how our desire is always caught up in pedagogy. What is ethical here, then, is precisely the declination to fall into the trap of believing we have formed critical, autonomous agents out of our students.

THE CLAIMS FOR CRITIQUE

The death of the avant-garde is not an end to its production, which continues unabated, but a theory-death, the indifferent circulation of its products in a critical atmosphere in which the very idea of cultural opposition is increasingly problematic, and no less so for being more shrilly proclaimed.

—Paul Mann, *Masocriticism*

In his 1996 chair's address at the annual Conference on College Composition and Communication, revised and published as "Literacy after the Revolution," Lester Faigley reminds us of the power formerly held to reside in education. He states, "That the good classroom could help produce the good society seemed self-evident when I began teaching college writing courses" (31). Faigley, of course, is referring to the 1960s and their legacy. The classroom then was considered a new space of possibility, ripe with the potential for improving the lives of students, if not the overall quality of social life. Yet not even two decades later, the faith that Faigley evokes is already clouded by the doubt and cynicism of another age, the one we call postmodern. Sloterdijk flatly states, "Basically, no one believes anymore that today's learning solves tomorrow's 'problems'; it is almost certain rather that it causes them" (xxix). Indeed, Sloterdijk's charge makes it easy to link cynicism with the general dismissal of the value of higher education—or, given cutbacks in state and local funding, attacks on tenure, the rise in adjunct teaching, and the proliferation of budget-priced community colleges, at least with the loss of the desire to pay for it. Which, cynically put, amounts to the same thing.

Despite all this, Faigley's statement that the good classroom can produce the good society embodies a faith long held by many educators that the achievement of critical consciousness is the means to effect social transformation. This idea has a long and winding lineage, reaching back at least to Socrates in his ancient Athenian gadfly role, including the Enlightenment's wedding of critique to reason (which was given reinforcement in the university by Kant's writings on the duty of the lower, or humanities-based, faculties to critique the higher faculties), and continuing with forms of cultural studies, post-Marxism, and other academic movements. In line with this, the 1980s saw the emergence of a new kind of critical practice in which first-year writing-course pedagogies were retooled to produce better students by teaching a more sophisticated and socially oriented form of rhetorical practice. In the field of rhetoric and composition, this orientation was first labeled social-epistemic rhetoric but rather quickly became tied to the burgeoning cultural studies movement. Many cultural studies writing pedagogies were developed, but they almost all shared a concern with teaching students to write by inculcating a critical attitude toward cultural practices and ideologies.

Above, we considered how the decentered classroom attempts to disrupt the customary flow of pedagogical power in favor of a more democratized, student-centered atmosphere. We found, however, that institutional authority is not easily sidestepped; it finds ways to return, perhaps in new forms, with its disciplinary traits intact. Often this occurs because of the structure of understanding that suffuses the decentered pedagogy; if one's notion of ideology is predicated on internal beliefs, this way of seeing occludes an understanding of how ideology can function otherwise in external practice. In this sense, it may well be that students are often far better "critics" of ideology than we might suspect. A cynical disinvestment from the products of their schoolwork may be one key symptom of their insight, but accompanying this symptom is their relative powerlessness to do much else about it. In other words, the students' cynicism may be one external formulation of their critique of the pedagogical fantasy permeating the classroom; however, at this point they may be largely unaware of why they are responding in such a fashion or have little idea of what to do about it.

Berlin has figured prominently in my discussion so far, and I am going to consider him again largely because of his close attention to the connections between rhetoric and ideology. His now-canonical 1988 *College English* essay "Rhetoric and Ideology in the Writing Class" is perhaps the key document in the consolidation and dissemination of critical cultural studies–based pedagogies. Berlin's essay demonstrates how ideology functions in and is negotiated by the rhetorics dominant in composition: cognitive psychology, expressionism, and social-epistemic rhetoric. Berlin thinks the attention to language elevates the importance of rhetorical considerations, especially in the way we construct and negotiate our world through writing; yet at the same time, he sees in the capacity for self-reflection the possibility for progressive social action and a critical democratic citizenry. Although this essay was widely lauded and hugely influential, it also met its fair share of criticism. In his "Comment on James Berlin," which followed Berlin's article a year later, John Schilb criticized Berlin for the reductive move of lumping together fourteen quite divergent rhetorical theorists as social-epistemic (769). Schilb then upbraided Berlin for presenting a contradictory understanding of ideology, at times viewing it as Marxist false consciousness, at others as a poststructuralist war of positions. Berlin in turn responded that his poststructuralist theory of ideology is neither contradictory nor predicated on false consciousness. More important, Berlin attacked Schilb for "the political consequences of the kind of skeptical critique Schilb [offered], consequences which would result in a paralyzed acquiescence to the status quo" ("James" 777). The task, as Berlin saw it, is not first of all to perfect our theories of culture, capital, subjectivity, and ideology, but rather to intervene with those imperfect theories we do have for the sake of students who, Berlin claimed, "pursue their burning visions of the unique, independent, and self-directed individual in the corporate fast lane" (777). For Berlin, it was of secondary importance whether or not his theory of ideology is contradictory or imperfect, especially since no theory is perfect. In the end, pedagogic utility should get first consideration.

Despite his claims to have moved beyond thinking of ideology as false consciousness—the notion that our perceptions of the world are misplaced but correctible through truth and consciousness-raising—it nevertheless seems that Berlin retains some trace of this orientation. Even if, as he claims, no viewpoint is ever innocent, if there is no pure nonideological point to which we could aspire, he nevertheless ties the power of critique to the idea of betterment. This cannot but create a hierarchy: the self-reflective subject is superior and can have a better life than the unreflective subject. Intriguingly, Schilb does not pursue this train of thought, presumably because he shares this assumption. Berlin sees his students as compromised subjects on fire for good corporate jobs, thereby setting up his own role as an intervening pedagogue. This rather Socratic stance is made even more clear in a discussion from a 1990 conference on resistance. After a paper given by Stephen North attacking critical, leftist pedagogies, Berlin claimed that he wanted "to show [students] a picture of themselves in a few years and how unhappy they're going to be" (qtd. in North 137). Setting aside the problem of the ethical/aesthetic superiority Berlin assumes, I want to focus on the oppositional relation that is an explicit part of his pedagogy. It is precisely this impasse of an oppositional relation that empowers students or turns them away from a false notion of the good life that requires closer examination, and not only because the call to oppose bears all the earmarks of an ideological interpellation. Further, such strong claims for the power of critique—that its inculcation in the classroom can help produce good citizens and a better society—resurrect the specter of false consciousness, on the one hand, and point to pedagogical problems with the use of poststructuralist theory, on the other. To sum up the problem: Berlin's pedagogue has access to a better, truer world than the students, and s/he will empower those students by giving them, through the inculcation of sustained critical reflection, their own access to this superior world. This belief in the powers of critical reflection on culture draws attention away from what is essentially a modernist orientation, in which a mandarin cultural critic sees clearly and truly where the masses are fooled, even if this modernist orientation is dressed out in fashionable postmodern garb.

BERLIN, CLASSROOMS, AND IDEOLOGY

As we have seen, Berlin presents a theory of ideology that is discursive and dialogic, as something that is always transmitted through language practices. Thus, rhetoric and ideology go together. Relying on Therborn, Berlin sees ideology as a discursive formation that predisposes us to act in prescribed ways; it "provides the structure of desire, indicating what we will long for and pursue," and it carries strong social endorsement, "so that what we take to exist, to have value, and to be possible seems necessary, normal, and inevitable—in the nature of things" ("Rhetoric" 479). Ideologies are multifold, and subjects often adhere to a mixture of ideological strands. Often these strands are conflictual, just as we in holding to these various ideological strands are conflicted. Because of this, Berlin believes the notion of ideology as false consciousness has been left behind. Since many ideologies exist and compete, and since no position can be nonideological, one can achieve no "true" position that would make another position "false." In this way, the ideological field, as mediated through language, becomes thoroughly rhetorical and agonistic. Furthermore, ideology is in this conception rhetorical in that it is always entwined with communicators, audiences, and formulations of reality.

In the classroom, Berlin's pedagogy amounts to identifying cultural codes and breaking them down so that they can be analyzed and critiqued. Here is how he describes this process in *Rhetorics, Poetics, and Cultures:* "Our main concern is the relation of current signifying practices to the structuring of subjectivities—of race, class, sexual orientation, age, ethnic, and gender formations, for example—in our students and ourselves. The effort is to make students aware of cultural codes, the competing discourses that influence their positioning as subjects of experience. Our larger purpose is to encourage students to negotiate and resist these codes—these hegemonic discourses—to bring about more democratic and personally humane economic, social, and political arrangements" (116). Thus, in an examination of cultural codes, such as in the popular 1980s TV show *Family Ties*, students are led to understand that although the show is superficial and dishonest, it is still enjoyable because "of the ways conflicts in cultural codes are typically resolved in television programs" (123). The goal is not to lead students to embrace or reject such cultural artifacts, but rather to encourage them to become "reflective agents actively involved in shaping their own consciousness as well as the democratic society of which they are an integral part" (124). Berlin, then, sees himself less as rectifying his students' erroneous understandings of the world than as empowering them by giving them techniques for critical reflection.

We see here that ideology connects with subjects almost exclusively at the level of identification, whether imaginary or symbolic. Thus, a program like *Family Ties* functions ideologically not only to shape the subjectivities of viewers but to "offer an imaginary fulfillment of desire" (*Rhetorics* 123). In other words, television shows and the like offer a fantasy with which we can identify in order to satisfy our desires, while at the same time coordinating or structuring them. In the classroom, after the hermeneutic process of identifying and interpreting cultural codes, students are asked through their writing to confront the conflicts and other problems that the ideology masks. Writing becomes the process whereby students attain a critical perspective necessary for the achievement of an active, sophisticated, and self-reflective form of democratic citizenship, and critique remains the central activity whereby what is only fantasy—what is only imagined and therefore to some degree false—can be unmasked for the achievement of a deeper truth. But the crucial aspect of this process of becoming a reflective agent is Berlin's assumption that students will share the same valuations concerning what is true or real versus what is false or imaginary and will act in the same way as he does concerning these valuations.

CRITIQUE AS SYMPTOMAL READING

The tenacity with which students, like almost everyone else, cling to the products of culture that produce and reinforce the "dominant ideology" should indicate that becoming a "reflective agent" is not only more difficult to achieve than suggested but perhaps already in itself insufficient for achieving ideological resistance. Indeed, it may be that such "reflectivity" produces a certain distance from ideology that, rather than creating the space required for critical distance, is actually necessary for an ideology to take hold. Žižek explains how this can be so through the example of Robert Altman's film *M*A*S*H*, in which doctors and nurses take every opportunity to mock authority, make practical jokes, and create mayhem—all interesting if established ways to resist the smooth efficiency of the military machine. Žižek points out, however, that for all this, the film is perfectly conformist. All these forms of resistance fail to interfere in any significant way with job performance. Indeed, these forms of resistance help enable the medical staff to continue their high level of performance; in other words, efficiency is maintained through their anti-disciplinary mayhem.

The lesson here is that the distance from ideology displayed in their shenanigans—which are taken to be antimilitarist—actually functions in the military's favor (*Plague* 20). Similarly, it is realistic, not cynical, to acknowledge that most people today—including students—already betray a modicum of critical distance toward school, work, and other daily practices. The achievement of critical distance, and the attendant minor activities of disturbance that would accompany such an attitudinal shift (including letters, movements, rallies, boycotts, strikes, speeches, articles and books, and so on), ultimately do little to disturb the smooth efficiency of the political-economic machine. This is not to make an argument for political quietism—far from it. Change is not just possible, it is inevitable, but such an assertion has little connection with teaching students about injustice, combining that with a phantasmatic notion of activism, and then expecting their new "knowledge" to lead them down the critical road to social justice. Considerably more likely is that these kinds of activities, including the small changes that they can achieve, are precisely what allow people to maintain their roles in keeping the larger system functioning. From this perspective, then, the ability to critique cultural artifacts and practices in order to ascertain what is more true or false, more real or imaginary, seems less persuasive as a means to empower students. We move here to what Sloterdijk calls "enlightened false consciousness," meaning that subjects may very well know that what they are doing is somehow "false" and from this "enlightened" position carry on as always. Let me say again what I have already argued: knowledge does not necessarily lead to actual change.

The interesting question for rhetoric and for teaching is why this is so. Note that I am assuming here that knowledge is not pure philosophical knowledge, but knowledge produced with some attention to rhetoric. So my question starts moving from the realm of pedagogy alone to touch on issues of what makes something persuasive. The insight I get from Žižek is that the knowledge produced from critique largely operates at the level of a "symptomal reading" (*Sublime* 125). Thus, in its postmodern formulation, ideology is read discursively in order to show how it is made up of a montage of codes and discourses that can all be realigned (in this sense they are "floating signifiers") or otherwise critiqued. For instance, Berlin sets out to produce "cognitive dissonance" in his students by getting them to see the constructed and conflicted nature of hierarchically arranged binaries. Certainly, there is some attention to affective factors, so it is not just a matter of ignoring how rhetoric operates beyond logic alone. Once they can create the hierarchy, identifying what is imaginary and what is true, they can and presumably will act on their newfound knowledge, not just because it is logically so but because they have investments in what is true and good. If this is ultimately insufficient, if this is ultimately unpersuasive, it is because there is a complementary step that must also be taken.

Žižek calls this next step "extracting the kernel of enjoyment." It entails "articulating the way in which—beyond the field of meaning but at the same time internal to it—an ideology implies, manipulates, produces a pre-ideological enjoyment [*jouissance*] structured in fantasy" (*Sublime* 125). Žižek illustrates how these two procedures work through an analysis of anti-Semitism. At the level of discourse analysis, one could demonstrate that Jews are set up in binary opposition to the rest of society: Jews become the corrupting element against which a sound social body defines itself. Or, similarly, one could say that the social antagonism around which society forms itself is displaced onto the figure of the Jew. In this way, Jews come to embody all those antagonistic features that are actually present in society but that society wants to deny and repress (*Sublime* 125). While such a critique can be accurate enough, even at some level persuasive, it is still insufficient. While it identifies the symptom and tells us what it means, it cannot explain how it captures our desire. Certainly, then, Berlin is correct when he argues that ideology structures desire. However, since he restricts himself to a discursive, symptomal reading of ideology, he is ultimately ineffective in explaining how it is that an ideology maintains its hold on our desire, regardless of our conscious, self-reflective understanding of its meaning and import and our desire for some notion of the good. This last point is key, since the whole classroom process of ideology critique is predicated on the ability of students to become cognizant of their ideological embeddedness, to compare it to an ethical standard derived from cultural studies or some other leftist politics, and on that basis to change their ideological orientation.

Continuing with the example of anti-Semitism, Žižek explains that to understand how Jews capture our desire, "we must take into account the way 'Jew' enters the framework of fantasy structuring our enjoyment" (*Sublime* 126). We need to keep in mind that fantasy is not just an illusion we need to see through; rather, it helps integrate us into the world, structuring our perceptions and coordinating our desires. One of Žižek's favorite examples of this point is the role of fantasy in sexual activity. Note how his explanation of fantasy differs from the commonplace of sexual fantasy (black leather, role playing, handcuffs, etc.): "In the middle of the most intense sexual act, it is possible for us all of a sudden to 'disconnect'—all of a sudden, a question can emerge: 'what am I doing here, sweating and repeating these stupid gestures?'; pleasure can shift into disgust or into a strange feeling of distance. The key point is that, in this violent upheaval, *nothing changed in reality*: what caused the shift was merely *the change in the other's position with regard to our phantasmatic frame*" (*Plague* 65). Such shifts are common, everyday occurrences, from a sudden feeling of being alone in a crowd when moments before you felt warmly connected, to a radical disengagement from a career choice that only yesterday seemed a dream job. These fantasy frames permeate our decisions, our social networks, our daily rituals. What is important to see here is how fantasy channels our desire and helps integrate it into our social activity.

Fantasy and ideology are aligned because they both help integrate subjects into the social, making reality itself a kind of escape from traumatic conflict.[18] We can clarify these ideas with a consideration of Laclau and Mouffe's slogan "Society does not exist" (see *Hegemony and Socialist Strategy*). "Society" is commonly taken to designate a really existing social organization inclusive of conflict and heterogeneity. Laclau and Mouffe want us to understand that society is always fissured by contradiction to an extent that forestalls inclusivity. To speak of society as a whole requires that this Real conflict be overlooked in favor of a phantasmatic sense that all of these conflicted and heterogeneous elements *do* fit together.[19] To speak of society as a whole inclusive of its conflicts is to make these disparate elements commensurable; to say that society does not exist is to give ontological weight to the idea that they are incommensurable.

Still, it could be argued that there are already understandings of society that resist seeing it as an organic whole, such as the postmodern version of society split by difference (often theorized in terms of race, class, gender, age, history, and other categories of identity and positioning). Such an understanding, however, presupposes a notion of society as the overarching, really existing conceptual frame within which these differences play themselves out. "Society" names that encompassing order gathering everything within its nominative reach, within which all conflicts can be seen as commensurable. Making an analogy with Derrida's famous statement that there is nothing outside the text, we could say that this postmodern conception sees nothing outside the social. The social thereby retains some—however nebulous—positive content. What Laclau, Mouffe, and Žižek claim instead is that while these understandings of "text" and "social" correctly apprehend the play of difference, they miss the constitutive role of conflict. The common idea of society is one that covers over the incommensurability of its antagonisms. Conflict, that is, doesn't so much play itself out within something we designate as society; rather, conflict determines what society is and will mean.[20]

This matters in our everyday activity because we act *as if* society is an actual thing, a really existing socio-symbolic entity that constitutes the a priori background from which we can then pick out disparate or antagonistic factions. Not only do we have a profound desire for this sense of organic social unity, but we are regularly confronted with situations that challenge it. While we may consciously acknowledge that our phantasmatic sense of social unity is in jeopardy, we tend not to follow up very rigorously on such insights. For instance, when two adolescent males scuffle, we might trot out the (sexist) commonplace, "Boys will be boys," indicating a conscious acknowledgment that boys fight. But in terms of our everyday activity, either we tend to assume the best (that boys do not really want to fight, that they are just going through a phase, etc.), or we create social mechanisms that externalize our belief in a scuffle-free adolescence. Žižek's emphatic point is that our conscious knowledge counts for little because in terms of desire, we crave this consistency and overcoming of strife. Boys continue to fight, but in terms of desire, they should not, or perhaps would not, if we could just find the right solution. To return to the example of ideology, we often cling to an ideological orientation less for its actual content than because we crave its consistency, the minimal harmony with the world and others it offers.

Responding to Berlin, we could say that one of the main reasons the knowledge achieved through critical reflection often fails to spur a change in ideological orientation is because that knowledge has little bearing on what the subject desires. The "correctness" of critical insight carries less subjective weight than the desire for coherence, stability, or social order. Simply put, rhetorical appeals are tricky, trickier sometimes than our rhetorical terminology lets us see. It is not that Berlin is unaware that authority or emotions frequently trump rationality: the notion of the good underpinning his ideology critique certainly engages more than logical sense. What we see instead is that terms such as *ethos* and *pathos* are insufficient to describe the complex affective investments at work here, just as we also see that Berlin, like so many others, underestimates the tenacity of an ideological hold. So the question becomes: if ideology frustrates our attempts to grasp its workings through rhetorical analyses and theories of subjectivity, and equally frustrates our attempts to extricate ourselves from it, where does that leave us?

GOING THROUGH THE FANTASY

Žižek's ostensible solution to the problem of ideology is simultaneously illuminating and anticlimactic. What he has to say about ideology and how it works is genuinely insightful, but it may leave one off where one does not want to be. Žižek argues that, above and beyond a symptomal (or discourse) analysis of an ideological formation, one must "go through the fantasy."[21] To return to our example of anti-Semitic ideology, Žižek states that we must "experience how there is nothing 'behind' [the Jew], and how fantasy masks precisely this 'nothing'" (*Sublime* 126). Žižek's use of the word *masks* is troublesome here, because it moves us back toward ideas of ideological illusion, but this is not really the direction being taken. Perhaps it is less that fantasy *masks* something than that it generates a prejudicial narrative out of irrepressible forms of social conflict. Repression, desire, and invention are all conjoined. The fantasy emerges as an inventive albeit troublesome displacement. The concept of society as an organic, harmonic whole is a base-level ideological fantasy, but it is continually beset by turmoil and struggle—what Žižek, following Lacan, would call eruptions of the Real. How is this discrepancy between the desire for harmony and evidence of dissonance accounted for in the symbolic? By an element that itself can stand in for, or replace, these eruptions, in order that the fundamental fantasy can be maintained. Thus, the Jew can be understood (from an anti-Semitic perspective) as the external, corrupting element threatening the sound social fabric. The impasses of society are displaced and acquire a kind of positive existence in the figure of the Jew, which allows the underlying fantasy framework of an organic social whole to continue. In other words, the maintenance of this fantasy requires collective psychic work. What makes this psychic work so difficult to apprehend and the ideology so hard to extricate ourselves from is the fact that at some level we obtain enjoyment, or *jouissance*, from it, much as our tongue incessantly worries a painful tooth or we perversely derive pleasure from watching a friend fail. The power of enjoyment in ideological investment and upkeep is substantial.

Žižek argues that what we need to do next is shift perspective on this "kernel of enjoyment." Using language reminiscent of an unpleasant medical procedure, he tells us that first we need to "extract" it, and then we need to identify with it. After doing so, we will thereby come to recognize in the ideologically constructed scapegoat (in this case, the Jew) a certain truth about ourselves. If the Jew appears as an intruder "who introduces from outside disorder, decomposition, and corruption of the social edifice"—and from this perspective, of course, the goal would be the elimination of this disruptive element—then "we must recognize in the properties attributed to 'Jew' the necessary product of our very social system; we must recognize in the 'excesses' attributed to 'Jews' the truth about ourselves" (*Sublime* 128). In a sense here, social criticism, or criticism of the Other, always comes full circle back to the one doing the critique. It is not that Jews or some other scapegoated figures (black welfare mothers, violent misfit children, antiwar protestors, and so on) manifest the corruption attributed to them; it is that all of us share in common this lack of coherence, stability, and order. We are defined by partiality, dependence, instability, and disorder, even if phantasmatically we reach for the opposite—completeness, autonomy, stability, and order. For Žižek, what is crucial here is not to stop with this insight but to press on to its fatal conclusion: not only do we not enjoy completeness, but neither does the Other. There is no final wholeness or harmony to be obtained; violence, conflict, disruption, and other social "ills" may very well be problems to be addressed, but they are equally implicit in any notion of the "human" and the "social." Which is to say, ultimately, that they cannot be made to go away. Since we all share in this lack of coherence and autonomy, the rational, critical procedure of fighting prejudice by demonstrating that the scapegoated figure "isn't really like that" is particularly ineffective. For instance, arguing that Jews are not like the stereotype is a failed strategy because it accepts as a priori the phantasmatic background that made Jews show up like that in the first place. Before one can target prejudice, one has to grapple with the phantasmatic background organizing social *jouissance*.

The upshot of this is that one needs to move toward a different sort of recognition—from symptomatics to abandonment.[22] This recognition gives us further insight into why cultural studies–based critical pedagogies seldom succeed in transforming students into critical agents of social change. Pedagogies like Berlin's retain the same phantasmatic vision of a harmonious society implicit in the ideologies that students bring to class with them. Asking students to trade one for the other by introducing cognitive dissonance, or inculcating a critical sensibility, simply introduces additional conflict that is threatening to the maintenance of students' own phantasmatic framework, but without calling attention to how that phantasmatic frame has constructed the problem. No wonder that when Berlin talked candidly about what his classroom looked like, he so often discussed student resistance. And Berlin is far from being alone on this score. So while I have reiterated the point that critical knowledge is not very effective rhetorically, of greater interest is the insight we have gained into how our affective investments structure our relation to the world and how rhetoric takes part in these investments.

Perhaps equally clear is that we have gained new insight into the affective investments of scholars. How are we to hear Berlin's claim that the "liberated consciousness of students is the only educational objective worth considering, the only objective worth the risk of failure[,] . . . [that] to succeed at anything else is no success at all" ("Rhetoric" 492)? Sure, training students to be perceptive readers of the ideological codes of power, exploitation, and injustice ultimately does little to liberate their consciousness, even though it may generate the cognitive dissonance Berlin describes. But notice that we also learn something here about the fantasy underpinning cultural studies pedagogies. Berlin steps back from the critical abyss that his classroom opens up: the notion that cognitive dissonance, holding multiple points of view, and being good readers of ideological codes are all part of a different ideological game. He remains strikingly unaware of the possibility that students perceive *him* as the problem to be surmounted—that pleasing him is the game they are playing. Thus, Berlin makes claims about not only what his students learn but what they internalize. Consider the following statement by Berlin: "Most students have deplored the dissonance manifested in these [class, race, and gender] codes, but others have attempted to justify them as economic or cultural expedients needed for a smoothly functioning social order. Since drafts of student essays are always shared with other class members, however, unreflective generalizations about the inevitability of class, race, gender, or age behavior never go unchallenged" (*Rhetorics* 129). Berlin unproblematically assumes that the successful completion of classroom assignments indicates a change in the subjective constitution of his students. Since Berlin is driven to transform his students' internal beliefs by challenging their ideologies, he is given to see their successful classroom work as proof of his pedagogical effectiveness. Manifestations of student resistance are in effect part of Berlin's own ongoing game, so that by the end of the course Berlin will claim of his students that "they begin to understand the coded nature of their daily behavior, and they begin to become active, critical subjects rather than passive objects of experience" (*Rhetorics* 130). Berlin understands his students' activity as confirmation of the pedagogical fantasy structuring his classroom, and accordingly he never takes the fatal step of questioning how his own desire is implicated in these interchanges.

Berlin tells us that "a way of teaching is never innocent" and that "every pedagogy is imbricated in ideology" ("Rhetoric" 492). However, the pedagogy advocated by Berlin effaces its responsibility to its own embeddedness by relying on its social-epistemic virtues. The lesson of Žižek is that Berlin misunderstands the tenacity of the hold of a given ideology by overestimating pedagogical power. Rather than identify student resistance as the problem to be overcome, Berlin must in effect extract the kernel of enjoyment from his own pedagogy — by which I mean that Berlin's social-epistemic pedagogy is already thoroughly ideological, and no more so than in its claims to achieve empowerment through self-conscious reflexivity. The operative fantasy in Berlin is that an intervention has the potential to disrupt the workings of capital and that this intervention will function through the students themselves. Indeed, this is further indicated by his reliance on the concept of identification; rather than see his students as subjects caught up in forms of ideological enjoyment (*jouissance*) that are nonrational, he sees them as capable of rationally choosing otherwise and consciously forming alternate identifications.

CAPITAL SNAGS

Social-epistemic rhetoric and cultural studies share a notion of community characterized by a multicultural approach that would respect difference and seek to include it. Ideology critique is one means to accomplish this. Some of the students for whom Berlin was mentor have formalized his approach, fixing elements of his pedagogy that were less effective and emphasizing its value for students in the postmodern world. In "Writing in a Post-Berlinian Landscape: Cultural Composition in the Classroom," Michelle Sidler and Richard Morris claim that, "after examining the points of view, expectations, stereotypes and cultural myths, and cultural positions involved in creating and consuming a text, the questions of who and what is privileged as well as how and why became more concrete to our students" (283). The *telos* of a Berlinian pedagogy—which is simply a highly influential version of many competing cultural studies–based pedagogies—is the schooling of students in where to plot themselves on the X-axis of privilege and the Y-axis of marginalization. The hope for the enactment of a genuinely democratic consciousness is understood primarily in terms of reducing social antagonism stemming from hierarchical organization.

Susan Miller nevertheless takes issue with this idea because "[student] writing is not positioned to enact [democratic] consciousness because they, as *writers*, are not taught that they have the power to do so" ("Technologies" 498). For Miller, there is no clear correlation between students' writing and the enactment of democratic consciousness. For one thing, as the above discussion of the decentered classroom has shown, it is difficult not to see students' adoption of the teacher's attitudes and modes of discourse as accommodation to a classroom situation over which they have no control. They can produce the required discourse without in any way internalizing the beliefs that these writings demonstrate. In other words, accommodation can function as a form of resistance. However, Sidler and Morris take issue with this claim, instead arguing that "democratic consciousness is a function of critical reading and writing" (288).

What lurks behind Sidler and Morris's counterclaim is an ideological faith in the power of cultural studies qua critical multiculturalism to reduce social antagonism across their chosen categories (privilege and marginalization). Such ethical values promote an all-inclusive multiculturalism that is believed to shift the traditional centers of power that deny the marginalized their voice and their place; these values also help generate questions about who gets privileged and why, thereby fostering critical consciousness. Some, of course, hold doubts about this program and the values underlying it. Deepika Bahri notes that "instead of expanding the limits of students' experience with difference and diversity, our efforts merely contain them through a managed encounter with otherness" (278). It is precisely this "managed encounter with otherness" that indicates multiculturalism's complicity with the cultural logic of late capital. The empty, universal position that "respects" all difference insofar as conflict is managed and superficial ("the toleration of otherness in its aseptic, benign form") mirrors the empty, global position of corporate capital free-floating over nation-states; nations, in turn, are beholden to and dependent on corporate capital, necessitating the allowance of any horror or injustice save those that disrupt capital's flow (Žižek, "Multiculturalism" 38–39). The social-epistemic/cultural studies practice of ideology critique, then, is founded on a misrecognition of its critical position. The attempt of Sidler and Morris, like other forms of cultural studies–based pedagogies, actually reproduces a form of violence precisely where it is supposedly evacuated. Otherness can only exist, true difference can only maintain its status, insofar as it accepts a priori a benign, pluralist, universal framework. But this very framework is already disempowering because it reduces otherness and difference to the benign framework of tolerance. Tolerance, while certainly a social good, is not an absolute social good. Difference and otherness cannot be thought exclusively in such benign terms—they must be thought in terms of all their particularities, including those less friendly to the multicultural project of benign tolerance.

Ultimately, multiculturalist pedagogies serve capital and the social status quo by eliminating noise, protest, violence, anger, and other frowned-upon reactions to otherness by means of the very gesture that would grant such otherness its "respect."

Given the above, it is difficult to accept at face value the claim of Sidler and Morris that "by using the post-Berlinian heuristic, students do not simply replicate capitalistic codes" (288). Rather, Sidler and Morris's pedagogy replicates many of the most common capitalist codes. Students learn that their critical thinking is possible only within a framework that forces them to void themselves of whatever particularistic impulses they might have, just as they must look forward to a corporate job in the near future that will induce them toward a similarly disciplined mode of being. What I highlight here is an implicit managerial violence that goes unnoticed.

Indeed, we might follow Žižek in suggesting that nonrational and abrupt manifestations of student resistance and disruption are linked—though not in magnitude—to other forms of violence in the cultural sphere that appear as a response to the generalized, managerial violence implicit in the multiculturalist framework. Žižek argues: "Hegemony designates usurping violence whose violent character is sublated. Democratic discourse exerts hegemony when even its opponents tacitly accept its underlying logic. . . . It is against this background that one should approach the problem of so-called terrorist *acting out*, of desperate attempts to disengage oneself from the double-bind of hegemonic discourse in which the highest violence poses as non-violent consent and dialogue—the true target of 'terrorist' *actings out* is the implicit violence that sustains the very neutral, non-violent frame" (*Metastases* 204). The lesson here is that violence inevitably returns, erupting in unexpected and unaccounted-for ways, even within a framework of pluralist respect and dialogue. Žižek calls such returns "eruptions of the Real" that demonstrate not so much that the social fabric has yet more problems that require fixing but that the social fabric is already itself defined by such impasses. That is to say, violence and conflict are woven into the social fabric, and attempts to mask them are but sophisticated applications of disciplinary force legitimated by phantasmatic narratives of a nonfissured, conflict-free society. These resistances, then, can be a way of returning to the pluralist, democratic framework its own violence—but in an inverted, unrecognizable, and traumatic form.

FAIGLEY AND IDEOLOGY

I would like to move toward a conclusion with one more example of postmodern ideology critique, this one from Lester Faigley, that highlights problems stemming from an investment in the power of cultural critique to enact political transformation. Faigley advocates postmodern pluralism as a way to resist or overcome problematic or unjust aspects of education and culture. Nevertheless, Faigley is careful in his deployment of cultural studies and postmodern thought, and what he achieves is often noteworthy. For instance, in his commendable analysis of the ideology underpinning *The St. Martin's Guide to Writing,* one of the more popular rhetoric textbooks on the market today, Faigley calls attention to the issue of emotion. Like many rhetorics, the *St. Martin's Guide* emphasizes rational values in writing and persuasion, but when it attends to emotion, it does so in a way that seeks the elimination of conflict or involvement. Faigley argues that the *Guide* "can leave room for emotional excess because it has the means of quickly reining in those excesses. . . . The appeal for personal disclosure is accompanied with a requirement for 'emotional distance'" (*Fragments* 158). Students are asked to disclose details about emotionally charged incidents, but the larger purpose in having them do so is to create narratives that rationalize what happened for tidy resolution.

To take one example, the *Guide* showcases an essay by first-year student writer Jean Brandt called "Going Home." These example essays, of course, are meant to illustrate the kind of writing that is desired, and as Faigley correctly points out, this oftentimes means that they model the proper subject position students are supposed to inhabit. Brandt, then, writes about how she was caught shoplifting a seventy-five-cent Snoopy button when she was thirteen. She was arrested and forced to call her parents from jail. Faigley writes: "Axelrod and Cooper fault the Brandt essay for lacking emotional distance. They criticize her for not including her present perspective, not explaining why she stole the Snoopy button, and not telling what she learned from the experience. Axelrod and Cooper speculate, 'Perhaps the reason her writing lacks insight is that Brandt still does not have sufficient emotional distance to understand the experience' (44). Although Axelrod and Cooper admit that not every autobiography should end with a moral lesson, they never mention that the significance of the experience might be contradictory nor do they discuss how she might have reflected more without moralizing" (159). Faigley's charge that Axelrod and Cooper are moralistic is essentially true, as is his insistence that Brandt may experience contradictory feelings about the event. Even more significant is his argument that such criticism induces attitudinal change in students, which is to say that at stake in such an example is the production of the proper writerly subject position. In this case, that means an orderly, self-reflectively rational writer who can make sense of personal emotional turmoil. Faigley's insight here is impressive, but at the same time, he misses something essential when he offers the possibility of students coming to inhabit alternate subject positions. He does not see that the problem with the strategy offered by Axelrod and Cooper cannot be fixed through recourse to a postmodern pedagogy. Faigley thinks that the strategies of multiple interpretations and a refusal of closure, such as opening up the scope of "possible responses in the ruptures," will allow for a more ethical stance toward what Brandt accomplishes, at least one that declines to school her in the obvious ways the *Guide* recommends.

While I think that what Faigley advocates is certainly an advance, the problem emerges that it does not engage the student's desire and for this reason in particular risks leaving the ideological bias of the *Guide*'s pedagogy unchallenged. Why? Because Faigley still sees Brandt's essay as an authentic attempt to write about an emotionally charged shoplifting incident. His postmodern pluralism and indeterminacy are still suffused by authenticity. His understanding of Brandt's rhetorical situation, in other words, neglects the extent to which it has been created from the start by the teacher and the assignment, by Brandt's own goals (which may have nothing to do with what the teacher expects), and by the university institution (which is not the same as the classroom). From this perspective, Brandt's desire is probably indeterminate, and what appears on paper a retroactive and especially artificial construct. And yet Faigley assumes that Brandt would be interested in the goals he sets out for her as alternatives to Axelrod and Cooper's. Thus, what Faigley misses is that, whether Brandt picks Faigley's admittedly more sophisticated suggestions or sticks to those offered by Axelrod and Cooper, she is still ideologically implicated by the very goals of institutional discourse that demand she offer up facets of thought and experience for scrutiny and evaluation. Disclosing identities, producing auto-ethnographies, critiquing binary codes—all these assignments and more are conjoined insofar as they remain part of an ongoing institutional process, another form of product for a grade. We might even highlight how many such assignments are profitable for teachers—they may be easy to grade, for instance. In some ways, then, Faigley's difference makes no difference or, indeed, is more obviously an ideological move to obtain from Brandt greater ease in accommodating herself to the disciplinary process of being a "student writer." Perhaps there is a sense in which Axelrod and Cooper are more honest and forthcoming about their ideological motives—although the irony is that if they are, it is most likely unwittingly so.

We can come to a better understanding of this problem by considering the constitution of the postmodern subject in relation to the advent of transnational capital. As Žižek explains: "Far from containing any kind of subversive potentials, the dispersed, plural constructed subject hailed by postmodern theory . . . simply designates *the form of subjectivity that corresponds to late capitalism. . . .* Capital is the ultimate power of 'deterritorialization' which undermines every fixed social identity, and [we should] conceive 'late capitalism' as the epoch in which the traditional fixity of ideological positions (patriarchal authority, fixed sexual roles, etc.) becomes an obstacle to the unbridled commodification of everyday life" (*Tarrying* 216). Žižek's point is centered on the question of how best to resist the dominant forms of ideology functioning in collusion with capital. Such ideological discourses are intimately bound up with institutions like colleges and universities. In other words, far from dislodging the ideological orientation that is transmitted through the pedagogy of the *Guide*, Faigley fine-tunes it to fit the postmodern age. This capacity to accommodate oneself to a fluidity of positions is what is most beneficial in the age of "fast capital."[23]

In this way, we return to the problem I broached at the beginning of this chapter, the problem Sloterdijk diagnoses as enlightened false consciousness. I do not see how Faigley gets very far beyond this impasse, although what he suggests is more aware and ethically nuanced than the pedagogies offered by Ebert, Jay, Berlin, and others I have discussed so far. Nevertheless, while it is self-aware, his approach stops short of finding a way to "go through the fantasy"; we can see this when we recall Faigley's statement in his 1996 address that the good classroom can produce the good society ("Literacy" 31). What we have learned from Žižek is that as noble a sentiment as this might seem, it is fraught with dangers. Postmodern cultural studies aspires to be ethical, noble, and good, of course, but in the end, it brings with it phantasmatic assumptions about society, harmony, and conflict that directly shape its sense of the good and its praxis. This gives it a critical edge that some find seductive, certainly. More troubling, however, is the fact that a baseline, watered-down cultural studies orientation is extremely common in new graduate teaching assistants—at least, that is my perception as a graduate instructor at a large Midwestern university. One might well respond, however, that this merely ties cultural studies to the liberal arts tradition or even rhetorical training. Did one not always learn about one's culture right alongside taking lessons in discursive sophistication—did the two not always go hand in hand? Yes, but the rhetorical training of old was not yoked to programs of critique, and therein lies the problem. And if new teaching assistants are bringing a cultural studies orientation to the pedagogical table, this means that the arguments of Berlin, Ebert, Faigley, and others still have purchase well past the 1990s—indeed, it is as if cultural studies has become lore. This suggests the relevancy of the issues raised in this chapter that may seem to have fallen by the wayside. I do not think they have waned, not in the least. So if the good classroom is to have anything to do with the good society, we need to abandon the idea that critique can get us there. As an index of that need, I might point to the ubiquity of the phrase "critical thinking" in composition outcomes statements, an empty phrase akin to the use of "excellence" (Readings 23–24). If we do not abandon them, we should at least interrogate, more fully than we have, the notions of the good and the good society that come with such a criticality. Psychoanalysis, I hope I have shown, can contribute greatly to working through these issues in times to come.

5

Breaking the Law
Resistance and the Problem of Limits

A man doubted that the emperor was descended from the gods; he asserted that the emperor was our rightful sovereign, he did not doubt the emperor's divine mission (that was evident to him), it was only the divine descent that he doubted. This, naturally, did not cause much of a stir; when the surf flings a drop of water on the land, that does not interfere with the eternal rolling of the sea, on the contrary, it is caused by it.

— Franz Kafka, "The Emperor"

T HE ISSUE OF RESISTANCE is still of great interest in English studies, and it shows up as a key topic in a good deal of work.[1] Pedagogical
theory reflects this concern by undertaking the time-honored goal of
making students critical thinkers. What critical pedagogues want resisted are
the various forms of power that complicate the achievement of a pluralist,
radical democracy and contribute directly to problems of injustice, oppression, and disenfranchisement. Oftentimes, what gets resisted is actually the
teacher's lesson as students opt for quietist, conformist positions legitimated by
the dominant ideological narratives. Furthermore, as forms of cultural studies
become more widespread and mainstream, they become lore. As I mentioned
at the end of the previous chapter, it is noticeable that new teaching assistants
enter graduate programs with a baseline level of cultural studies understanding not dissimilar from a commonplace understanding of rhetoric as *ethos-
pathos-logos*. These students are asked to conduct critical readings of cultural
objects and narratives, sometimes as tied to some larger cultural studies–

derived political project. Given this status, we should not be surprised that many undergraduates arrive in our classrooms with a lore-driven grasp of what cultural studies is about, along with predispositions toward what it will ask them to do. Cultural studies has even become moderately well-known in its lore form in the wider cultural sphere, and it has developed its share of enemies. For instance, David Horowitz, a right-wing critic of today's university, writes books and runs a Web site attacking the leftist orientation of many humanities scholars, and organizing resistance to cultural studies in the classroom is perennially on his to-do list. We might note, with irony, that such programs from the right often follow the same grassroots, critical, consciousness-raising strategies utilized by leftist cultural studies programs. All in all, such complex shiftings in the flow of power should cue us that considerable theoretical nuance is needed to explain what allows one strategy to work, another to fall into disrepute, and so on.

Still, if we want to obtain greater insight into the matter, we will have to begin with where we are, which in contemporary theory is with an understanding of how power works to instigate or produce resistance. More directly, we might say that resistance must in advance know something about power in order to formulate itself in concrete practices, and this foreknowledge necessarily shapes what is valued or recognized as "resistance." Indeed, as James Kincaid reminds us, "the power of power is sustained by belief," meaning that how power shapes us is inseparable from the processes of coming to know the ways in which we already believe in power's power (1328). Further, we see a split emerging between attempts to foster critical, resistant scholarship and pedagogy and the eruption of counterresistances that take the form of limits or laws that seem remarkably difficult to grapple with or dissolve. Is there not something still uncanny about power and its relation to resistance, something we have yet to apprehend, much less come to grips with? It is not enough to say that power is diffuse, multiple, and agonistic, in line with the "power produces counterpower" mantra. We must further add that power is internally fissured by its own limitations. Put differently, just as previous chapters argued that we cannot reduce the social realm to its historical givenness, I am now arguing that resistance cannot be reduced to its immediate network of power relations. This is one of the reasons for the attention afforded law in psychoanalytic theory, but the case for the importance of law is also a contention at odds with contemporary theories of power indebted to Foucault. The tendency of such postmodern theories of power is to see law only at the level of its contingent historical relations. I argue instead that law is far more slippery than this and cannot be so reduced. These complications suggest that we need a reexamination of law's relation to the "wonder twins" of power and resistance, one that declines to collapse law into a field of immanent power relations.

FROM POWER TO POWER-STUFF

It is more than a curious coincidence that the academic fascination with resistance arose at the same time that the humanities began to assimilate poststructuralist thought (including new theories of power) in the 1970s. Looking back, we see that one key concern was developing an awareness of the ways power functions in the socio-political field. The centrality of Michel Foucault for these debates is well-known. His theory of power as decentered, diffuse, relational, and productive was at the center of controversies about how power shapes us, what liberatory possibilities we have, and what forms of resistance are possible. Many critics were dismayed by Foucault because they thought his theories shut down the potential for resistance: always being caught in the flow of power allowed no escape from it. Despite the efforts of many to demonstrate that Foucault's theories of power did not preclude resistance, or worse, efface agency entirely, such criticisms remain common.

In fact, they are widespread enough that they have provoked a reengagement with the issue. For instance, John Muckelbauer considers the ways Foucault is read as theoretically deficient on resistance but then teases out a contrary thesis: while all the criticisms of Foucault's theory of power are true, they are unproductive, since their understandings of resistance adhere to principles that Foucault challenges. Singling out three principles held to be necessary for resistance to take place—"a space outside of power, a unified subject, and normative foundations"—and labeling them "programmatic," Muckelbauer demonstrates that Foucault does in fact deny each one of them (73). There is no space outside of power, there is no unified subject, and there are no normative foundations. Although in this productive engagement with Foucault our understanding of resistance necessarily changes, resistance is still possible. Power becomes "a collection of actions on other actions," and resistance simply "the term for the encounter of multiple and conflicting forces of power" (80).

While the theoretical terrain Muckelbauer covers is significant, it undertakes a flattening out of the key terms *power* and *resistance* that is on the one hand useful for identifying the common albeit nonprogrammatic occurrence of resistance but on the other hand risks falling into banality. Resistance may be more common than is recognized. Nevertheless, we should consider carefully the implications of the theory of power subtending this theory of resistance. Power can take on overarching, metaphysical attributes, becoming both "monolithic and ungraspable" (Kincaid 1328). Not only do power and resistance lose their specificity beyond any given convergence of power, but all other terms begin to function in relation to power qua ur-term. It is tempting to see this definition of power functioning as an ontological claim—who we are as speaking beings is at any given moment defined by an un/identifiable matrix of power relations, including the resistances that not only inevitably arise but are part and parcel of what is meant by the term *power*. From this perspective, and punning off Carl Sagan, we might say we are "power-stuff," or "resistance-stuff": they have become two sides of the same coin.

Nevertheless, if the idea of resistance is to have any usefulness beyond our acknowledgment of its ubiquity and pervasiveness, then it requires closer scrutiny. One insight is already provided in *The History of Sexuality*, where Foucault notes that great radical ruptures happen only occasionally; "more often one is dealing with mobile and transitory points of resistance, producing cleavages in a society that shift about, fracturing unities and effecting regroupings, furrowing across individuals themselves, cutting them up and remolding them" (96). So if abrupt, sweeping change rarely occurs, that does nothing to forestall the countless local resistances that are continually happening. Foucault himself was intimately involved in such local struggles, and even his scholarship was usually focused on particular socio-historical problems (madness, medicine, incarceration, sexuality, and so on).

Such a view of power, and the analyses that derive from it, are thus oriented quite differently in regards to particular socio-political formations. As Foucault points out, if we want "to analyze power within the concrete and historical framework of its operation," we must jettison the theoretical privileging of law and sovereignty (*History* 90). Upholding notions of law and sovereignty diverts attention away from power understood as an all-pervasive, immanent set of conflicting and in/congruent forces by reifying particular aspects of power as ahistorical and/or transcendent. We should, however, tread this path warily. This is one of the lessons I take from Franz Kafka's *The Trial*. In the section entitled "Before the Law," Kafka tells a parable about a man who journeyed far seeking entrance to the Door of Law. Initially denied admittance by the Doorman, he waits his whole life there in anticipation of entering, finding out right before he dies that the door was in fact open for him, though he never did enter, and that now, at his death, it will be shut. Paul Mann comments, "As K. knew, we are always *before* the law because it never appears" (239). Law in this sense is never just immanent; law cannot be fully explained in terms of its particular socio-political circumstances. Being "always on the way" gives it a certain intangible force, and it is this manifestation of force, which is an a priori to any particular content or socio-political context, that establishes law as "Law" in its blunt, ultimately inexplicable presence. This is the aspect of law that we are always "before," the aspect that makes us subjects of and to law.[2]

This understanding of law has significance for contemporary debates about resistance. The disjuncture between law as an always historicizable *materialization* of power and as a *limit* to what is historicizable speaks to radically different conceptions about the relations between law and power, with significant ramifications for how we are to understand what is possible to accomplish in the world. Consider: when a law is unjust, remedy is sought. Oftentimes this is successful. Where legal, established remedies are difficult or denied, it becomes preferable to resist the force of law in a variety of ways, regardless of whether or not such resistance is ultimately successful. Law, however, remains a problem. It is quite difficult to separate out law from "Law." Jettisoning a law because of its particular content does not necessarily pose a threat to "Law" in general. This is noteworthy because oftentimes the way to resist a particular law involves questioning Law in toto. This is common in postmodern discourses. Hegemonic practices are called into question by demonstrating how they are constructed, situated, or historical, showing that they achieve their effects through matrices of power/knowledge. This is the strategy underlining, for example, Susan Miller's *Textual Carnivals*. By demonstrating how composition's devalued status is the product of particular historical practices, confluences of power, and institutional misapplications of knowledge, Miller effectively calls this devaluation into question. Again, however, the insufficiency of this approach is indicated by the title of her last chapter: "On Seeing Things for What They Are" (177). In the end, Miller is forced by the very logic of her argumentative strategy to appeal to something beyond the historical play of knowledge, power, and practice. Miller's analysis of the plight of composition is sophisticated, well researched, and acute, but she nevertheless reinscribes law in the form of truth when her corrective strategy throughout has depended on destabilizing the rhetorical power of truth and law.

More is at stake than demonstrating the intricate conundrums of seeking a better, more ethical form of power than one's opposition. One key difference between postmodernist (especially those derived from Foucault) and psychoanalytic approaches hinges on issues of power, law, and their interrelation. Integral to the example of Miller is that making law an immanent, historicizable practice does not in fact dispel its transhistorical, transcendent force. Any theory of resistance that we might offer should be able to address why this is so. Accordingly, I turn now to the theory of resistance offered by Judith Butler, who has been significantly inspired by poststructuralist thought, Foucault in particular. Butler, of course, is not a stand-in for Foucault, and since I focus on Butler, my comments on Foucault should be considered provisional.[3] Further, what follows is not meant to be a rebuttal of their work but rather an attempt to think through one small aspect of their theories as they pertain to resistance, contrasting them with the psychoanalytic perspective. Foucault, Butler, and Žižek provide a means for investigating concretely certain possibilities for rhetorical action in contemporary theory, as well as the construction of two different modalities of the suasive subject. That is, their theories of power and resistance assemble different notions about how the subject emerges in or through power and therefore different conceptions of what it means to act and speak within limits, specifically how those limits become figured as law.

BUTLER AND THE LAW OF SEXUAL DIFFERENCE: FROM PERFORMATIVITY TO CITATIONALITY

In her now-classic work *Gender Trouble,* Butler proposes a novel theory of sex differentiation: the male and female sexes are to be seen as performances, meaning that there is no *essential* component to their respective constitutions. The body retains its materiality, but it is *discursively* materialized; for Butler, there is no recourse to a purely natural sexed body. As Veronica Vasterling notes, for Butler, "the body is always already linguistically constructed" (19). Taking the idea that sex is performative even further in *Bodies That Matter,* Butler focuses more concretely on the (feminine) material body.[4] Sexual difference, Butler points out, "is never simply a function of material differences which are not in some way both marked and formed by discursive practices" (*Bodies* 1). Thus, following Foucault, Butler sees sex as a norm, "a regulatory ideal whose materialization is compelled, and this materialization takes place (or fails to take place) through certain highly regulated practices" (*Bodies* 1). In this sense, gender as performative precludes any active choosing; the "regulatory ideal" functions more in the sense of what Žižek calls a "forced choice," in which one has the freedom to choose so long as one chooses correctly.[5] Butler makes clear that sexual difference is performed, but this "performance" cannot be separated from the matrix of compulsory discourses that materialize the sexed body in culture. The sexed body materializes as the confluence of multiple folds, both internal and external, of discourse, law, and matter, and it is constituted temporally as a constant yet symbolically coerced reiteration (*Bodies* 10). In order to underscore how the subject is decentered as a performative agent of gender, Butler introduces the Derridean concept of citationality: "The forming, crafting, bearing, circulation, signification of that sexed body will not be a set of actions performed in compliance with the law; on the contrary, they will be a set of actions mobilized by the law, the citational accumulation and dissimulation of the law that produces material effects, the lived necessity of those effects as well as the lived contestation of that necessity" (*Bodies* 12). The movement from "compliance" of the body to "mobilized" action underscores the shift in the meaning of performance from obedient theatricality to a practice that "enacts or produces that which it names" (*Bodies* 13). Common examples of these kinds of phenomena are the opening of a meeting and the launching of a ship. In each of these cases, the words and deed merge, so that the discursive "performance" of the ceremony is already its enactment. In Butler's theory, this narrow understanding of discourse is greatly expanded, so that the entire matrix of sexual markers becomes available for this process of citationality. However, since what is being cited in the performance already exists in the form of regulatory laws and norms, and hence derives its power from what is already preexistent, there can be no subjective "author function" ascribed to the performance. As Derrida explains it, "the category of intentionality will not disappear; it will have its place, but from that place it will no longer be able to govern the entire scene and system of utterance" (qtd. in *Bodies* 13; see also Derrida, *Margins* 326).[6]

Central to Butler's appropriation of the notion of citationality is a concern with what is understood by "construction." Poststructuralist narratives are often accused of robbing subjects of any capacity for agency by ascribing to institutions, practices, and discourses the constitutive and active powers formerly held to reside in the humanist subject—in effect, a form of determinism. Lester Faigley, for example, argues that "postmodern theory offers an ongoing critique of discourses . . . but it does not supply a theory of agency or show how a politics is to arise from that critique" (*Fragments* 20). However, Butler understands construction as "neither a subject nor its act, but a process of reiteration by which both 'subjects' and 'acts' come to appear at all. . . . There is no power that acts, but only a reiterated acting that is power in its persistence and instability" (*Bodies* 9). Citationality, then, stands as a kind of performance that works in and through subjects grounded—insofar as this unstable flux can be considered to be grounded or placed at all—twofold—in the existent discourses of power and law and in their constant manifestation as such due to their continual reiteration.

If "construction" thereby comes to mean a process of materialization whereby the body appears in a properly sexed form that is itself dependent on its own continued repetition, then this is also the precise locale for situating the potential for disruption. The importance of citationality for Butler lies not only in providing a means for (re)understanding how the body is culturally normatized, disciplined, and materialized but in (re)formulating how the possibility of resistance is already inscribed in that very process itself.

Resistance is to be located internal to the social production of subjects; resistance is not a matter of proper theorization but of adequate recognition. As Butler explains, "This instability is the *deconstituting* possibility in the very process of repetition, the power that undoes the very effects by which 'sex' is stabilized, the possibility to put the consolidation of the norms of 'sex' into a potentially productive crisis" (*Bodies* 10). Resistance is complicated, however, by the fact that the subject that would resist normatizing cultural law is simultaneously enabled by those very same norms—they are integral for bringing the subject into its social being and are accordingly difficult to apprehend, much less resist. Any act of resistance must stem from, and thereby take part in, those selfsame norms. Butler's best-known example of performativity is the phenomenon of drag, whereby one gender impersonates, performs the other gender, or "cites" the law of sex differentiation otherwise. Indeed, it is precisely this capacity that makes the performative a priori to any particular manifestation of the sexed body in society. Judith Halberstam's *Female Masculinity* extends these insights and demonstrates the cultural power of such performances.

LIMITING THE REAL

A key element in Butler's understanding of resistance is the idea that all law is contingent and historicizable. Nothing transcends the immanence of human interaction. If the specifics of Butler's argument about citationality seem to owe more to Derridean deconstruction, here we sense the Foucauldian notion that power constitutes the matrix of human interaction, including its beliefs and practices, such that nothing transcends this plane of immanence. The radicalness of Butler's position stems from her extension of this argument to include sex differentiation. As the male/female split has a long history of being thought in terms of biologic or transcendent law, and as these ideas are still prevalent in culture and politics today, it is easy to see why Butler is controversial. The law of sex differentiation is unlike other forms of law in that it is a site for massive social investments. These investments cannot be limited simply to the realm of ideology. They are inscribed so pervasively on the body and in culture, in discourse and action, in myth and science, that ideology can be at best only a partial explanation for the staggering cultural investment in gender boundary maintenance. Butler's suggestion of the possibility of resistance to this vertiginous "being caught up with" sexuation is thus a landmark. At the risk of oversimplification, we might say that Butler posits a radical constructivism and in so doing demonstrates that something like sexuation, no matter how pervasively and powerfully it shapes us, our world, and our interactions, can be deconstructed, or at least constructed otherwise (see Vasterling). Butler tells us plainly that while discourse is not the last instance of or sole element for composition of the body, nevertheless "there is no reference to a pure body which is not at the same time a further formation of that body" (*Bodies* 10). This must be understood to include her own discourse, which tells us that new formations of the sexed body are not just possible but inevitable. Resistance is inscribed into the very scene of production.

Throughout her work, Butler utilizes aspects of psychoanalytic theory, but in the end she remains critical of what she sees as its biases (on the side of patriarchy, law, and norms). It is beyond my scope here to unravel all of these intricacies, but I do want to focus on a few of Butler's criticisms of Lacan, which have taken shape in the literature primarily as a debate between Butler and Žižek. Rather than simply present Lacan's and Žižek's positions, followed by Butler's critique, I will start with Butler's portrayal of the Lacanian position. I do this, first, because Butler and Žižek arguably agree about more than they disagree, as can be seen in their collaborative collection *Contingency, Hegemony, Universality*. Second, Butler's description of the Lacanian position is not only lucid and insightful in its own right but significant for demarcating clearly lines of contention that can otherwise appear murky. As I have intimated above, at stake in these debates is the problem of resistance and limitation. Given the largely social-constructivist narratives dominant in cultural and rhetorical theory today, what can be said to elude construction and, hence, to suggest a limit to what resistance is or can accomplish? This question applies not only to active forms of resistance, whether resistance of a willing agent or Butler's productive notion of resistance inscribed into the scene of materialization itself, but also to what resists us—our socio-political interactions, theory building, knowledge construction, and so forth. It is in this list that we should hear the title of Butler's chapter on Žižek: "Arguing with the Real." We have not only competing theories about the scope of resistance but radically different views on the connection between knowledge and world, on the very nature of what we speak of as reality and how transformation is enacted within that "reality."

The specifics of Butler's critique of Žižek involve rewriting and restating Žižek's Lacanian position on sexuality, salvaging what Butler finds useful but arguing strongly against elements in his thinking that she sees as defending and serving patriarchal power. She finds useful the way Žižek's work underscores how identity functions phantasmatically as a political rallying point because this theoretical position dovetails with her own attempts to demonstrate the constitutive instability of sexual division (*Bodies* 188). As Butler explains, political signifiers like "democracy" and "woman" unify disparate elements under one identity-creating signifier; in this way, such signifiers come to unify *and create* the constituencies that they claim to represent. The unifying and constitutive function, however, is not inherent in the signifier, which is itself empty. Instead, subjects come to invest in these empty signifiers on their implicit promise that they will represent and unify political subjects. It is this phantasmatic component that imbues political signifiers with the great rallying power they possess. However, as Butler emphasizes, this kind of investment itself stems from a fundamental misrecognition (*meconnaissance*); she claims that "it produces the expectation of a unity, a full and final recognition that can never be achieved. Paradoxically, the failure of such signifiers— 'women' is the one that comes to mind—fully to describe the constituency they name is precisely what constitutes these signifiers as sites of phantasmatic investment and discursive rearticulation" (*Bodies* 191).

The usefulness of Žižek for Butler lies in the correlation Butler makes between the empty signifier that retroactively creates identity by naming and her notion of the performative as citationality. In both cases, the act of nomination identifies something because it has an ontologically constitutive role in the formation of what will have been identified. And in both cases, what is named or cited is tied to (or perhaps framed within) the already existing matrix of culture, symbolization, and law. Of course, as Butler has argued, such processes can easily go awry. Thus, the political usefulness of Žižek for Butler lies in how what is foreclosed in the creation of identity becomes the site for resistance and potential rearticulations.

Butler takes issue with Žižek's concept of the Real on the notion of foreclosure. Butler ultimately sees Žižek as the defender of the law of sexual difference that functions to legitimate patriarchal domination and compulsory heterosexuality. As she puts it, "Is the textual defense of originary foreclosure, designated by the real, itself a *re*articulation of the symbolic law; does Žižek's text enact an identification with that law, and speak in and as that law?" (*Bodies* 198). Butler follows these leading insinuations with some concrete examples from Žižek's text. Specifically, she focuses on his argument that the hard kernel of the Real announces itself through the patriarchal family. Butler charges Žižek with speaking for the real of the law, when the real is supposed to be that which is foreclosed from symbolization.[7] As Butler wittily puts it, it is as if Žižek "receives the word from the rock, and brings it down the mountain to us" (*Bodies* 201). In tying religion, tradition, law, and patriarchal authority together in this encapsulation, Butler presents Žižek as a defender of patriarchal, Oedipal structures—structures that, it hardly need be said, have long been the targets of feminism.

The ease with which Butler achieves her characterization of Žižek is both instructive and commendable, and it may well be that his breezy deployment of Lacanian neologisms helps her case. Nevertheless, Butler's argument in a sense wins the battle at the cost of losing the war. Her upbraiding of Žižek obscures his essential point about how ideology and law function. I must note that this criticism of Butler is not a matter of correction, as if there were some "right" reading of Žižek that she missed, but part of a project of "working-through" the implications of their positions. Thus, we certainly have to ask, along with Butler, what could possibly be gained by "defending" the traditional, patriarchal family structure—and all that goes with it—that would not be reactionary and thoroughly ideological. A succinct answer would be the rhetorical process of distinguishing limitable limits from illimitable limits (see Dean). Žižek is less interested in defending the patriarchal nuclear family than in demonstrating how overrapid historization is just as ideological a procedure as overrapid universalization. Putting it differently, Žižek is asking why there is such a disconnection between theories that open up spaces for wondrous multiplicity and the reality of dogged adherence to traditional binary divisions, reactionary identities, and so forth. Is it the case that people are duped or coerced? Is it only a matter of resituating our understanding of resistance in theory and practice? If so, and we successfully redress these problems, will transformation then follow?

Butler's critique of Žižek illuminates these questions. She cites a passage from *Sublime Object* that she reads as defending the "threatening force of law" and patriarchy, wherein Žižek equates the "patriarchal family" with the "Real of the Law" (see *Bodies* 201; *Sublime* 50). Butler is quick to take Žižek's example as a reactionary defense of universalized, patriarchal normative laws. Intriguingly, she omits the passage that immediately follows: "If over-rapid universalization produces a quasi-universal Image whose function is to make us blind to its historical, socio-symbolic determination, over-rapid historization makes us blind to the real kernel which returns as the same through diverse historizations/symbolizations" (*Sublime* 50). Rather than seeing Žižek's position simply as antiprogressive, we should recognize this debate as opening up a clear fault line that separates Lacanian from Foucauldian (or Derridean) understandings of the relation between subject formation and social laws, a fault line that shows the Lacanian position to have a distinctly different understanding of change. From Žižek's perspective, then, "fundamental antagonism" refers to a constitutive fissure that returns again and again in countless cultural and symbolic permutations. It is not the particular content that is being defended, but the way particular contents manifest a universal, formal category of the Real—without, however, relinquishing in any way their unique or pathological particularity. Žižek's argument is that the Real, in the form of a fissure, deadlock, or antagonism, is not a description of the array of conflicting forces immanent to the social plane; rather, it is a description of what constitutes the social plane *as such*. Being the constitutive element, it is precisely what drops out, despite the fact that it is still symbolizable and historicizable. But the grasp of the symbol and the scope of practice are insufficient to eliminate it since this antagonism is the very condition for what *is* in the first place.

From Žižek's perspective, what is "announced" through the nuclear-family triangle is "the rock of castration"—the fact that neither men nor women have "it," that which would make them whole and complete. This is commonly characterized as lack, which has served as a point of critique against Lacan (see, e.g., Deleuze and Guattari; Vitanza; Nealon; Widder). It is important to recall, however, that Lacan insisted that nothing was lacking in the Real. The upshot is that "lack" is not a fundamental ontological feature of human beings but the result of the emergence of the subject through language. To put it otherwise, "lack" refers to the fact that we can never be entirely autonomous beings. We need other people; we are always dependent on others. Language is constitutive for becoming who we are because it allows us to articulate what we need from others; yet the implicit promise of language—that it can realize our autonomy and desire—is false. What it makes possible is only partial. But, in the sense that we are driven to become autonomous, and that identity is predicated on the misrecognition that we are or could be autonomous, we efface this a priori dependence in the fulsomeness of language's promise. In the Lacanian lexicon, castration refers to a priori dependence, but only—and this is crucial—from the perspective of the desire to efface it, to become an autonomous subject. Further, this notion of castration cannot be thought of simply as a limit; rather, it is the tension out of which erupts desire as a striving to obtain or achieve an originary wholeness or satisfaction (typically referred to as *jouissance*). That this originary wholeness or satisfaction was never originary and is entirely phantasmatic does not dispel the desire for it.

Yet it is precisely on this point that Butler stages her next argument against Žižek. Just as he argues that the Oedipal family illustrates the real of (symbolic) castration, she points out, Žižek also utilizes the example of concentration camps to illustrate another irreducible form of antagonism. Žižek argues that the procedure of overrapid historization would make concentration camps the product of a particular—and pathological—social order (fascism,

Stalinism). Butler counters that Žižek thereby trivializes the traumatic quality of all these examples by making them equivalent, such that "the historical becomes what is most indifferent to the question of trauma." She continues: "The political or historical effort to understand the institution of the family or the formation of concentration camps or Gulags cannot account for the 'traumatic' character of these formations. . . . But insofar as the real secures this lack, it postures as a self-identical principle that reduces any and all qualitative differences among social formations (identities, communities, practices, etc.) to a formal equivalence" (*Bodies* 202). Intriguingly, Butler's argument rehearses in its formal properties one frequently used against those who invoke truisms that seemingly contradict themselves. Nietzsche's (in)famous argument that language is a mobile army of (lying) metaphors that only have the appearance of truth because of long usage has been discounted by pointing out that if Nietzsche is "correct," then his argument is paradoxically false.[8] As Robert C. Solomon asks, "How does Nietzsche escape the paradox in which one asserts but at the same time undermines the truth of the claim that 'there is no truth'?" (Solomon and Higgins 10).[9] Butler's argument follows a similar trajectory: she argues that if overrapid universalization is an ideological move, then Žižek's charge that instances of socio-historical trauma like the patriarchal family and gulags are examples of the manifestation of the Real is itself ideological *because it too quickly assigns a universal underlying principle to historically contingent phenomena.* This point is crucial, and it has come to be an impasse between Butler and Žižek, to the extent that the bulk of *Contingency, Hegemony, Universality* hinges on precisely this same question. Nevertheless, the problem with such arguments—Solomon's reading of Nietzsche, Butler's of Žižek—is that they assume that the truth value of a statement is immanent to the statement itself. As in the paradox of the liar who states that everything s/he says is a lie, the key to avoiding the discrepancy is to posit a second position from which the statement's value will be adduced.[10] At stake for Butler is the necessity of historicizing everything in its particularity so that the possibility of rewriting and recoding the social can take anything and everything within its purview. However, her argument assigns to Žižek a metaposition that he is at pains to discount; it is not that he is pontificating from the "rock of the Real," claiming that patriarchy and gulags manifest socially universalized content or that they are somehow inscribed in the Real itself. Instead, in his view, they are particular cultural/political responses to an internal, constitutive limit. The universal deadlock exists at the level of the impossibility of a whole and harmonious society that is free of conflict, not at the particular and perfectly historicizable level of male privilege or Nazi genocide. Žižek argues that what Butler cannot master or overcome is precisely the deadlock that prevents the achievement of wholeness and free-dom from conflict and strife.

Note that we would have to include Žižek himself in this charge as well. What are Žižek's numerous books if not endless variations on dealing with and palliating the very social antagonisms he theorizes? Insofar as we can think of them symptomatically, they can be viewed as attempts to grasp and control the very deadlock that he describes as impossible to grasp and control. That is, rather than portraying him as a "wannabe" theoretical master, with the (Lacanian) truth in his grasp, we should see him, especially in light of his excessive publication record, as just as caught up with this "fissuring" logic as anyone else. Indeed, if we separate Žižek the author from the theories that he deploys, it may very well be the case that we betray at the level of the per-formative—as I think Butler's critique suggests—a disjunction between what Žižek the author says through theory and the point that the theory itself makes regarding the impossibility of mastery or control. I would only note that this disjunction should be read speculatively: it is another, inevitable manifesta-tion of the Real deadlock that returns again and again through the symbolic. Žižek's theories are not "it," the magic formula that will resolve our personal and social conflicts; instead, their worth lies in how they set us along a path that suggests the possibility of knowledge at odds with any particular manifest content and, as one consequence, real limits to social transformation. In other words, Žižek upholds a palliative "working-through" and declines the kind of utopian possibility Butler retains, this difference between them hinging on what one puts forward as subject to human intervention.

RESISTANCE AND PEDAGOGY: CLASSROOM SCENARIOS

Just as rhetorical theory has engaged the problem of resistance, so too has ped-agogy. And yet, in all these arenas, an oft-noted and recurring problem with resistance is that it tends to reinscribe the very powers and structures that are objectionable. Thus, the goal is to find forms of resistance that achieve suf-ficient equity and stability for freedom and happiness to proliferate. This goal underwrites many criticisms of Foucault; in making us all inescapably subject to power, no free space remains that resistance can achieve. Conversely, Fou-cault's defenders turn the inescapability of power into an affirmation: since power defines our common space, everyone in turn has power. As I have demonstrated above, Butler plies the latter path. But does resistance mean the same thing as we are accustomed to thinking in these models? Judith Fetter-ley suggests it does not in her foreword to *Composition and Resistance*, a book otherwise convinced of the usefulness of pedagogies that foster resistance to dominant culture. Fetterley reflects on the success of her first book, which fo-

cused favorably on resistance, noting that in retrospect she has grown ambivalent: "Perhaps it is the case that resistance, at least of the kind I practiced in
The Resisting Reader, serves an essentially conservative purpose. The stance of
the antagonist is classically male; the voice of the critic, rational, angry, ironic,
in sufficient command of the material so as to critique it, is essentially male;
and the act of resistance finally serves to foreground and reassert the very
material being resisted" (ix). For Fetterley, resistance, which once seemed a
promising terrain for pursuing socially progressive goals, has fissured and now
seems masculinist and conservative. Fetterley is compelling about being wary
of fetishizing resistance: resistance is everywhere; it is ongoing; and it often
serves contrary, nonutilitarian purposes. Resistance is, ultimately, not all, and
as soon as we see that resistance is everywhere, including in our forms of resistance, our valuation and investment in resistance must change as well. In
this way, Fetterley evokes keenly a primary thesis underpinning Butler's (and,
by extension, Foucault's) work: resistance and the resistant agent are mutually
implicated with/in power relations, which endlessly complicates projects of
"social transformation and resistance to regimes of power given that agency
itself is an effect of power" (Mills 265).

It is illuminating to examine some specifics concerning these dangers
and challenges. In her foreword to *Composition and Resistance*, Fetterley describes an intrusive dynamic in a class that introduced students to issues of
sexism and racism, frustrating her attempts to deconstruct sexism:

The majority of the students in the class were women, but the loudest voices, even
when they were silent, were those of some men in the class, not all, whose agenda
eventually took over. Unfortunately, the very model I proposed of the class as a community of learners worked against the goals I had in making such a proposal, for the
male students were able to present their complaints as consonant with the genre of
problem posing and to present themselves as sharing and representing the interests
of the larger community. They positioned themselves, not as men concerned with
the implication of the issues we were discussing for their own current and anticipated
privilege, but rather as sensitive fellow feminists resisting the agenda of a power-hun-
gry professor. (xi)

Fetterley further notes that many female students sided with the men as well,
seeing the opposition as one of students against teacher. Sharon Crowley tells
of a similar event in a class from which she received a substantial number of
bad student evaluations because, as she found out, several white men in the
class had felt silenced by her (*Composition* 225).[11] As in Fetterley's case, female
students joined in voicing the concerns of the "silenced" but still disruptive
men. Fetterley and Crowley understandably share an interest in these rein-

BREAKING THE LAW

scriptions of sexism. In trying to fathom what went wrong, both Crowley and Fetterley conclude that males effectively still hold more power than females and that this power differential effectively silenced women and disrupted the potential social good offered by the course content.

What intrigues me in these two otherwise well-balanced accounts is the fact that what underlies the male students' sexism remains unclear. Fetterley says nothing of the male students' motivations, leaving one to believe they were moved by culturally received sexism, pure and simple. Crowley suggests that one possible reason for her trouble is that the male students were resisting her teacherly authority because she is an "old woman," a figure culture typically depicts as powerless (*Composition* 226). Sexism is presented as a socially sanctioned discourse manifesting itself in students who feel threatened or otherwise challenged by the course material. The ambivalent role of the teacher further confounds the situation, leading many females to choose sides in the conflict based on allegiances to antiauthority narratives rather than antisexism narratives. Although this argument runs very smoothly, it nevertheless accomplishes little that would suggest a way out of the impasse it describes. Fetterley hedges on what resistance has to offer (xii), and Crowley says there is little she can do but challenge the situation (226). Little attempt is made to theorize the situation or account for it in any way other than a binary (male/female) opposition operating in a cultural background of really existing sexism. What this suggests about these teachers' attitudes toward and constructions of (young) male subjectivity is additionally troublesome.

These accounts need a way to explain the mechanisms whereby sexist behavior can return, as if through the back door, even in a feminist classroom that is directly addressing sexism—one that avoids falling into a simplistic model of subjectivity to explain away a traumatic occurrence. What should be avoided, in other words, is the trap of explaining the situation by coding the disruptive males as either cases of pathological male resistance, on the one hand, or mere representatives of received sexist narratives, on the other. Such explanations reduce them to male "wild cards" in the former case, in which their disruptions are disconnected from larger contexts, and unwitting dupes in the latter, in which they become agentless vehicles for culturally sanctioned sexism. These scenarios are unconvincing theoretically and practically, reducing (male) subjectivity to a caricature. While we may want to move beyond these explanatory models, however, to include more complexly various contextual factors, such as agency, motivation, and power, it remains for us to explain how.

We might begin with the immediate context, which is the classroom. The students were in feminist classrooms, and in both Fetterley's and Crowley's narratives, the male students are seen as resisting the content of the class and soliciting female support in doing so. But it is illustrative to listen closely to what the students claimed.[12] They did not see themselves as resisting the particular course content but as resisting something within the pedagogical situation that in turn spilled over to include the content. The first problem we run into, then, is distinguishing specific course material from the classroom forum in which it is disseminated. For Fetterley and Crowley, at least in the narratives they supply here, pedagogy is framed in a traditional form, one that Ellie Ragland describes as "the act of acquiring or dispensing knowledge as a content put in a context" (50). Explanations for resistance emerge within this understanding of education. Given that we live in a sexist culture, that the content of the course was the means to disrupt that sexism via knowledge, and that the students were resisting this process, they can be seen only as resistant subjects who embody sexism.

PEDAGOGY AS SYMBOLIC RESIGNIFICATION

From Butler's perspective, we would understand pedagogy, à la Foucauldian theory, as a site where various strands of power intersect and conflict. More precisely, the classroom is a disciplinary nexus for producing docile, compliant student subjectivities. Students internalize the overt and covert forms of power that are in circulation, taking them on and "citing" them as part of the ongoing process of "schooling." But, as the above discussion of Butler makes clear, these "citations" can always be cited differently. This means that at the level of subjective production, the possibility exists for students to move beyond normative sex divisions, to resist hegemonic cultural practices that proscribe proper behaviors, and so on. The cultural, symbolic laws that define and discipline normative sexuality can be resisted at the level of subjective performance, meaning that what makes such a classroom progressive is the concrete possibility it offers for sexual resignifications. Indeed, Fetterley's and Crowley's dismay at the resistance they met with arises because it directly threatened this possibility. Their counterhegemonic resistance was itself resisted, and successfully so. This corresponds with the contemporary understanding of power: despite the fact that this was an unwanted result, it was nevertheless entirely in keeping with power's operative principles. Power necessarily produces counterpower, and thus, in a conclusion entirely congruent with Fetterley's, we see that resistance is inherently unstable. If our relations are all power, we cannot object *theoretically* when our attempts to produce change are in turn disrupted, though we are perfectly free to object on other grounds (e.g., ethically).

What, then, about the discrepancy between the form and the content of

BREAKING THE LAW

the course? The pedagogical disconnect occurs as the male students react to female and/or pedagogical power. Their enlistment of the allegiance of the female students indicates that they were rhetorically successful in presenting the issue as one of pedagogical power, not sexual power.[13] This is not to say that we can redescribe these scenes as genderless, however. If performativity "describes this relation of being implicated in that which one opposes, this turning of power against itself to produce alternate modalities of power" (Butler, *Bodies* 241), that still does not dissolve the cultural discourses and histories that come with what is being performed. As Butler reminds us, "neither power nor discourse are [sic] rendered anew at every moment; they are not as weightless as the utopics of radical resignification might imply" (*Bodies* 224). But if progressive classrooms are predicated on the possibility of contributing to the resignification of gender difference, power relations, and so on, we must come to understand more comprehensively the "weight" of signification, or, as Butler might put it, the compulsion to cite the law in accordance with cultural norms. Butler and Žižek have much to agree on here. Both would share the idea that pedagogy cannot so easily transform students. Both would agree on the necessity of accounting for the passionate attachments or *jouissance* that provide the psychic drive for identity formation and maintenance. Indeed, Butler makes explicit the need for psychoanalytic contributions like Žižek's in understanding why people choose paths, allegiances, and identifications that are inimical or oppressive for them (see Butler, Laclau, and Žižek 149; Butler, *Psychic* 87).

Nevertheless, as described in detail above, Butler and Žižek part company on the limits they see accompanying such understanding. Žižek, like other Lacanians, maintains that there is an irreducible fissure that eludes historicization, precisely because it defines the emergence of history as such, whereas Butler would in turn historicize that very figuration of the fissure and thereby put everything back in play for possible resignification. Perhaps we could say that at stake is nothing less than the limits of rhetoric or, more sweepingly, the vertiginous implication that rhetoric emerges *because* of limits. We can see this limit at work in Fetterley's and Crowley's classrooms. If we cannot necessarily specify its exact contours and characteristics, we can certainly see it through its effects: student resistance. If in the teachers' eyes the classes were not successful, we should ask why they were not persuasive enough. Why were the materials presented in the two classes insufficient to achieve student transformation and consensus? If rhetoric emerges because of fundamental socio-symbolic impasses, as Žižek argues, then resistance to rhetoric cannot be "only" rhetorical resistance; it must also trace the limits that define existence.

Timothy Dean takes up this point against Butler in his essay "Bodies That Mutter." He notes the curious fact that advertising maintains its persuasive power despite attempts to disrupt it. We can be easily enough persuaded about the ways in which ads function, how they sell us sexual and social relations rather than just products, how they manipulate us, and on and on in accordance with contemporary strategies of critical analysis and deconstruction, but this knowledge does little to dissolve their allure (82). Dean points out that the fact of mediation is not sufficient cause for concluding that whatever is mediated is thereby open to change (or resignification). The lesson is not just that subjects are more complex than theories of resistance suggest but that law itself, as that which is to be resisted, cannot be reduced exclusively to the realm of the historical and mutable. This would counter Butler's claim that "citationality" includes at the level of the production of the subject the ability to "cite" the laws of gender difference. An understanding of how people undergo change should include the notion that resistance to law is complicated by the fact that not all aspects of it are apprehensible in theory and language. From Dean's neo-Lacanian perspective, then, the law is not purely contingent; or, put differently, what is in language cannot be reduced to what is strictly linguistic. Language is characterized by its excessiveness because it alone cannot explain language and its operations (even if the predicament can be described).

Dean, like Žižek, argues that desire, *jouissance*, and law function in a way that exceeds the plane of historical and linguistic immanence. He shows how this occurs by contrasting Butler's phrase "bodies that matter" (which underscores how the material body and the subject are united and politically recognized) with the phrase "bodies that mutter." A muttering body is a body attempting but failing to find a signifier to articulate its desire. As Dean explains, the "difference between muttering and speech concerns the distinction involved in a notion of desire as something *in* language but not itself linguistic. While speech comprises signs and signifiers, muttering comprises the symptom, which represents an unspeakable desire involving *jouissance*. . . . If symptoms were simply signs or signifiers, they would be spoken or written. It is precisely because the speaking subject is a disembodied subject that the body mutters" (102). Dean's "disembodied subject" does not literally mean that the subject has no body, but that there is a fundamental disjunction between the subject's body (as, say, a discursive materialization) and the subject who has his/her body as an object that cannot be smoothly reduced or translated into discourse. Thus, if poststructuralist accounts of the subject are grounded in language, Lacanian psychoanalytic accounts are grounded in the object (Dean 101). Butler's account of the subject elides the loss that founds desire, substituting instead the possibility that loss can be effaced by means of the resignification of the imaginary and symbolic orders. "Bodies that matter" are bodies that have access to corporeal meaning, that can make matter speak and signify in such a way as to resist the normalizing effects of hegemonic, heterosexual determinations. A muttering body is one that is constitutively out of joint, dissonant, striving, and struggling to be heard. What is crucial to me here is the hope offered by Butler of "assisting a radical resignification of the symbolic domain" (*Bodies* 22). Butler's faith in the resignification that she desires bears strong similarities to the modernist drive to reengineer society; Butler desires an alternate production of sex difference in order to rewrite the codes of bodily recognition. Butler sees that the political is present in all aspects of human interaction and that even at the level of sex production, there is room for choice and power shifts, at least in the symbolic domain. But Dean's lesson—the lesson of a body that mutters—is that the desire to resignify the symbolic domain is both less (this desire is not "it," the key to satisfaction; it will not bring about the harmony and recognition it purports to) and more (the project cannot go as planned; it will go awry, producing unforeseen consequences) than it is.

For Dean, the possibility of resistance stems not from the ability to reformulate or resignify our constitutive discursive chains, but instead from the recognition that loss in the socio-symbolic order is constitutive of subjects and desire. As Dean argues, to recognize that the Other does not have what it takes "is to recognize that loss is constitutive of subjectivity rather than the consequence of an oppressive regulatory regime that has arranged the world to one's disadvantage" (103). It is the attribution of a greater satisfaction and power to the Other, in his/her differentiated otherness, that actively forestalls the emergence of resistance. Nevertheless, this is a common tactic, further aggravated by the belief that the resentment that develops toward the Other who has "it" can be alleviated by rearranging the socio-symbolic order. As has been argued throughout, rearrangements of the socio-symbolic order as suggested by Butler continually run into the socio-symbolic order's constitutive limits, limits that, not being of the same order, cannot be reintroduced and therefore remain outside direct control. Change, of course, is occurring continuously; it defines the human condition. But what further defines it is that such change does not, cannot occur as we would like or plan and, further, that the attempt to make change so conform is fated to go awry in accordance with the logic of fissuring.

The classroom situations described by Fetterley and Crowley show this logic being played out. The students who resist are not mere sexist dupes of a sexist culture; instead, their behavior allows us to trace a constitutive limit defining any pedagogy that has as its goal the resignification of the social symbolic. Note, however, that this does not deny that the male students may have been sexist. But their ability to resist in the manner they did and to enlist female support demonstrates that their behavior exceeds the explanatory narrative of culturally received sexism, pointing to a fundamental limit faced by pedagogy, a fissure internal to its operations that I have characterized as law.

CONCLUDING DIS/INJUNCTIVE POSTSCRIPT

I have argued that Žižek and Dean describe a fundamental fissure that structures human existence and that this fissure manifests itself in countless permutations, including gender difference and pedagogy. This fissure or deadlock takes the form of law, although it is an uncanny (*unheimlich*) form because of its slippery, mutable nature. The attempt to grasp or get a handle on it, rather than allay its effects, instead allows for its variegated reproduction at another level. In this sense, law functions as a limit. In contradistinction to Žižek and Dean, the theories of Butler (and, at times, Foucault) suggest the possibility that this limit can be reintroduced to the plane of immanence, politicized, and thereby resisted. Fetterley and Crowley implicitly subscribe to this model, in terms of both their pedagogies and their accounts of what happened. Thus, I have described their pedagogies as operating out of the notion that power produces normalized bodies, that it in fact materializes bodies, and that pedagogy provides one means for counterproduction (i.e., resistance). Instead of simple counterproduction, however, their pedagogical projects go awry, in part because their pedagogies are enacted (or performed) as a means of transformation or as a way to cite normatives differently. Accordingly, the male students are simply guilty of bad power, even if this is to be expected because they are choosing to reproduce (to cite conventionally) the discourses of normative sexuality and thereby uphold standard (or sexist) notions of binary sexual division. From the Lacanian perspective, there is a fissure between teacher and student that cannot be bridged, not so much despite the specific content as because of it. The students are not learning what the teacher directly wants them to learn. They are learning from, and reacting to, what emerges in excess of the specific content. This is most commonly understood to mean the pedagogy itself, but given the dynamic and complex connections among teaching procedures, subject matter, and larger contextual factors, "pedagogy" can only function as a vague metaphoric condensation of what is being enacted. Nevertheless, this pedagogic "excess" illuminates a limit that cannot be transcended solely by means of course content or, to put it otherwise, by means of knowledge inculcation. In terms of pedagogy, the upshot is that the content of the course is split, and this split emerges as a disjunctive law whose symptom is resistance.

And this brings us to my final point. My discussion of the differences between Žižek's and Butler's theories of power finds itself played out in classrooms, where important implications for their positions can be worked through. Examples of classroom resistance are especially telling, and not only because student resistance—as troubling, problematic, and angst inducing as it can be—needs to be rethought. If our sense of the classroom is akin to a social microcosm, an arena for staging in miniature the development of critical citizenship and social transformation, we are mistaken on a number of counts. We misrecognize the extent to which pedagogy itself is circumscribed by limits that materialize in countless permutations as disjunctions between form and content. We code resistance as a problem needing resolution, and the resisters as suspect. This is especially easy to do in cases such as sexism, where there are clearly delineated normative values underpinning leftist, academic perspectives. Thus, Crowley suggests that in the eyes of her students she was an old woman, a figure culturally powerless and therefore not to be taken seriously; Fetterley merely acknowledges that resistance can work both ways, so watch out. What neither of them does, and what we might do, is acknowledge this limit not as a hindrance to our pedagogical goals but as our most crucial sign of hope. If students resist us, this means that resistance is always ongoing, always present, and that it functions as an emergent limit qua law beyond the immanent play of power. Not everything is power, even if the fissure traced by this statement inevitably finds its particular manifestation within such play. But its particular manifestation is never exhaustive. The reserve that remains opens the space for resistance even as it necessitates the fundamental role of rhetoric in all our affairs.

6

"Hands Up! You're Free"
Pedagogy, Affect, and Transformation

One of the lessons which Hitler has taught us is that it is better not to be too clever. The Jews put forward all kinds of well-founded arguments to show that he could not come to power when his rise was clear for all to see. I remember a conversation during which a political economist demonstrated—on the basis of the interests of the Bavarian brewers—that the Germans could not be brought into line. Other experts proved that Fascism was impossible in the West. The educated made it easy for the barbarians everywhere by being so stupid. The farsighted judgments, the forecasts based on statistics and experience, the comments beginning "this is a subject I know very well," and the well-rounded, solid statements, are all untrue.

> —Max Horkheimer and Theodor W. Adorno, *Dialectic of Enlightenment*

At all events, it is better to be controlled by someone else than by oneself. Better to be oppressed, exploited, persecuted, and manipulated by someone other than by oneself. . . . In this sense, the entire movement for liberation and emancipation, inasmuch as it is predicated on a demand for greater autonomy—or, in other words, on a more complete introjection of all forms of control and constraint under the banner of freedom—is a regression.

> —Jean Baudrillard, *The Transparency of Evil*

I believe in Jesus, I just don't have belief.

> —The House of Love, "Fisherman's Tale"

CYNICISM AND VIOLENCE have come under increasing scrutiny by political agencies, the media, and educational organizations. According to Henry Giroux, if the professional pollsters are correct, we live in a "culture of cynicism" ("Cultural" 505). Associated with a postmodern sense of the futility of critique or of attempts to substantially change the world for the better, this pervasive cynicism undercuts collective and individual engagement in socio-political activity, reducing the investment necessary for sustained and vibrant public commitments.[1] Meanwhile, social violence and its media amplification are also perceived to be pressing issues requiring redress. Indeed, our "culture of cynicism" could as well be described as a "culture of fear." Fear of violence underwrites the battery of security mechanisms that shape postmodern life: surveillance, monitoring, guards and patrols, gates, procedures, and the like. Violence and cynicism together produce a climate of resignation, the sense that any attempt at social transformation will yield more of the same, or perhaps something worse.

This debilitating cynicism began emerging in the 1980s and 1990s as a new generation came of age. It is useful to compare this cynicism with the sensibility of the 1960s, as evoked by Lester Faigley (see chapter 4). Faigley, again, characterizes the 1960s as marked by a utopian confidence that the world could be changed for the better. A large gulf separates that conviction from our contemporary zeitgeist. Consider the iconic alternative rock group of the early 1990s, Nirvana, who articulated their generation's cynicism with the unlikely anthem "Smells Like Teen Spirit." Its lyrics—"I feel stupid and contagious / Here we are now, entertain us"; "Oh well, whatever, nevermind"—were rambling, disjointed slices of angst-ridden ennui. Little comparison to the utopian spirit of the 1960s is possible. In fact, that sensibility was itself mocked by Nirvana in the song "Territorial Pissings," prefaced by a shrill, atonal rendition of the chorus to the Youngbloods' baby-boomer anthem "Get Together": "Come on people now / Smile on your brother / Everybody get together / Try to love one another right now." In an age when nobody really seems to want to "get together," there also seems to be an escalation in violence at the social and personal levels. The 1960s and 1970s saw greater media violence than previous decades, in the form of riots and protests, Vietnam and other war footage, and greater interest by the entertainment industry in depictions of violence for profit. This interest in and deployment of violence through media channels has continued to grow. All this is readily apparent in the media, from the news to film to music to games; it is readily apparent in its effects, from discussions of the dangers of violence, especially as an influence on children, to the culture of fear in which we live—the culture of the gated community, intrusive surveillance, engineered safety, and threats of terror.

Because of their cynicism, apathy, and predilection for violent behavior, youth have become an object of concern for political pundits and educators. Neil Howe and Bill Strauss note that the reputation of the young has become a "metaphor for America's loss of purpose, disappointment with institutions, despair over culture, and fear for the future" ("New" 79). Complaints about their stupidity, hatred, laziness, and antisocial behavior abound.[2] The litany of grievances paints a picture of cynical, violent youth who lack the discipline or knowledge to overcome their shortcomings. These negative portrayals have only become more pervasive in the media following a string of school shootings—Pearl, Mississippi; West Paducah, Kentucky; Jonesboro, Arkansas; Edinboro, Pennsylvania, Springfield, Oregon; Littlefield, Colorado; and Red Lake, Minnesota. Such events have fostered in the public imaginary a conflation of images of bored, disaffected youth with incidents of violence and crime.

It is perhaps inevitable that educators find themselves confronted with these problems of cynicism and violence in their teaching. Peter Sacks's bestselling account of the current state of education, *Generation X Goes to College: An Eye-Opening Account of Teaching in Postmodern America*, openly proclaims that cynicism is a direct response to the pervasiveness of media culture and the delegitimation of knowledge and power. Reluctance to complete any assignment not tied to a grade, the relativist slogan "It's just your opinion," and a distrust of teachers and schools are commonplaces. Overall, Sacks claims, students' indoctrination by media culture, which leads them to expect to be entertained; their internalization of attacks on science and reason, which delegitimates large swaths of knowledge; and their loss of faith in authorities and institutions, which erodes trust in the possibility of effective socio-political action, are indicative of the paralytic effects of large-scale, deep-seated cynicism. These are the students who give teachers The Look: the blank, bored stare of utter disengagement (Sacks 9).

The problems of cynicism and violence, while certainly not new and arguably not as severe as media coverage might suggest, are nevertheless noteworthy for being symptomatic of larger cultural shifts.[3] These shifts, often described as "postmodernism," can also be described in terms of what Deleuze calls the "society of control" and Žižek calls "de-Oedipalization." These two otherwise disparate theories of the social connect since they both argue that Foucault's concept of the disciplinary society no longer carries sufficient descriptive force. Deleuze and Žižek suggest that power is no longer organized primarily through institutions to produce compliant, useful, and productive bodies; instead, institutions are breaking down, and forms of external regulation are withdrawing. However, as has been noted by numerous cultural theorists, there has not been a concomitant resurgence of liberatory practices. The usefulness of Deleuze and Žižek is that they provide two ways to model the flows of power and highlight their modes of control. Žižek further suggests that the withdrawal of the body of external social regulations and constraints—what is referred to as the big Other—has initiated post-Oedipalized forms of subjectivity no longer keyed to the Oedipal scene. Lacking libidinal,

"HANDS UP! YOU'RE FREE"

internalized attachment to authority (typically in patriarchal forms of the Father and its substitutions), subjects now are prone to disaffected attitudes and behavior, including cynicism, apathy, disregard for others, and violence.

Interest in the problems of cynicism and violence has extended to rhetoric and composition, not only because cynicism and violence are implicated in rhetoric. Apropos in this regard is Michael Blitz and C. Mark Hurlbert's *Letters for the Living: Teaching Writing in a Violent Age*, which might be described as a casebook about post-Oedipal subjects in the classroom. In one narrative, Blitz writes to Hurlbert about a student, Matthew, who snickers throughout class, "making cynical remarks about the project proposals, choosing the paths of least resistance in [his] writings, and spending, at most, 10 minutes per short assignment" (30). Matthew waits until the last minute to do his project, and when he finally turns it in, it is less than half the required length. In his paper, Matthew relates his experiences as an emergency medical technician (EMT) who has witnessed many traumatic episodes of the type that most people do not see, except on TV. He recounts a time when he was the first EMT on the scene where a man had brutally raped and killed his girlfriend's daughter, a toddler; the perpetrator had then himself been brutally beaten by the police while in lockup (30–32).

Blitz is, understandably, at a loss: how does one evaluate such work? It is filled with superficial errors, and Matthew's conclusions are neither apt nor particularly well considered. Blitz sees that Matthew is simply "at his limit for sensitivity" (32), but at the same time, how can he give him credit simply for going through a harrowing experience? Blitz's problem is noteworthy for the larger issues it illuminates. To what extent can Blitz offer Matthew anything that will undercut or sever the tight connection between violence and cynicism or allow him to "make sense" of what he has witnessed? Blitz's problem, I suggest, is of importance to education in general, and composition in particular, if we attend to the ways pedagogy is implicated in forms of social control and violence and is called to engage, intervene, or otherwise grapple with such problems.

In what follows, I use Deleuze's and Žižek's ideas concerning the global society of control and de-Oedipalization to argue that many writing pedagogies manifest an authoritarian violence that restrictively re-Oedipalizes students. I suggest that we might theorize a postpedagogy that recognizes the inventive possibilities already inherent in post-Oedipal subjectivities in order to promote writing Acts that shift control of the dominant loci of contention from the teacher to the student.[4] This would not be a decentering of the classroom so much as a remodulation—in terms of content, practice, evaluation— that refuses to mirror the society of control with a pedagogy of control. The goal is to resist projects of re-Oedipalization and avoid the dismissal of writing Acts that have unacknowledged value, whether transgressive, inventive, or otherwise productive.

TOWARD THE ACT

Implicit in pedagogies centered on cultural critique is a faith that teaching writing can resist dominant social practices and empower students, and in this way, it is argued, cynicism can be overcome. As I have been proposing throughout the book, however, the notion that we can actually foster resistance through teaching is questionable. Paul Mann takes this idea even further, suggesting that "all the forms of opposition have long since revealed themselves as means of advancing it. . . . The mere fact that something feels like resistance and still manages to offend a few people (usually not even the right people) hardly makes it effective" (138). From Mann's perspective, opposition in the postmodern world has been co-opted, with the implication that other strategies are to be sought or developed. In light of Mann's statement, I urge us to take the following position: teaching writing is fully complicit with dominant social practices, and inducing students to write in accordance with institutional precepts can be as disabling as it is enabling. By disabling, I do not mean that certain skills—typically those most associated with current traditional rhetorics, like grammatical correctness, basic organization, syntactic clarity, and such—are not useful. Such skills are useful and are often those most necessary for tapping the power that writing can wield. Nor should my statement be taken to mean that we should abandon these writerly precepts. What I am suggesting is that they might be inhabited differently.

Thus, as students learn the things we ostensibly teach, we might also ask what students are not learning. What other forms of writing and thinking are being shut down or distorted—forms of writing that have their own, different powers and inventive allure? We might consider this question to have greater heuristical than critical value, but from the perspective I am working from, this only adds to its importance. So if one of our goals as teachers of writing is to initiate students in rhetorics of power and resistance, to get them to see the motivated nature of the word, we should also be equally attuned to rhetorics of contestation—which is not necessarily the same as opposition. Indeed, this issue of contestation is a consequence of my earlier argument that "there is no pedagogical relationship." Sure, there is no correlative, harmonious teacher-student relation, but perhaps this pedagogical fissure can be seen to work for us, to enable us in productive ways. We might then take seriously the impossibility of knowing the areas of contention and struggle that will be most important in our students' lives or of assuming that our lines of contention will be theirs. Pedagogy could reflect this concern by promoting the idea that each student's life is its own *telos:* the individual struggles of each student cannot and should not necessarily mirror our own. This is but one reason for rethinking cultural studies pedagogies and their focus on oppositional and ultimately Oedipalizing strategies, moving toward less critical and more inventional pedagogies. Or, to look at the matter from a different perspective, students must sooner or later overcome *us*, even though we may legitimate our sense of service with the idea that we have their best interests in mind—a position, I hardly need add, that we enjoy. There is something suspicious about this presumptive ethic of service through knowing best; as Paul Mann argues, "nothing is more aggressive than the desire to serve the other" (48). In other words, in our desire to do what is best for students, we often have difficulty moving outside our own frames of contestation, our sense of what is important or at stake, and this makes it difficult for us to grasp how these matters will be to greater and lesser degrees different for our students. It is inevitable, then, that we too will have to be superseded, contested, or abandoned at some point.

The next step for writing pedagogy, however, cannot be that we just stop teaching writing as we have been teaching it; given the institutional and cultural fetishization of thesis statements, grades, and grammar, this would be well-nigh impossible anyway. Nor can we take such fetishization lightly; attending to these facets of writing is necessarily a part of our everyday pedagogy. But, going further, we might inflect our own particular pedagogies with insight into education's general culpability, to the extent that we grant students possibilities for a writing that would be their own Act. This asks us to acknowledge that we do not always know best how to rectify social problems for *them*, and this further necessitates a partial relinquishing of control and learning from students. Not only could student knowledge be incorporated into the subject of the pedagogy (as in class discussions), but it could be incorporated into the pedagogical structure itself, so that content, methodology, and affective comportment all become intermeshed with student knowledge and experience. Nowhere is this more pertinent than in cultural studies–based pedagogies that seek the disruption and politicization of hierarchies of power and privilege, especially in terms of race, class, and gender. Problems arise in part because of the continued reliance on critique as a means for personal and social transformation. That is, despite the good intentions and soundly reasoned groundwork underlying many of these pedagogical approaches, they can nevertheless produce new forms of power and privilege that in turn produce new resistances, further alienate already cynical students, and (re)produce the possibility of violence.

In *Fragments of Rationality*, Faigley wrestles with Baudrillard's theories as emblematic of postmodern culture. Faigley sees Baudrillard as a controversial figure, a combination of court jester and astute observer, simultaneously ironic and blithe about the traumatic and often lamentable events of the postmodern age. Faigley notes that what most disturbs Baudrillard's critics, however, is his denial of the possibility of criticism. He adds that Baudrillard's arguments pose dire problems for pedagogies that are centered on the possibility of critique, such as social-epistemic rhetorics and cultural studies, and on student writers themselves, who are expected to produce effective critical writing. Such claims—Baudrillard's arguments and Faigley's warnings—have direct bearing on my project insofar as the effort to establish a critical sensibility in students seems to find its limit in postmodern cynicism.

Faigley understands this danger and explains how Baudrillard poses a danger to teachers and scholars who are invested in achieving political progress via critical approaches to culture. He writes:

If Baudrillard's claim is valid, then the key assumption of a cultural studies pedagogy—that students can usefully investigate how mass culture is produced, circulated, and consumed—is called into question. Baudrillard's critique is far more extreme than merely arguing that students are situated within their culture and that any conclusions they reach will be circumscribed by that culture. Baudrillard rejects the idea that we can somehow get outside the flow of codes, simulations, and images to discover any space for social critique. Instead, the process is just the opposite: as society is increasingly saturated with ever expanding quantities of information, objects, and services, the space for the autonomous subject with a capacity for critical thought collapses. (213)

Academics who maintain the necessity for critique, then, are from Baudrillard's perspective wallowing in nostalgia for a time when it was possible to find a space for social critique and maintain faith in its transformative potential. Faigley resists Baudrillard's arguments, claiming that this position is one of "unrelenting cynicism," but let us highlight what he tells us next: "I find Baudrillard valuable particularly in one respect: students often sound very much like him" (212).

Who are these students that Faigley aligns with Baudrillard? It is important to emphasize that Baudrillard is often seen as easily dismissable, ethically objectionable, and politically irresponsible, someone whose work is a cartoon-like caricature of perspicacious scholarship (Faigley, *Fragments* 207–9). How does Faigley link such a characterization to his students? In his discussion of the networked classroom, Faigley supplies the transcript of an online class discussion about a *Ladies' Home Journal* article on sexual politics. He describes the dialogue that his students produced as "coming from outer space," adding "that beyond the giggly, junior-high-school-bus level of the discussion of sexuality, it had a ghostly quality, an image of the dance of death on the graves of the old narratives of moral order" (196). Similarly, Faigley later presents a student essay that details how a female student effectively transformed her high school sister into an acceptable collegiate package over the course of a weekend. Faigley is so amazed by the narrative's brand-name consciousness that he at first suspects it is a parody; he links the paper's total capitulation to consumerism-as-identity to Baudrillard's claim that we, as subjects, would rather be taken profoundly as objects (214–15).

Faigley points out that what links all these scenarios involving his students—the Bugs Bunny–level understanding of sexuality, the Tommy Hilfiger–inspired equation of brand names with identity—is a certain "cynical energy that Baudrillard calls an 'evil genie' because it undermines all narratives of human progress and rational systems of morality and science" (*Fragments* 215). The drive to be an object is aligned with the desire to achieve a sense of self exclusively across the perceptions of others because in both orientations the sign's role is central, to the extent that a sense of individual agency can be covered over by the object-sign qua student. It is a kind of defensive cynicism that has its own power, its own form of revenge, against those who would make them subjects, that is, subjectivized through meanings and narratives that they have to assume and in which they come to invest. According to Faigley, what Baudrillard's point illustrates is that "what fascinates everyone and thus what drives our society is the debauchery of signs" (216). The sign is debauched because it transcends all social codes, practices, and institutions that would regulate values, regardless of whether or not these values are yoked to notions of social utility and justice. Signs are therefore slippery, multivalent, normative one moment, oppositional the next. Unstable and ungrounded, they nevertheless exude a seductive pull that functions as the central mode of being, as the "ungrounded ground," operative in the contemporary world. When students-as-objects take on this logic of the sign, they thereby submit themselves to this same debauchery of meaning. There should be little wonder that teachers of writing would find this extremely frustrating, when writing is predicated on controlling the flow of signs.

Faigley conveys well the difficulty of bringing students who are so immersed in consumerist media culture to critical consciousness, but he does not emphasize the extent to which critique is threatened by a transformation in the way the sign functions in postmodern culture. In other words, not only the impossibility of escaping the code but the reversibility of all signs defang critical discourse. There is no sign upon which critical discourse can depend that is not itself jeopardized by reversals and transformations in meaning. This point was underscored for me in a memorable composition class. It was the late 1990s, and we were reading Ronald Collins and David Skover's essay "The Death of Discourse" in the first-year composition reader *Signs of Life*. The authors argue that mass-media consumer discourse, to the extent that it disrupts the possibility of effective political discourse by catering to the lowest common denominator and providing endless distraction, should no longer be given full protection from the First Amendment. My students' response was massive apathy, summed up by one female student with the trenchant explanation, "But we're happy." Setting aside all the counterevidence that could be brought up to demonstrate otherwise, the point underscored in the resulting class discussion was that the First Amendment, as a *sign* (of the guarantee of free speech, of American freedoms in general), was no longer stable for them. Not only did Collins and Skover's argument depend on a reversal of the First Amendment as a sign (the guarantee of free speech in the form of the First Amendment is now producing the opposite effect by obstructing forms of free speech), but my students' apathy indicated the extent to which the First Amendment no longer signified American freedom in general (hence the apathetic response to Collins and Skover's attack on this most prized amendment). Several students, for example, indicated that they would prefer other people to make social and political decisions so that they would not have to be bothered thinking about them. What this episode seems to indicate, if it is possible to extrapolate from it, is that there is a sharp break between the worldviews of teachers and students in the postmodern age that has little precedent, and one of the key fault lines falls along the role of critique.

Victor Vitanza has also attended to the crisis of critical discourse. In contradistinction to Faigley, Vitanza deploys Baudrillard to show that the drive to generate determinate meanings for cultural objects and practices, a procedure necessary for critical consciousness to awaken, can also produce a reversibility of the sign that renders critical discourse unstable. In other words, the sign is liberated from the requirement that it maintain some semblance of stability. In "The Hermeneutics of Abandonment," Vitanza explains that, as in the case of the First Amendment example, facts have become interpretations; he argues that this state of affairs has yet to be adequately confronted, so that critical facts are continually deployed in the effort to generate liberatory activity with little acknowledgment of how precarious this practice is. Vitanza writes: "And yet, still ever *again*, some of us insist that we see the lack of liberation everywhere. However, enlightened false consciousness, and radical technologizing (all the world's simulation), and the *loss of categories* (sign/signifier, privileged/supplement, public/private, male/female, good/evil, just/unjust)— all these and more make it impossible for 'any radical critique'; that is, make it difficult for us to help others *see* injustice, and, if seen, to get others to want to change the world in which we all live" ("Hermeneutics" 134). Vitanza notes that it was already quite difficult to effect change in the world when it was believed that the sign maintained some stability and granted some semblance of truth; given the fate of the sign as described by Baudrillard, however, he claims that all modernist enterprises—all that would depend on the stability of the sign or the (critical) truths extracted from the sign—are "impossible" ("Hermeneutics" 134). It is instructive to compare Faigley and Vitanza on this issue and delineate where the "impossible" lies. Faigley emphasizes the extent to which it is impossible to elude the code, thereby preventing the possibility of achieving critical distance, whereas Vitanza calls us to note the transformation in the processes of recognition and persuasion. That is, Faigley sees the problem of the sign as described by Baudrillard as one of spatiality—a question of the proper critical position whereby it would be possible to regain critical effectiveness. Thus, he retains the modernist hope for overcoming the instability of the sign. Vitanza, conversely, understands Baudrillard as describing not only a socio-political but a discursive transformation: the way discourse functions, its effects and effectivity, has mutated. The fate of the sign is that it is no guarantee at all; rather, it twists upon itself, moving from use value to exchange value to sign value to what Baudrillard calls fractal value, in which meaning radiates out, unstable and immanently reversible.[5] The structures that were formerly reliable for establishing the proper perspectives, values, and determinations are thereby dissolved, mutated, transformed, multiplied. The postmodern age is one that must deal with the insufficiencies of modernist strategies for stabilizing the sign. Of course, investments in modernist strategies and critical hermeneutics still abound, even if various postmodern discourses have suggested that they will not deliver on what they promise and have accordingly offered alternate strategies. It is for this reason that Vitanza advocates abandonment—abandonment of those critical enterprises that ultimately depend on interpretive procedures motivated by the desire to control signs. What Vitanza sees so clearly is that invention, intervention, and resistance will emerge in other ways and that cultural studies pedagogies tend to delimit if not obstruct them.

CONTROL AND THE CRITICAL DRIVE

If the postmodern age is in part characterized by a new recognition of the sign's instability, then it makes sense that so many theorists would be interested in alternate understandings of subjectivity. If the sign is unstable, then so is the subject. For this reason, among others, many theorists seek a conception of subjectivity no longer predicated on Oedipalization (the process of internalizing repression as enacted by the law) but on multiplicity, whereby an individuated, Oedipalized subject becomes the de-Oedipalized, dispersed subject. This additionally suggests needed innovations in pedagogical strategies and intents. Rather than bemoan the difficulties of achieving a critical distance that will revitalize our hopes for making the world better, I suggest that we rebegin from an abandonment of that critical drive, at least as it is currently defined and practiced, and especially in the way it informs and structures pedagogies and the subjectivities that they invoke and police. If, as Vitanza states, we live in a world where it is more difficult than ever to get others to see injustice, or if they do see it, to actually do something about it, we might well ask how our pedagogies are implicated. The temptation, of course, is to ignore such complications; in the name of justice and the good, pedagogies are to enact the desire to accomplish positive change in students, to liberate and empower them. In the classroom, this too often comes to mean, as D. Diane Davis puts it, "that students (and scholars) rush to judgment in the name of the Conclusion, that they simplify complexity in the name of clarity, and they rein in their own multiplicitous sites of exploration in the name of *The* authoritative voice" (*Breaking* 16–17). And when it comes to pedagogies that are predicated on instilling the properly critical attitude in students, that "authoritative voice" is usually the teacher's, the subject who knows (best), whose voice the students will dutifully reproduce in the proper discursive format.

We are left with the question of what kind of pedagogy would be resonant with the postmodern world, seeking a performative mode that does not depend on reproduction of the authoritative/authorizing voice. It would be hasty, however, to intimate that we could simply abandon the critical drive and things would be better. First, such a project would not be easy. The critical drive remains; it is not just going to disappear. Indeed, my argument that critique is part of the problem already takes part in that same critical drive, an irony that is not lost on me. This irony concerning criticism is well explored in Mann's *Masocriticism*, where it is argued that critical interpretation is ultimately a futile exercise, a fact that ultimately does nothing to detract from the pleasure (*jouissance*) it evokes—hence *masocriticism* equals *masochism* plus *criticism*.[6] But this too must be a (re)beginning place: the host of inner contradictions, impossibilities, failures, and other setbacks on the road to something better—better pedagogies, better theories, better students, better world—should be understood as being part of the road itself, not setbacks on the road.[7] In part, then, abandonment might mean a redistribution of one's investments; in this case, seeming setbacks might be thought of differently. Though coded negatively, they are not of the negative. They mark the failure of any inherency in strategies, practices, and projects, and as such, they are just as much a guarantee for the possibility of change.

Indeed, these "setbacks" can only appear as such from the utopian perspective of wholeness and harmony for people and for the world. This idea is, I think, at the heart of John Brereton's charge, shared by Richard Miller, that the many reformers who work in education, from E. D. Hirsch and William Bennett to Cary Nelson and Michael Berubé, are often "blind to the fact that they work in constrained circumstances, with imperfect students, an unenlightened administration, and financial limits" (qtd. in R. Miller, *As If* 495). The critiques leveled and the calls made have in common a fundamental idealism and a corresponding will to actualize the vision grounded in that idealism. Implicit in such a utopian view is a profound and extensive faith in the power to effect control, and indeed, as D. Diane Davis reminds us, the field of composition is a "control freak" (*Breaking* 8). For me, this insight already suggests the beginnings of another kind of pedagogical orientation: one that would relinquish faith in the pedagogue's power to control. This does not return us to a vision of the decentered classroom evacuated of power; the teacher still has power, but that power is no longer deployed toward the idealized actualization of an empowering critical consciousness in students. Perhaps what we are really confronting here is the fact that this goal was always precarious, the faith that invested it largely ideological. Student resistance would be one index of that precariousness.

But this problem has still more nuances. In short, we cannot reduce the problem, as Laurie Finke suggests, to a "simple dichotomy between conformity and resistance" (7). Indeed, it is not even enough to suggest that student resistance is a complex interplay among varying modalities, from resistance to authority to resistance to being freed from authority (Finke 20–21). This is so because it is not resistance qua resistance that is at stake but how the dialectic of resistance and conformity structures and informs student thinking and writing and how that dialectic is interpreted and evaluated by composition teachers. That is, compositionists are doubly implicated in the problem of resistance in that they provide the forum and impetus for the actions and thoughts of students while simultaneously providing the very criteria by which those thoughts and actions will be evaluated as critical, or resistant, or some other category. However, despite all of this complex interplay around authority—the reproduction of the proper critical stance, conformity, resistance, and the establishment of pedagogical criteria that provide the hermeneutic framework for understanding all these concepts in their particularity—

despite all that has been theorized as a collection of impediments to learning (to write), it nevertheless happens here and there, in the best classrooms and the worst classrooms, that students learn, and learn writing. Writing happens. Thinking happens. Critical attitudes emerge. It is important not to forget this. But it is equally important to remember that it could be happening more often, that composition's drive to establish and maintain control can actively prevent writing and thinking from being more than the mechanical reproduction of general commonplaces in *the* proper, thesis-centered essay format in *the* proper critical mode. Or, conversely, it may be that good, challenging writing is ever present, but our pedagogies limit us so that we cannot see or acknowledge it.

The point, ultimately, is not that we should immediately change the pedagogical road we are on. This would risk falling into the same critical mode I am discussing, whereby psychoanalytic critique becomes the new authority underwriting more sophisticated control pedagogies. Rather, I suggest that we come to see the road differently, to think about it afresh, and perhaps to try detours or other routes, not by replicating the latest new pedagogies but by reinhabiting current pedagogies through an evolving sensibility.

TOWARD A POSTPEDAGOGY

One significant marker of postpedagogy would be the element of surprise. Although this is hardly a determinate or even precise concept, I submit that it is useful precisely because of its generalized nonspecificity. The fact that other concepts could just as easily be substituted for it (such as creativity, the new, insight, and so on) traces the arc of the ephemeral that I want to convey and seek to introduce into pedagogy. The fresh miracle of surprise can erupt anywhere, out of any circumstances—in a sense surprise evokes *kairos*, while at the same time maintaining its elusive quality. We see that surprise on our own part, for example, when we see good writing come out of a "bad" class.[8] But surprise must also inform pedagogy. As Gilbert D. Chaitin states, "Surprise is the mark of that unpredictability which betrays the operation of the subject as a 'cause' opposed to any law" (236). Surprise, in other words, is the mark of the unique opposed to any general form. Insofar as control is linked to the general (the application and enforcement of a generalized mode or practice on others), we can understand surprise as an indicator of the failure of control, on the one hand, and the subject's ability to extricate itself from a prefabricated discourse acting as a container, on the other. Surprise and control, however, are not diametric opposites, and surprise, being unpredictable, remains uncodifiable. This means that it violates one of composition's most dearly held imperatives—that, as D. Diane Davis, following Vitanza, puts it, "every theory be immediately translatable into workable classroom practice for the pedagogue" (*Breaking* 222; see also Vitanza, "Three" 160–61). Surprise cannot be orchestrated in advance as the glittering pedagogical prize achieved by means of good theories devoted toward just ends. Rather, the pedagogue is just as implicated as the students in the *kairotic* moment(s) that *may* arise; further, it is this mutual implication that makes of the pedagogy a unique moment beyond the possibility of repetition or control. Another though somewhat different way of putting it is, as Theodore Reik claims, that "it is not at all difficult to find words for what we think. . . . It is much more difficult to find out what we think" (qtd. in Chaitin 234). It is the disadvantage of good theories deployed toward just ends that they favor the former, placing it on the side of truth, and not the latter, fearing the risks it entails.

From a psychoanalytic perspective, something is always out of place, sticking out, slipping, in error. A postpedagogy acknowledges this as a starting point and affirms it rather than "fixing" it. Thus, such a postpedagogy can be read as critical to the extent that it challenges the dominant desire to fix things by instilling in students a critical aptitude that is expressed within institutionally defined strictures of what counts as acceptable writing. Faigley's attitude toward his student who demonstrates a glib brand-name consciousness betrays Faigley's own desire to be critical of such a culture, a desire that he seems to want to see replicated in the student. One might further surmise that Faigley enjoys his critical position. To some degree, this aligns Faigley's pedagogy with the process of Oedipalization. Indeed, it is probably the case that Faigley can provide detailed arguments to support his position against his students, and I could further surmise that students, so confronted, would have difficulties marshalling an adequate defense. Of course, I am not suggesting that a teacher must now, in an orgy of self-policing, accept and affirm everything or always agree with students. A postpedagogy would be concerned, however, with transmuting the pedagogical situation to short-circuit the possibility of its becoming what Vitanza calls a "programming session" ("Three" 162). That is, a postpedagogy advocates a shift in what is understood by the word *critical*, moving from a negating or opposing position (which we could call a "negative deconstruction") to an excriptive position that would transform the entire discursive matrix.[9] In other words, postpedagogy is, as I will elaborate, a pedagogy of the Act, in which the goal is not a reversal of valuation (as in a binary reversal or negative deconstruction) achieved through oppositional strategies, but a transvaluation (in the Nietzschean sense) achieved through production.[10]

But it is also the case that such a postpedagogy cannot remain inherently critical. Given that the nature of discourse has shifted to the extent that all signs are reversible, we should be attentive to how shifts in culture, subjectivity, and politics transform a pedagogy—its reception, operation, and efficacy. I am specifically moving toward a consideration of some central postmodern characteristics: a particular kind of violence, characterized by Lynn Worsham as "wilding," and a certain detachment or waning of affect, often categorized as "cynicism" (see Worsham 214–15, 228–29; Bewes 3–7; Sloterdijk 3–8). In terms of the path this chapter is charting, I am looking for the moment when ambiguity becomes apathy. My suggestion is that the production of that apathy by both hegemonic and marginal pedagogies challenges us all to consider how the instruction of writing is deeply implicated in global trends, including those trends that a given pedagogy is designed to resist.

I also want to note that the dilemma I am staging here by means of Faigley is an ancient one that goes back at least to Plato's *Gorgias*. Socrates and Callicles argue concerning rhetoric that it should be placed in the service of justice and the good as defined by philosophical discourse (Socrates) or should serve the individual strength and desire of the powerful (Callicles). How should we understand Faigley in terms of this binary situation? On the one hand, we can see him as inhabiting the Socratic position, having greater knowledge of what is good and what is not and putting that knowledge toward obtaining change for the better in the student. On the other hand, we can see him modeling Callicles's position, in that he uses his strength (as a sophisticated and powerful rhetor/pedagogue) and desire (to achieve critical distance toward consumer culture for himself and his students) for his pedagogical and personal ends. Ultimately, both positions have validity. My argument is that the postmodern era makes it increasingly difficult to tell one of these positions from the other or to determine which is better, more effective, or more ethical. Thus, I return again to Vitanza's point in "The Hermeneutics of Abandonment," derived from Baudrillard, Deleuze, and other postmodern thinkers, that all depths implode into surfaces, or, to put it another way, that there currently exists an imminent reversibility of the sign (126, 128). The questions I want to turn to now are directed toward the issues that arise when pedagogy confronts ambiguity, apathy, and cynicism. What kind of pedagogy obtains from these postmodern conditions and attitudes? Who are its subjects? What are its modes of operation?

De-Oedipalization might be considered as being but a different modality of what we generally call postmodernism. As I have argued, de-Oedipalization has direct bearing on what pedagogies are used, how they are practiced, how they are received, and what they achieve in terms of their effectiveness. I should emphasize that both critical pedagogies and postpedagogies are implicated—it is not my intention to proffer the latest pedagogy as a simple solution to our post/modernist ills. Although I favor a postpedagogy, I do not want to stop there. Instead, I want to ask how it would be possible to achieve a pedagogy that retains a critical sensibility—or, better, how it is possible to transmute it into an/other pedagogy that forestalls such a question, that achieves a perspective from which that question would appear less meaningful or important. Specifically, this pedagogy would not fall prey to the desire to reproduce itself in the student, would not ask students to join the Cause, would not ask them to seek out the (one) truth as the answer that will make the world a better place, and would not school them into a protracted cynicism. Or, as Geoffrey Sirc states in "Godless Composition, Tormented Writing," a "composition assumes satisfaction, success, desires satisfaction"; accordingly, a postpedagogy for composition can only appear as a kind of *Summa Atheologica* where writing happens "without the God of Meaning, without the Commandment of Project" (545).

What is staged, then, is further evidence that Oedipalizing projects do not work as intended. The postmodern "waning of affect" makes it increasingly difficult, Worsham argues, "to bind meaning to feeling" and thereby to obtain from others the emotional commitment and motivation to do the work necessary for concrete social change. The idea that affect is actually "waning" is problematic; what is really being suggested is that de-Oedipalization involves different or redistributed affective investments. The question would not be, "where did affect go?" but "what are its new patterns?" This further suggests that a postpedagogy cannot be a trouble-free solution to the problems facing pedagogies invested in Oedipalizing forms of "schooling." Although I, like Davis and Vitanza, consider a postpedagogy to be an approach that redefines the pedagogical scene in ways that decline the oppositional, Oedipalizing politics of radical, critical pedagogies, I also argue that we need to ask what effects de-Oedipalization will have on a postpedagogy. It will also be important to discern the different ways in which de-Oedipalization can occur and to be especially sensitive to the way certain forms of de-Oedipalization can perpetuate dangerous, destructive, and disempowering practices in the postmodern era. Finally, it will also be necessary to ask how it is that some forms of de-Oedipalization lend themselves to further refinements in the control of subjects, despite the fact that de-Oedipalization is ostensibly a process describing the dissolution of external prohibitions.

THE GLOBAL SOCIETY OF CONTROL IN A DE-OEDIPALIZED AGE

In *Fugitive Cultures: Race, Violence, and Youth*, Henry Giroux discusses some of the transformations that have occurred in youth's relation to the process of schooling. He argues: "Youth . . . often find themselves being educated and regulated within institutions that have little relevance for their lives. This is expressed most strongly in schools. . . . Schooling appears to many youth to be as irrelevant as it is boring. . . . In a rapidly changing postmodern cultural landscape, the voice of authority no longer resides exclusively in the modernist spheres of the school, family, and workplace" (13). Giroux suggests not only that schools too often present a curriculum that fails to address real student needs and interests but that institutions like schools have lost some of the authority and power they once had. Giroux's argument resonates with the post-Foucauldian work of cultural theorists who claim that the modernist society of disciplinary institutions is waning as new forms of social control emerge.

The transformation from a disciplinary society (Foucault) to a global society of control (Deleuze) ensures "the decline of the mediatory functions of the social institutions" (Hardt 140).[11] Institutional, or disciplinary, control is predicated on a certain stability of subject and discourse, as in the dialectical play of inside and outside. Yet what may have been clearly defined spaces and flows in modernity give way to a smooth space in which "there is no place of power — it is both everywhere and nowhere" (Hardt 143). As Hardt explains, "the walls of the institutions are breaking down in such a way that their disciplinary logics do not become ineffective but are rather generalized in fluid forms across the social field" (139). However, the breakdown of institutions has not yielded a corresponding breakdown in forms of control. Rather, the matrices of control have themselves been transformed, finding flexible, less discernible modalities from which to operate. These remodulations in the flow of power have certain concrete effects on the kind of subjectivity that is produced, which further changes the social and discursive fields within which strategies of control operate.

Nikolas Rose describes this transformation in terms of the movement from individuals to "dividuals" (see also Deleuze, *Negotiations* 180). We are not dealing "with subjects with a unique personality that is the expression of some inner fixed quality, but elements, capacities, potentialities. These are plugged into multiple orbits, identified by unique codes, identification numbers, profiles of preferences, security ratings and so forth: a 'record' containing a whole variety of bits of information on our credentials, activities, qualifications for entry into this or that network" (234). Control becomes dispersed and distant, concerned with actual conduct rather than with a "self." Since changing people's beliefs is difficult and costly, the focus of control mechanisms shifts toward actual behavior. Management strategies deemphasize direct contact in favor of preemptive structures of prevention. Such control strategies, Rose states, are "based upon a dream of the technocratic control of the accidental by continuous monitoring and management of risk" (235). Rose further notes that as control strategies shift loci of contention away from individual subjectivities and groups, the possibilities for resistances organized through identification (with an individual or group) lose vitality (236). Modernist forms of resistance through identification with a subject position (criminal, patient) or ideology (Marxism) lose political effectiveness when power no longer operates along those lines of contention. Control dissolves its investments in any particular group or strategy, finding renewed vigor in a highly generalized effectiveness: what matters is whatever works.

Žižek, like Deleuze, is also interested in exploring transformations in subject formation initiated by the breakdown of institutions and the dispersal of power. He argues that changes in social and discursive fields indicate a lessening of the structural influence of what Lacan calls "the big Other," the social discourses and institutions that mold and discipline subjects (*Ticklish* 332). Žižek suggests that once the big Other withdraws from the scene of meaning, the perspective from which the sign is approached becomes determinant, as opposed to any broader social assignment of meaning. The big Other no longer functions as the guarantor of the modicum of consensual agreement that works to stabilize meaning. Instead, we enter the world of multiplicities, *technes* of the self, dispersed subjectivities, performances. It is a world that slip-slides out of Foucault's disciplinary society in which institutions (church, school, family, hospital, prison, state) fashion particular modes of subjectivity by means of internal and external conjunctions of power and knowledge. As the big Other withdraws, so also the repressive, Oedipal forces withdraw. We are left in a world of multiplicitous possibilities, embodied flows that are not now quite what was meant formerly by the term *subject*, which, it should be recalled, cannot exist without repression (Deleuze and Guattari, *Anti-Oedipus* 26).[12] Žižek argues that the subject that emerges in the postmodern world is post-Oedipal, meaning that it is not produced via the same modernist mechanisms that produced the properly "humanist" subject. In this way, too, Žižek insinuates that identification with external institutions and subject positions has lost its formerly preeminent place in political practices.

The idea of a de-Oedipalized subjectivity is not especially new, but its characteristics, aesthetics, practices, and ethics are still to be fully explored. Fred Pfeil suggests, though, that a post-Oedipal form of subjectivity was being broached in 1980s music, theater, and film. Paradigmatic for Pfeil is the film *River's Edge* (1986), based on a true story about a group of high school adolescents who hid the murder of one member of the group by another. Pfeil analyzes the film and its portrayal of "a social field characterized by the decline of the Oedipal/patriarchal authority" that is "without replacement by any other psychic and social principles for meaning, individuation, and order" (218). The world depicted in *River's Edge* resonates with other descriptions of the decline of orienting metanarratives and consensually established, guiding criteria. Pfeil comments, "In such a morbid situation, marked by the devaluing of both private and public figurations of significance and signifying power, *pathologies run rampant*, especially insofar as, for men, the dissolution of the Oedipal 'solution' to the task of separation and individuation from the female mother opens the way to a vast outpouring of fearful misogynist rage, and a desperate, protofascist attempt to restore patriarchal authority in the private and public realms at all costs" (218; my emphasis). The waning of patriarchal/Oedipal/symbolic authority has been greeted with a variety of responses, from glib celebration to dire predictions of violence and lawlessness. It is not my purpose to join in any of the responses that lie along that continuum but to suggest instead that there is a certain fait accompli about the transformation. We should explore what is entailed by such a transformation in order to ascertain its potentialities as well as its dangers. Pfeil addresses this issue by expressing doubt about the continued viability of socialist goals. A new strategic project of attaining socialism without "any ordering principle or *a priori* category of the Real" is problematic not because he doubts its validity, especially "given the exhaustion of all the strategies of immanence we have seen," but because he cannot see how, "in the world we share with the kids in *River's Edge*, it could ever work" (222). I read Pfeil as falling into cynical accommodation since he is unable to articulate an effective social strategy for these newly emergent posthuman subjectivities.

More than likely, however, multiple forms of post-Oedipalization are possible, allowing theorists to develop a variety of de-Oedipalizing strategies. Deleuze and Guattari's attacks on Oedipalization, for example, are designed to produce schizo-subjects who can resist the territorializing effects of family, state, and capital. This form of de-Oedipalization—literally an anti-Oedipalization—is not congruent with the forms of de-Oedipalized subjectivity currently emerging. Deleuze and Guattari want de-Oedipalization to occur through a concrete realization of the schizophrenic desire that is inherent in capitalism; for them, resistance is thus not a form of opposition, per se. They are not as concerned about the resistance to or withdrawal of external regulations as they are about the acceleration and proliferation of desire *within* social systems. Unfortunately, as forms of external regulation withdraw in favor of other forms of social control, it is difficult to see a corresponding acceleration and proliferation of desire. What this means, perhaps, is that capitalism has found ways to counter the possibility offered by Deleuze and Guattari, or at least to make it more difficult to achieve, and has thereby made possible the reterritorialization of de-Oedipalized subjects by means of an internal master unsupported by any direct, external regulation. If this is so, then we must be wary of supporting practices and theories that offer the promise of liberatory hope while in fact opening up the possibility for even greater forms of control and repression. Deleuze, I think, was well aware of this problem, as some of his last work was centered on the possibility of resistance in the new global society of control.

Delueze and Guattari are in the minority concerning the positive aspects of de-Oedipalization. Most cultural critics cast a dubious eye on de-Oedipalized subjects. Pfeil calls them "paradigmatically decentered subjects, individually and collectively slipping and sliding around on an ever more loose and gelatinous field of 'discursive positions,' none of which is strong enough to secure the subject, or to be articulated with any other discourse to form a general framework or guide for action" (222). Pfeil's description corresponds with that of the multipositioned poststructuralist subject, and consequentially it suggests problems with writing pedagogies predicated on stable identifications and articulations as the means for practicing critical resistance. Linda Brodkey, for example, underscores the importance of articulation as a "crucial notion" that makes "distinctions between the intentions of discourses (which have to do with positioning people as subjects) and the effects of discursive practices (which have to do with whether people identify themselves as the subjects of a discourse" (*Writing* 14–15). Brodkey retains an investment in producing a discursively stable subject. This subject is predicated on an identification in which the writer is called on to create a stable position vis-à-vis another person, group, or discourse. These attachments *to* specific subject positions necessitate the ability to make clear distinctions *between* positions, which in turn requires students to make affective investments in the creation and demarcation of subjective boundaries. Problems arise, however, in climates of rampant disinvestment, especially where the distinction between intention and effect can no longer be readily discerned. As Pfeil explains, "the gap between affect and effect, between feeling and its meaningful, significant, effectual articulation, is massive" (220). The problem with projects of articulation is that they neglect to account for this gap and thereby can leave entirely excluded from the pedagogical situation the distance the student sets up between his or her notion of self and the discursive products that are required in the class. Indeed, assignments directed toward this kind of subjective identification can actively produce cynicism and apathy in students who are well aware of the language game they are playing for the sake of teacher and grade. However, this pedagogical failure is often projected onto the student, so that the student is held responsible (for not being good enough, not working enough). Such strategies of blame, whether directed toward student, teacher, or pedagogy, are all ultimately insufficient.[13] All should be considered together, as each is implicated with the other and as each is situated in and forced to negotiate with the unique matrix of effects that is postmodernism.

As I argued earlier, oftentimes as teachers we forget the significant discrepancy between the intention of our pedagogy and the larger lessons that our students derive from it. What we (think we) teach is not quite what they learn. In the context of Brodkey's project of articulation, another way of making this point is that students can be strikingly aware that symbolic articulations and rearticulations do little to change the status quo. Instead, they are variations on a fundamental (fantasy) structure that remains undisturbed (Žižek, *Ticklish* 266). Regardless of the nature of the articulation or the sophistication brought to the analysis of the identification, the actual ensemble of social practices and institutions being challenged continues unabated and unchanged. This ensemble includes the university itself and by association the writing classroom. The incitement to challenge disempowering practices by means of the analysis of identifications and articulations is itself already complicit with practices designed to exercise control over students in ways synonymous with other mechanisms of control at work in postmodern life.

Grades are one obvious example of how this complicity manifests itself; whatever the content of the course, evaluation still serves to initiate students into the competitive, hierarchically structured job market they will soon face. The writing classroom thereby perpetuates the continuation of practices of valuation and exclusion, often, as is the case with radical, cultural studies–based pedagogies, the very same practices that are being challenged. Furthermore, many classrooms offer a pedagogy of slackening in which the strict rules pertaining to organization, grammar, and format are relaxed in favor of an emphasis on critical thought. These strategies can backfire when students develop an inflated sense of the importance of the deemphasized elements. We can see here how the writing classroom becomes complicit with the generalized strategies ongoing in a society of control; the withdrawal of direct external regulation does not of itself create the conditions for liberated, creative, and critical writers. Instead, other control mechanisms emerge to mold student conduct: assessment, credentials, and competition produce anxieties concerning class grade, academic development, and/or job future. Students are thereby induced to police their own writing, even if they are not very good at it, or suffer the possible academic and vocational consequences. Additionally, their goals may well be given primary shape by the strategies of risk management to which they are subject, so that they become preoccupied with "identification, assessment, elimination or reduction of the possibility of incurring" penalty or failure (Rose 261). The critical content of the writing pedagogy is reduced to a disaffected form of "whatever works" for the student,

"HANDS UP! YOU'RE FREE"

a situation often accompanied by a preoccupation with superficial forms of correctness.

The impassive challenge to pedagogies that require a certain amount of emotional investment—as, for example, in an assignment that requires students to care about injustice, misfortune, inequality, or other social ills—is the extent to which many students are disinvested, not because they are just "apathetic" or "bored" but because de-Oedipalized subjectivities may have a structural predilection for such attitudes. Now this is not to argue that all students are uncaring or apathetic, but in the social realm alternate patterns of affect are emerging, and an inability or reluctance to tie emotional investment to people and practices in conformance with cultural studies' ethical norms may be one symptom of this.[14] New subjective forms will likely have different affective modalities. Perhaps this also exacerbates the difficulties involved in getting others to see or care about injustice, at least in the way that we want them to.[15] The withdrawal of standard forms of pedagogical regulation has not produced engaged, liberated students, nor has the opportunity to develop and explore a critical sensibility resulted in a slew of good, politically engaged social critics. As James Berlin notes, with a significance that has yet to be given the attention it merits, the most remarkable effect of critical, cultural studies–based courses has been "the intensity of resistance students have offered their teachers, a stiff unwillingness to problematize the ideological codes inscribed in their attitudes and behavior" ("Composition and Cultural Studies" 52). Berlin goes on to say that eventually he had to forbid certain strategies of accommodation on their part, such as turning personal hardship into a narrative of growth. The question that arises is, from where does this resistance spring? Berlin and other cultural studies pedagogues would argue that it indicates a mystified investment in ideological narratives. Thus, their pedagogies espouse a process of demystification; if students can be forced to acknowledge how ideology disempowers them, they will in turn become responsibly critical. What are the consequences for pedagogies that try to empower students through critique, but at the risk of authoritatively re-Oedipalizing students who have other means of resistance that too often go unrecognized and undeveloped?

VIOLENCE, CYNICISM, AND PEDAGOGY

In "Going Postal: Pedagogic Violence and the Schooling of Emotion," Lynn Worsham argues that links exist between critical pedagogies and violence. Worsham suggests that postmodernism can be considered a kind of pedagogy that generates disaffected forms of behavior (229). I understand her to mean that culture does not simply construct subjectivity but continually schools subjects. Worsham writes: "If it can be said to be a pedagogy, then postmodernism is a wild pedagogy; the subject it educates, a wild subject. As such, it inculcates a kind of ultimate estrangement or dissolution from the structures that traditionally have supported both self and world. More specifically, the 'waning of affect' is one of the defining features of the new epoch. . . . The waning of affect is the liberation from the structures of recognition that bind meaning to feeling" (229). Worsham points out that the de-Oedipalizing effects of postmodernism have helped authorize many of the progressive social movements that have developed since the 1960s, including feminism, civil rights, environmentalism, and gay rights. However, on the other side of the equation is a bored and apathetic subject, one who experiences "the total defeat of desire" and who "feels its power only in feeling too much or in feeling for the sake of feeling, in the absence of the possibility of anything more significant" (Worsham 228–29).[16]

Worsham further makes the argument that postmodern violence, which she calls "wilding," is derived from this kind of boredom and apathy. While Pfeil claims that the dissolution of the "Oedipal solution" leads to rampant pathologies, Worsham establishes the wellspring of violence in the dissolution of affect, which is compounded by pedagogy's emphasis on a limited emotional scope. As she puts it, "wilding is perhaps the predictable form violence takes when meaning is cut loose from affect: free-floating violence, so to speak, and its apparent randomness makes it seem purely anonymous and impersonal" (231). She recognizes that this representation of violence is a mystification that masks the "othering practices that we call gender, race, class, and sexuality" (231). Radical pedagogies that seek to empower students by obtaining from them critical understandings of the discourses and practices that disempower them—which, typically, are aligned along the cultural studies axes of gender, race, class, and sexuality—thereby perpetrate a particular kind of authoritarian violence on the student.

An example of this link between violence and pedagogy is implicit in the notion of being "schooled" as conceptualized by Henry Giroux and Peter McLaren. They explain that "fundamental to the principles that inform critical pedagogy is the conviction that schooling for self- and social empowerment *is ethically prior to questions of epistemology or to a mastery of technical or social skills* that are primarily tied to the logic of the marketplace" (153–54). A presumption here is that it is the teacher who knows (best), and this orientation gives the concept "schooling" a particular bite: though it presents itself as oppositional to the state and to the dominant forms of pedagogy that serve the state and its capitalist interests, it nevertheless reinscribes an authoritarian model that is congruent with any number of Oedipalizing pedagogies that "school" the student in "proper" behavior. As D. Diane Davis notes, radical, feminist, and liberatory pedagogies "often camouflage pedagogical violence in their move from one mode of 'normalization' to another" and "function within a disciplinary matrix of power, a covert carceral system, that aims to create *useful* subjects for particular political agendas" (*Breaking* 212). Such Oedipalizing pedagogies are less effective than they are claimed to be; indeed, the attempt to "school" students in the manner called for by Giroux and McLaren is complicit with the malaise of postmodern cynicism. Students will dutifully go through their liberatory motions, producing the proper assignments, but it remains an open question whether they carry an oppositional politics with them. The "critical distance" supposedly created with liberatory pedagogy also opens up a cynical distance toward the writing produced in class.

Concerning the Oedipalizing effects of liberatory pedagogies, Worsham argues, they triangulate "the pedagogical situation and [give] the teacher the authority to stage the kind of Oedipal conflict that the de-Oedipalized family and postmodern society no longer provide. The authority that has become disembodied and abstract as a consequence of the bureaucratization of postmodern space is re-embodied in the (impersonal) figure of the teacher" (236). In the face of the waning of affect and the dissolution of institutional power, then, the call to achieve a critical position toward authority unwittingly reinscribes these quite traditional forms of adherence to authority. Furthermore, such pedagogies reduce the full spectrum of human emotions to a very few, such as pleasure, desire, and anxiety. The consequences are continual processes of redirection and redescription in which the emotions, especially those evoked by disempowerment, are actively elided, forestalled, or otherwise refused recognition. Thus, not only are expressions of disempowerment like "boredom, apathy, bitterness, hatred, anger, rage, generosity, nostalgia, euphoria, sorrow, humiliation, guilt, and shame"—and many more besides—excluded from the general pedagogical scene, but the authoritarian structure of this kind of pedagogy "offers a re-Oedipalization of emotion" that "requires a reassertion of the dominance of emotions of self-assessment" (Worsham 236–37). Just as students are immersed during their entire period of schooling in external matrices of assessment, so now pedagogies that are explicitly or implicitly authoritarian demand that they self-reflexively internalize assessment.

Worsham argues that the schooling of emotion can lead to eruptions of postmodern violence because students "are arguably acting out the kind of omnipotence and rage that results from the failure of mutual recognition and a thwarted sense of agency" (240). Pedagogies that predicate their modes of operation on the continuation of Oedipalizing processes, then, are complicit with structures that contribute to the production of postmodern violence qua wilding. Additionally, they demonstrate little success in staging for analysis, discussion, and exploration in the classroom the mechanisms that allow the eruption of such violence. In such a scenario, incidents of schoolyard slayings, or "going postal," will continue to be misrecognized as the purely pathological, criminal, or evil acts of those who are isolated, disaffected, or crazy (Worsham 240). The legacy of the shootings at Columbine is exemplary here: Eric Harris and Dylan Klebold were lambasted in the media as "natural-born killers" who listened to questionable music (gothic and industrial), dressed inappropriately (too much black clothing), and were steeped in media violence (video games and films). Public and media discussions did little to understand Harris, Klebold, and similar violent killers in ways that declined simple narratives of blame and condemnation. I take this to mean that the array of generative social forces, especially as regards the production of violence, remains largely beyond understanding, much less significant pedagogic intervention.

BETWEEN TWO LAWS; OR, FATHER DOESN'T KNOW BEST

Let us pause a moment to take stock. What is clear is that postmodern students are the most commodified generation the world has yet seen, and as such they are uniquely "schooled" to be subjects of late capitalism; indeed, Deleuze states that the primary instrument of social control is now the operation of markets (*Negotiations* 6). Such forms of control, it should be emphasized, depend on integration and participation rather than on prohibition. Thus, many prohibitions have become more flexible, in keeping with the drive for new forms of production and the continual search for new, larger markets. Instability and flow are the keys to growth, which means that if these strategies formerly had oppositional power, that power has undergone a transformation such that it can often serve capital more readily than it can resist it. Thus, new generations experience both more and less freedom than previous generations as they make their way through a world where power is, as Hardt claims, "both everywhere and nowhere" (143). Slippery and unstable, signs shift and cynicism reigns—we are all in on the joke, we acknowledge the simulacrum with the knowing wink, and we hunker down to necessity and work with the suspicion that there is little else to be done. Meanwhile, the big Other qua regulating symbolic order is receding in favor of flexible, continuously modulating flows of power and control, making every strategy of resistance provisional and temporary at best and ineffectual or recuperated in advance at worst. Most pertinent, pedagogy's challenge is to find ways to grapple effectively with the unique particularity of this highly commodified global society of control. Accordingly, we have been considering the complex

"HANDS UP! YOU'RE FREE"

interrelations and intersections between the postmodern era and pedagogy, the desire for justice and the inertia of cynicism, the administration of subjectivization and the eruption of violence. Radical pedagogies that offer alternative "schooling" practices are to be applauded for their intention to meet such challenges, but unfortunately they remain enmeshed in authoritarian and Oedipalizing practices that little disturb the structures of domination and/or replicate them at another level (such as the level of unacknowledged practice).[17] As Vitanza reminds us via Deleuze, "a deterritorialization followed by a reterritorialization does not bring the expected liberation" ("Hermeneutics" 127). Similarly, trading the Oedipalized subject for a de-Oedipalized subject does not necessarily bring about a liberated subject in an era where the processes of de-Oedipalization are too easily made to serve capital.

This claim should not be taken to mean that there are not forms of de-Oedipalization, specifically those described by Deleuze and Guattari, that retain transformative potential. It may be that they allow transformation, but only to the extent that de-Oedipalization is accompanied by a corresponding denegating of subjectivity. So long as subjectivity emerges as schooled by the Negative, especially as it emerges within the logic of the globalized market, de-Oedipalization will find new loci of control in the internal master (the injunction to enjoy), which can be described as just another form of the manifestation of the Negative in a different modality. Another way of saying this is that Deleuze and Guattari's project of negating Oedipus cannot be said to emerge unproblematically within the logic of the global market. Or, as Vitanza argues, capitalism may in fact produce "schizos" (de-Oedipalized, schizophrenic subjects of desire) that it cannot in turn control or re-Oedipalize (*Negation* 118). But not all forms of post-Oedipal subjectivity correspond to the denegated schizo. The schizo-subject may no longer be subject to the logic of the market, whereas other post-Oedipal forms have been reterritorialized by the market. This effect of reterritorialization is seen by Berlin when he describes his students as being on fire to achieve the good life despite their classroom "schooling" about its complicity with social injustice (Hurlbert and Blitz 137); it can also be seen in the resurgence of identity politics and hate crime in an era of multicultural pluralism. The waning of external regulations and prohibitions can intensify the desire for the benefits of capital or identity formation rather than encouraging the exploration of other possible subject positions outside such restricted economies. In short, despite the fact that forms of de-Oedipalization are engaged in the dispersal of desire, the logic of the market reterritorializes the majority of subjects in the proscribed forms, including even the oppositional margins, which actually begin to function as an advance guard for the center (Mann 106). Although schizo-subjects may operate outside the logic of the market, for other post-Oedipal forms the logic of late capital returns as the injunction to enjoy, erupting out of the withdrawal of external forms of prohibition and law.

If, as Žižek argues, Law is nothing but crime taken to an extreme, there is irony in reframing the postmodern condition as two forms of Law. Žižek argues via Lacan that there are two kinds of Law (the two Fathers), external and internal. External laws, Žižek claims, are the ensemble of social regulations that make peaceful coexistence possible, whereas internal Law is the call of conscience, the perfectly subjective moral law that manifests itself as a kind of traumatic injunction disruptive of external laws. We know the form well: it is Martin Luther nailing his ninety-five theses to the church door in 1517, or claiming, "Here I stand; God help me, I can do nothing else." Žižek's suggestion is a curious reversal of the standard claim that we need external laws to maintain order over and against the inner call for disruption, such as hedonism, violence, disregard, rebellion, and all the other joyous forms it takes. Instead, Žižek asks: "What if the subject invents external social norms precisely in order to escape the unbearable pressure of the moral Law? Isn't it much easier to have an external Master who can be duped, towards whom one can maintain a minimal distance and private space, than to have an extimate Master, a stranger, a foreign body in the very heart of one's being?" (*Ticklish* 280). External laws can be, and always are, justified and/or justifiable — belief is a subsidiary and often irrelevant consideration. The inner call of conscience, however, does not partake of reality in this way and cannot be so easily justified; it is of the order of the Real and is, hence, unconditional, inescapable. It is also unsubstantiated by any direct external, explanatory narrative. Instead, it takes the form of being "in you more than you," a traumatic demand: "God help me, I can do nothing else."

The question regarding pedagogy invokes relations to both of these manifestations of Law. If we apply an authoritarian, Oedipalizing pedagogy, then we run the risk of promulgating cynicism or replicating the same social structures that contribute to the social production of violence. However, Pfeil and Žižek both argue that with changes in our investments in the socio-symbolic edifice, particular forms of pathological behavior increase in frequency. There are two ways to look at this. First, escalation in the particular, idiosyncratic behavior associated with post-Oedipal subjectivity has accomplished little toward achieving an increase in general freedom and justice or forestalling the smooth operations of the global society of control. Second, it seems that the ground is now cleared for the eruption of further pathological behavior, including violence, and this situation is only aggravated by the emergent society of control. In this way, we return to the question asked by Wilhelm Reich, considered at length in Deleuze and Guattari's *Anti-Oedipus*, about why the masses choose oppression and servitude: "After centuries of exploitation, why do people still tolerate being humiliated and enslaved, to such a point, indeed, that they *actually want* humiliation and slavery not only for others but for themselves?" (*Anti-Oedipus* 29). It is not, as Reich attests, that people are stupid or fooled. Rather, Deleuze and Guattari argue, as subjects produced though Oedipalization, people are predisposed to reinscribe through their everyday behavior the same subjectivizing processes that produced them as subjects. This is to say, "no, the masses were not innocent dupes; at a certain point, under a certain set of conditions, they *wanted* fascism, and it is this perversion of the desire of the masses that needs to be accounted for" (*Anti-Oedipus* 29). In an era of de-Oedipalization, we must ask again this very question: why, given the possibility of occupying multiple subject positions or reformulating capital, do subjects choose to do otherwise and thereby contribute to their own continued subjugation? How have their desires been perverted on the very brink of deterroritialization?

Žižek takes this idea from another angle and attempts to demonstrate why it is that in an era when Oedipalization is no longer the primary means of subjectivization—that is, in the era of the de-Oedipalized, dispersed, multiplicitous subject—people are still ever and again choosing servitude and domination, while at the same time manifesting new and virulent pathologies. Or, as Žižek pointedly asks, "Why does the decline of paternal authority and fixed social and gender roles generate new anxieties, instead of opening up a brave New World of individuals engaged in the creative 'care of the Self' and enjoying the perpetual process of shifting and reshaping their fluid multiple identities?" (*Ticklish* 341). Žižek's argument is that we should be wary of seeing this problem as an indicator that postmodernity is an incomplete project. The argument runs that once postmodernity has achieved its goal of a fully de-Oedipalized subjectivity, the self-fashioning, dispersed, multiple subject will come into full flower. This form of subjectivity corresponds with the decentered, pluralist subjectivity of poststructuralism, not the de-Oedipalized, schizo-subject theorized by Deleuze and Guattari. That said, it is easy to see that the logic displayed here for the poststructuralist subject is in principle (and ironically) the same that is claimed for modernity, which is also labeled an incomplete project by apologists like Habermas. The problem with conceiving postmodernity as something incomplete until a total break with modernism has been achieved is that the hindrance actually lies elsewhere, "in the obscene need for domination and subjection engendered by the new 'post-Oedipal' forms of subjectivity themselves" (Žižek, *Ticklish* 360). For Žižek, then, the recession of the socio-symbolic order, the matrix of regulating norms and prohibitions, clears the ground for the eruption of an internal master, what he calls the "superego injunction to enjoy." The price, as he sees it, is an increase in individual perverseness without a corresponding increase in real social progress or freedom.

This injunction to enjoy can occur at either the individual or the group level. Jenny Holzer's famous dictum "Protect me from what I want" describes the operation of this injunction on the individual level: what "I" want, or most profoundly desire, is of course already the desire of the Other erupting from the unconscious or the inner injunction to enjoy erupting as a form of self-reflexive fascism. The unconscious cannot be considered as a pure resource for resistance. This constitutes Berlin's main criticism of Marshall Alcorn Jr.'s "Changing the Subject of Postmodernist Theory," to which Alcorn concedes, admitting that "libidinal structure *is* always ideological" (345). Although I consider Alcorn somewhat mistaken in this assertion—the libidinal is not necessarily ideological even though it may find its modes of expression through the ideological—the point illustrates how there is no recourse to some pure scene that would underwrite resistance. Or consider Nick Land's charge: "[The unconscious] howls and raves like the shackled and tortured beast that our civilization has made of it, and when the fetters are momentarily loosened the unconscious does not thank the ego for this meager relief, but hisses, spits, and bites, as any wild thing would" (124–25). Alcorn and Land are expressing not opposing views on the unconscious but two sides of the same coin. The unconscious, insofar as it is produced by and operates within a restricted (repressed) economy, is the already colonized other scene to consciousness, and when it erupts, it erupts with the force of Law, regardless of whether that force is on the side of orderly accommodation or reactionary wildness. Thus, we should reconsider the narrative that has consciousness as the dupe of restrictive, repressive Law. Žižek says, "it is *consciousness*, the conscious *ego*, which is the agency of the imaginary misrecognition of and resistance to the unconscious symbolic Law" (*Ticklish* 307 n.18). This move leaves the door open for resistance to occur at both conscious and unconscious levels, while it simultaneously shows the precariousness of theories that hold out unqualified resistant potential for the unconscious.

This precariousness is demonstrated every day through capitalism, which provides not only a climate conducive to the eruption of the injunction to enjoy but also a spectrum of strategies that can appropriate it. A way to illustrate this point is by considering how capital has moved toward collapsing the distance between work and hobby. Žižek points out that this is the case with computer hackers. Hackers who are hired by corporations must follow "the injunction to be who they are, to follow their innermost idiosyncrasies," even if this means ignoring social norms of dress and behavior; in other words, corporations target the subject's special, creative, idiosyncratic core, and the minute that this imp of perversity is lost, the minute the countercultural edge is supplanted by "normal behavior," the employee becomes useless (*Ticklish* 368–69). The point is that this kind of appropriation is made directly possible by the lack of symbolic prohibition—the kind that would prevent the entrance of countercultural perversity into the corporation, both at the level of the formerly conventional corporation (in which that kind of employee would not be considered hirable) and at the level of the conventional employee (who would have to conform to specific normative codes). It could be said that teachers ask something similar when they direct students to be creative and original for the fulfillment of conventional grade requirements. Students will typically be penalized for not finding their authentic voices or using too bland a style. What we see in such scenarios, then, is the dissolution of the conflict between the Institution and the uncanny, idiosyncratic person who must be properly disciplined. This conflict has vanished to be replaced by the demand of the inner master to be what you are, and capitalism, operating as flexible accumulation, has responded by finding modalities of appropriation.

This corresponds to the thesis behind Thomas Frank's *The Conquest of Cool: Business Culture, Counterculture, and the Rise of Hip Consumerism.* The modernist conflict between the repressed behavior required in the workplace (the Protestant work ethic) and hedonistic consumerism (buy, buy, buy!) is resolved, at least symbolically, by hip consumerism. Frank argues: "However we may rankle under the bureaucratized monotony of our productive lives, in our consuming lives we are no longer merely affluent, we are *rebels.* Efficiency may remain the value of daytime, but by night we rejoin the nonstop carnival of our consuming lives. . . . Our celebrities are not just glamorous, they are insurrectionaries; our police and soldiers are not just good guys, they break the rules for a higher purpose" (232). The lesson is that rebellion is both hip *and* useful, that resistance to capitalism has been effective only to the extent of becoming "good business," and that this transformation in the way capitalism functions was in part initiated by the loss of Oedipalizing symbolic structures. Keeping in mind Marx's formula that the limit of capitalism is Capital itself, the waning of the Oedipal father and its authoritarian substitutes might now be seen as a problem from which capitalism has found ways to benefit. Indeed, we can take this thesis another step into the classroom: the rise in the popularity of cultural studies–based pedagogies of critique can be seen to follow the same logic. Critique is a form of hip schooling that corresponds to the hip consumer; we may be going to work or school as normal, but we can tell ourselves that underneath this surface appearance, we are radical critics.

I understand Žižek to be saying that ultimately we are between two Fathers, between internal and external manifestations of Law. However, Father—whether as the matrix of Oedipalizing prohibitions or as the inner master qua injunction to enjoy—does not provide the coordinates for any substantial action that would maintain a critical capacity not co-opted in advance and made to serve what it purportedly resists. Father, it seems, does not know best.

WRITING THE ACT

How might we address post-Oedipal forms of subjectivity in our pedagogies, and how might we develop strategies that circumvent, forestall, or resist the replication of authoritarian or protoviolent modes of control? In the interview "Control and Becoming," Deleuze responds to this issue concerning the possibilities for resistance in the society of control with doubt about the effectiveness of communication as a strategy: "Maybe speech and communication have been corrupted. They're thoroughly permeated by money—and not by accident but by their very nature. We've got to hijack speech. Creating has always been something different from communicating. The key thing may be to create vacuoles of noncommunication, circuit breakers, so we can elude control" (*Negotiations* 175). Since postmodern society operates primarily through continuous, modulating control and instant communication, Deleuze seizes on the idea that one way to elude control is to break up the circuits of communication that are key to monitoring, tracking, and administering. Thus, current forms of computer piracy and viruses could be understood as breaking up the logic of the communicative circuits (which is increasingly tied to production as corporations continue unabated their Internet feeding frenzy) in much the same way that factory slowdowns, sabotage, and strikes were the disruptive forms of the modernist age.[18] Breaking up the circuits of communication is precisely what the schizo-subject does; its inability to communicate "effectively" curtails capitalism's drive to make it a *productive* subject congruent with the *productivity* of the market. Instead, the schizo-subject is desirous, *producing* according to a logic that cannot be effectively utilized by the global market. However, Deleuze acknowledges the difficulty of resistance in the society of control, noting that "a snake's coils are even more intricate than a mole's burrow"; elsewhere he warns, "compared with the approaching forms of ceaseless control in open sites, we may come to see the harshest confinement as part of a wonderful happy past" (*Negotiations* 182, 175). In short, the means for achieving resistance through subjective transformations are fleeting and provisional; the dominant forms of post-Oedipal subjectivity remain co-opted and controlled.

Furthermore, it is important to keep in mind that our students are entering a world in which increasingly their every utterance, their every communicative act, is noted, saved, utilized, screened, deployed. School transcripts, church records, credit ratings, shopping habits, browser cookies, the "*69" code and caller ID on the telephone, surveillance cameras, police records, electronic transations, medical records, polls and surveys, mailing lists, licenses, evaluations—all these things and more identify and gather information about people, circulating it in databases that are open to those who are granted access. In such a world, we should not be surprised at the cynical detachment toward the writing that we elicit from students since assignments are part of larger ongoing projects of assessment and information gathering. Asking students to take a critical attitude toward, say, advertising, does little to dissolve advertising's persuasive power, but it does provide yet another forum in which they will be evaluated and ranked, a procedure that is most useful for their future employment opportunities.[19] The language game of criticism seldom attains the level of personal affect because students understand all too well that their writing ultimately only services their own continued servitude. This is the world of what Deleuze calls "continuous assessment": from school to workplace, one is always being monitored and tested (*Negotiations* 202 n.7).

It is in this context that I want to examine the (in)famous student essay David Bartholomae describes in "The Tidy House: Basic Writing in the American Curriculum." Geoffrey Sirc, too, makes much of it in "Never Mind the Tagmemics, Where's the Sex Pistols?" Over the course of a brief paper, a student named Quentin Pierce negates himself, his writing, his composition course, and his world in general. Bartholomae, it should be noted, kept the paper for eighteen years before he wrote about it and considers it one of his most memorable papers. Bartholomae admits that at the time, he was not prepared for the paper, that it could not be brought into the class he was teaching, that he did not know how to read it (6). I suggest that we can read Pierce's paper as an Act that has sophisticated transgressive potential. I emphasize here at the outset, though, that I do not want to romanticize the paper. Although I read it as transgressive, its quality of transgressiveness is not inherent. Rather, its transgressiveness emerges with the advent of post-Oedipal subjectivities, perhaps because its field of contention derives largely from that particular subjective experience. Furthermore, its transgressive quality is itself predicated on the background Sirc provides, tying Pierce's strategies to those utilized by punk rock, which is itself often grounded in post-Oedipal logics of resistance. With these qualifications in mind, here are excerpts from Pierce's paper:

> Man will not survive, he is [an] asshole.
>
> The stories in the books [are] mean[ing]less stories and I will not elaborate on them[.] This paper is mean[ing]less, just like the book, But I know the paper will not make it.
>
> STOP.
>
> I don't care.
>
> I don't care.
>
> about man and good and evil I don't care about this shit fuck this shit, trash and should be put in the trash can with this shit
>
> I lose again. (Bartholomae 6)

Who is Pierce? Where did he come from? What possessed him to write this piece? Bartholomae compares lines in the essay to *Leaves of Grass* or *Howl* (6). Sirc compares them to the lyrics of a Sex Pistols song, calling it the excess that our pedagogy cannot process (26). (I would note Sirc's pun on "process" as a statement on the limits of process pedagogy.)

A careful reading of Pierce's paper shows that it disrupts the exchange circuit on which successful communication depends. First off, most extant writing pedagogies would evaluate Pierce's work as poor at best if only because of its excessive grammatical problems or failure to complete the assignment. And yet Bartholomae's response, followed by Sirc's, makes something significant of this paper. Certainly it can be considered memorable and, for Bartholomae, even haunting. More pertinent, the failures the paper graphically performs stage some of the fundamental contradictions that define and constrain writing pedagogy. It is not so much that pedagogy fails as that pedagogy is implicated at every turn in the structures that contribute to Pierce's nihilism and daily humiliation. Pierce knows all too well that "effective communication" is a trap for him; his defense is to relegate it all to meaninglessness and apathy. Cynicism is here taken to an extreme, becoming a willful nihilism used to portray the failure of the class, of the material he reads, of his writing, perhaps even of his existence (he loses again). It is in fact likely that this extreme cynicism betrays an even deeper sense of care—not a waning but a realignment of affects. But again, even if this is so, the classroom is arranged so that such care is difficult if not impossible to invest.

We cannot, however, stop here. For the fact remains that Pierce's paper marks a very specific movement that is transgressive in yet another sense. We could consider his paper an exemplary mark of perversity and, as such, illustrative of post-Oedipal writing. The question we need to ask is if this writing, which is made possible by the withdrawal of the external matrix of social prohibitions, manifests its counterpart, the inner master qua injunction to enjoy. My suggestion is that it does not, but neither is it the writing of that other de-Oedipalized subject, Deleuze and Guattari's schizo-subject. However, Pierce's paper can help us delineate between the eruption of the inner master and the passage to the Act. The injunction to enjoy perpetuates servitude in a new, personal key from which there is no escape (as opposed to the external master, who is easier to dupe). Writing pedagogies can easily replicate these two permutations of Law. A pedagogy that coincides with external laws will say, "You must write well and conform to all the established conventions for determining quality: grammar, organization, clarity, and all the other usual characteristics of correctness." Conversely, a pedagogy that corresponds to the inner Law will say, "Although you know what kind of writing is rewarded in the university and the corporation, you are free to write in these other exploratory and liberating ways if you want to." It is easy to see how the choice is rigged: it is actually a "forced choice." What makes the inner injunction to enjoy appear so slavish for the subject is precisely the fact that one is being forced to enjoy what one has to do anyway. Thus, if a liberatory pedagogue teaches students that they can critique the various institutions that disempower them, the "forced choice" imposed on them is *freely* to choose to present forms of writing that service *institutional* assessment and ranking procedures. The institution thereby hijacks for its purposes the alleged primary goal of having students learn to write well for their own advancement. Is there any wonder that students will decline to respect and value this writing as "empowering"?

Furthermore, the unconscious, as the discourse of the Other, is every bit as caught up in Law and ideology as the external world (which is also the Other). As Žižek argues, the inner injunction to enjoy is ultimately akin to speech acts because it gains its performative power from "the pre-established set of symbolic rules and/or norms" (*Ticklish* 263). Although this inner injunction is not in itself a priori ideological, it becomes so in its performative expression. Thus, the symbolic rules and norms structuring action and discourse would include codified forms of transgression as well. A certain amount of transgression is always taken account of in advance by society and thus hardly disturbs it all. This is especially the case with intellectual opposition, which, Mann reminds us, is not oppositional, but a form of "systems maintenance" (98).

What makes Pierce's paper transgressive is not that it opposes Bartholomae or the classroom but that it challenges the fundamental, phantasmatic core that underlies writing pedagogy in general, thereby moving beyond symbolic accommodation into the realm of the Act. Pierce refuses to find his writing act empowering; he sees that he is being called to enjoy, through his acts of writing, his own continued servitude to the institution and the state. However, it is precisely his ability to cut through that servitude, to refuse to believe in a fantasy of writing for the university as being somehow liberating, empowering, or even meaningful, that allows him to traverse the fantasy at the level of performance—which is to say, to make of his writing an Act. Pierce takes on the risk of failure, even anticipates it, by negating the writing fantasy in such a way as to challenge any and all readers to reconceive what good or valued writing is, as well as its place in and relation to the university and the world at large.

The Act in this sense is not just transgression but transgression tied to the creative transformation of the very field of social regulations and prohibitions. In this sense, every Act is both personal and social, and there can be no separation of the two. As Sirc reminds us about the punk rock movement of the late 1970s, "it's a gamble, of course, to refuse to reproduce old writing, to be so seized by the desire to create a new thought that one is desperate enough to try to wring meaning out [of] even such nothing junk as safety pins" ("Never" 23). Pierce may not have seen himself as being "so seized by the desire to create a new thought," but he nevertheless predicated his writing on little more than a "fuck you" to his teacher and a sheer hatred of writing itself—on what writing is in the academy, on what we make of writing in our pedagogies.

I would note that this intense hatred of writing is debilitating to the extent that Pierce cannot ultimately celebrate his Act, and he thereby denies himself the fulsomeness of productive desire. Still, this does not entirely delimit what can be done with his work. Composition studies, argues Sirc, mostly "are interested in clarifying the day, further articulating the day, bettering the day, never rupturing the day" ("Godless" 560). The Act is interested in rupturing the day, in transforming the entire discursive field that determines what is proper and valued. The Act refuses accommodation in favor of radical transformation despite the risk of total loss. Ultimately, this is what most pedagogies refuse to do: they do not teach "risk" ("Godless" 561). Even the most radical pedagogies, which would wage war on capital itself, betray the servitude that underwrites their success: "if you do this, then this will happen; if you plan ahead, you will save time; if you are critical of power, you will be empowered." It is all predicated on success in the very economy that defines success in terms of production and accommodation. Pierce, however, haunts

Bartholomae and Sirc because he refuses this notion of success; he refuses to equate it with a kind of writing that is worth doing. In this way, he sets out the possibility for a writing that would be otherwise, that would not display in each grammatically correct line, in each thesis proved and supported, in each ending skillfully reached and concluded, the utter slavishness and impoverishment of what counts as "good" writing in the academy. And, as far as Pierce is concerned, this possibility does not even exist; he hates what he has produced just as much as he hates the conditions and forces that were aligned in calling to make him produce it. In the end, Pierce challenges and dismisses the existing writing economy, but, at the same time, he cannot imagine, create, or otherwise point to a way out, to an alternate writing economy.

This is useful for my purposes to the extent that I can note that he never sets out from any established criteria, nor does he try to establish criteria afterward. There is no model, no "school" here. In this sense, any writing pedagogy that could learn from Pierce's Act would have to accept in advance that pedagogy cannot be orchestrated directly to produce forms of writing that would be Acts. To do so would be to reinscribe the pedagogical fantasy of control. As pedagogy is currently practiced, and as writing is currently evaluated, writings that would be Acts can only arise out of risk and chance. Most students, I suspect, will actively decline to take such risks. However, this does not mean that pedagogies cannot foster a climate for invention. Such postpedagogies would themselves have to take on the character of an Act and would be nothing less than disruptions on the way to becoming transvaluations of what pedagogy is and how it functions in the academy. Thus, elements of surprise, chance, and risk would be brought into consideration, with all the possibilities for deterritorialization and reterritorialization that go with them. As Gilbert Chaitin argues, "Surprise is the mark of that unpredictability which betrays the operation of the subject as a 'cause' opposed to any law" (236). Surprise, like other aleatory elements, expresses a uniqueness often covered over in general pedagogical forms.

Just as Worsham claims that the de-Oedipalizing effects of postmodernism have helped authorize many of the progressive social movements that have developed since the 1960s, so too I am suggesting that post-Oedipal subjectivity is conducive for a postpedagogy of the Act. Such a pedagogy would be many things. It would be what Sirc labels a punk pedagogy, predicated on DIY (do it yourself) ("Never" 21). It would be a pedagogy of risk. It would refuse the reproduction of the everyday, or, better, seek to reenchant the everyday via the new, the unthought, the unaccommodatable. It would decline accommodation in favor of an abandonment that seeks to squander its energy through forms of desiring production.[20] Declining accommodation, I should note, is not a form of opposition. Rather, it is a redistribution or alternative investment of energies, a way of inhabiting one's pedagogical locus otherwise.

It is not enough for post-Oedipal pedagogies merely to decenter stable subjects. The war on identity is not enough because it leaves the door open for the return of the inner master that merely replicates servitude at a different level. The inner master says, "You may," but demands that you thereby enjoy. Although it allows a subject to enjoy the rejection or transgression of social norms and prohibitions, it is nevertheless strictly correlative with them: these things the subject had to renounce in submitting to traditional patriarchal symbolic Law are transgressive only to the extent that they have in advance been produced by that very same Law. Otherwise, they would not be transgressive; their transgressive qualities are defined within the field of contention set up and ultimately governed by the regulating social norms. In other words, the narrative that sees the two Fathers as oppositional misrecognizes that this is a false front. The two sides are mutually dependent.

Indeed, we might even go one step further and say that every oppositional practice or strategy, to the extent that it defines itself as oppositional, is already structured by fantasy. I do not see how this structure can be dissolved; it strikes me that it is implicit, and hence complicit, in everything we do and say. Given this structure, and given that every opposition is to a certain degree phantasmatic, we can say that strictly speaking there is no oppositional relationship.[21] Every attempt to oppose is already caught up in, or brings with it, a certain accommodation. It is perhaps this point—difficult as it may be to accept—to which we should abandon ourselves. This is one of the tasks for a postpedagogy: an abandonment to the idea that despite our desire for it, "we cannot achieve absolute knowledge" (Nicol 47). I would argue that we transform this negative inability into a positive ability and see in our inability to achieve absolute knowledge the hope for growth in others and in those who come after us. In this sense, then, a postpedagogy warns us, "Hands up! You're free"—meaning that we must take on the responsibility for our inability to control everything, but not by succumbing to the pressure to conform to the internal master that arises from the vacuum created by the withdrawal of external regulation. The abandonment of the drive for control does not necessitate a corresponding surrender to other forms of control.

A postpedagogy, insofar as it declines to participate in the dialectics of control, is an exhortation to dare, to invent, to create, to risk. It is less a body of rules, a set of codifiable classroom strategies, than a willingness to give recognition and value to unorthodox, unexpected, or troublesome work. Indeed, it is finally only in this way that we can see Pierce's paper as an Act. Writing the paper matters to the extent that it has borne fruit and achieved a social effect. As Deleuze reminds us: "It's jurisprudence, ultimately, that makes law. . . . Writers ought to read law reports rather than the civil code" (*Negotiations* 169). To the extent that the social works within the modern—which would here correspond to the negotiation and transformation of social laws—Deleuze seems to indicate that lines of flight are best discerned in the actual arguments that transform the laws, not in the static codes of law themselves. Thus, change will be wrought in the journals and forums devoted to discussions of writing. At this conflict-ridden microlevel, transformations in how we teach and conceive writing at a broader level will occur. Of course, reterritorializations will occur in these forums as well. There are no guarantees, and in fact, at a practical level, given the restricted economy within which writing pedagogy functions, the prospects for change cannot be said to be shining brightly. Nevertheless, we cannot ignore the fact that Bartholomae and Sirc were called to challenge the conventions of what counts as writing by Pierce's paper. Pierce can be seen to stage Andrew Ross's description of punk rock—"a surprising reinvention of the ordinary, the trivial, and the marginal is creatively transformed into a volatile micropolitics" (111). To the extent that lessons gleaned from Pierce's paper can inform composition pedagogies, and thereby create conditions of possibility for producing and valuing alternate forms of writing, this volatile micropolitics can be said to be more than just a fantasy. But perhaps only to that extent, and no further.

Ultimately, writing the Act, or a pedagogy that would create the conditions of possibility for Acts, must abandon the drive for explanations that would control and codify what happens and what is written and abandon the attendant faith that is placed in these explanations. Where the Act comes from, or where it leads, can only be a transvaluation to the extent that it is understood as a *moment*. As Deleuze says, speaking of a new kind of event as opposed to a new kind of subject, it is the event that matters, if only for a moment (*Negotiations* 176). But it is *this* moment that matters, and it is *this* chance that must be seized.

There is a sense in which my reading of Pierce's paper may be misread as implying that only certain, special works can function as Acts, events, or transgressions. On the contrary: inventive resistance to control is always happening. Perhaps key here is less the necessity of trying to produce its possibility—which in any event harkens back to strategies of control, of orchestrating flows and powers to produce a certain, specified result—than trying simply to recognize it. We might aspire to see how these "Act-ive" moments are already present in student writing in countless different ways, making classroom practices a forum for lighting up the thousand tiny resistances that irrepressibly emerge. We should, I think, seize these moments as much for ourselves as for our students. We need Act-ive moments as much as our students do, and it is this creative transformation that can offer so much to revitalize pedagogical work.

Retrospective

An interpretation whose effects are understood is not a psychoanalytic interpretation.

—Jacques Lacan, *Television*

I N THINKING ABOUT AND working at the intersections of cultural studies, pedagogy, and psychoanalytic rhetoric, I want to make clear that such work should not be converted into a static hermeneutic framework. Freud was firm about this in *The Interpretation of Dreams*. Although dreams produce symbols, and symbols can become cultural commonplaces, one should avoid falling into the trap of creating overly stable symbolic commonplaces. Our markets are stuffed with popular, self-help literature proffering watered-down Freudian dream analysis. Such books codify dream symbols into standard meanings and easy taxonomies. One looks up one's dream or symbol, and voila, it is all explained. For example, a dream of being naked in front of others indicates anxiety, and so on. In such an approach, the interpretative work has all been done in advance and is presented as mere information one looks up.

In actuality, Freud suggested nothing of the sort. Instead, a dream's meaning emerges through dialogue in an analytic situation. Dreams can have many meanings, not just one (*Interpretation* 253). Further, the analyst/interlocutor, in playing the proper role and by means of the intersubjective event of transference, becomes an *aid* to the analysand/dreamer's own interpretation of the dream (*Interpretation* 130 n. 2). The analyst is not to impose an interpretation of the dream. Freud himself may have stumbled on this point in some of his most famous cases (Anna O., the Wolf Man), but perhaps this just means that sometimes he was more insightful as a writer than as a practitioner. In any case, we can learn from him; we need not emulate. The larger point is that eventually it is the dreamer who has to come to know the validity of a dream's interpretation because the dream's rebus emerges from the dreamer's own un-conscious processes. However, just as crucially, the dreamer needs help—an intersubjective network—to do so. The emergence of meaning requires an Other, suggesting that communication is not simply the transfer of informa-tion but a complex process involving (mis)understanding, affective engage-ment, and dialogue.

A psychoanalytic approach to rhetoric, then, must retain an inventive, so-cial, and heuristic mind-set that takes on these communicative complexities if it is to remain vibrant and avoid the rigidity and stagnation common to formu-laic approaches. Perhaps this also requires a certain faithlessness to, or even betrayal of, psychoanalysis's founding figures and the grounding concepts they developed. Thus, it may be quite useful to look toward work like Deleuze and Guattari's in *Anti-Oedipus*. Such an approach might be considered—to use a Deleuzian locution—a kind of "becoming Lacan" that shows up, critiques, moves beyond, and makes freshly productive what had become static. In this way, the dangers of the programmatic are avoided. Indeed, it is important to recall that Lacan himself rebuilt and reframed Freud, jettisoning Freud's lin-gering biologism, adjusting his theories of gender division and the Oedipus complex, and grounding his work in sophisticated theories of discourse. Yet all the while Lacan reiterated that he considered himself a faithful follower of Freud. In what sense faithful, however, if he initiated so many changes and implicit critiques? Faithful in the sense of capturing something of the spirit or essence of Freud's work, something that could not be contained by the concepts, theories, cultural context, and terministic screens within which he worked. Lacan, then, might be more Freud than Freud, but precisely by unleashing what was only begun or implicit in Freud. *Anti-Oedipus* might be read similarly, as an unleashing of what was only implicit in Lacan, beyond what Lacan himself could do. Implicitly, I have argued that Žižek also does this for Lacan.

My larger point is simply this: a static, stagnant, rote, schematic, call-it-what-you-will application of psychoanalysis to rhetoric is precisely what we do not need. If psychoanalytic rhetorics have a future, they will need to be inven-tive, and rigorously so. Certainly, they should be amended and extended by other work. One area for exploration is work on affect, and another is complexity theory; although I touch on both in the book, there is much more still to be done. This lesson was borne out for me as I wrote: it has become increasingly clear to me—it was far murkier when I began writing—that psychoanalysis has always attended to the complex enmeshment of (what we posit as) inside and outside, discourse and not-discourse. Filling out the realm of the nondiscursive is affect. Psychoanalysis deals with affect in perhaps peculiar ways. *Jouissance* and *fantasy* are not simply familiar terms for conceptualizing the emergent affective links between sensation and feeling as they impact consciousness, attitude, and behavior; as I have attempted to show, *jouissance* and *fantasy* suffuse all we do. *Jouissance* in particular underpins our activities and in a very real sense makes them worthwhile.

For example, in *Changing the Subject in English Class*, Marshall Alcorn Jr. conducts an extensive analysis of the infamous Stanley Milgram experiment, in which test subjects were asked to punish difficult learners. Urged on by the experiment leader, over two-thirds of the test subjects were willing to administer dangerous if not lethal electrical shocks to their screaming "students." Alcorn's lesson is a spin on Lacan's old adage that desire is the desire of the Other. In this case, desire takes a pernicious turn, becoming authoritarian. Indeed, this is in part how authority works: the follower wants to please the authority by doing as s/he demands, regardless of whether the demand is explicitly intended. Alcorn points out that in stressful scenarios such as these, where followers are reluctant to carry out a demand because it is objectionable, when they finally do submit, they integrate their acts, no matter how repugnant, "into an understanding of work that fulfills the subject's sense of purpose and personal dignity" (*Changing* 44–45). Although Alcorn does not make the point directly, it is clear that we see the emergence of *jouissance* here. This principle applies even to the greatest contemporary cultural commonplace of evil, the Holocaust. Žižek, drawing on the work of Hannah Arendt, writes that most of the Nazi executioners "were well aware that they were doing things that brought humiliation, suffering and death to their victims. The way out of this predicament was that, instead of saying 'What horrible things I did to people!' they would say 'What horrible things I had to watch in the pursuance of my duties, how heavily the task weighed upon my shoulders!'" ("Depraved" n.p.). In other words, even in the case of what we might customarily think of as the greatest of evils, the most extreme inhumanity one could inflict on other human beings, a kind of satisfaction emerges. Further, part of what allows individuals to continue in diabolical work is how this satisfaction in duty, even horrible duty, fortifies them against the temptation to care about suffering. Of course, this is an extreme example far removed from everyday life, but it does illuminate the sheer and sometimes perverse scope of enjoyment, as well as its power. In terms of contemporary problems and issues that occur in academic work and classrooms, we see the role a person plays in actively entangling him- or herself in ideological and discursive nets of culture. Thus, it is not enough to say that we are "produced" or "disciplined" without taking a further step and acknowledging the subject's complicity— which is to say, without working through the psychic mechanisms energizing our attitudes, beliefs, and activities. In this sense, we could argue that affect, far from being a subsidiary notion, takes center stage.

Alcorn's example stages how one of rhetoric's perennial concerns, persuasion, is diffused across disparate experiential realms. The discursive act of the experiment test leader telling the test subject to zap the difficult "student" is only one slice of the persuasive pie. Indeed, this base-level understanding of discourse is woefully inadequate for obtaining a sophisticated understanding of what actually occurs to initiate change or the desired behavior. The test subject needs to be in transference with the experiment leader, meaning that the experiment leader must be someone the test subject is prepared to accept. The fact that approximately one-third of the Milgram experiment's test subjects refused to carry out the leader's demands shows that this phantasmatic frame is crucial for persuasion to occur. Note that this is not a simple matter of *ethos*. One can be credible and still fail to obtain obedience. Instead, what we see is that *ethos* is itself a complicated matter fully caught up with fantasy, in fact depending on it for success. *Ethos* is nothing unless it is considered from the perspective of its entanglement in the various affective processes that constitute our intersubjective relations. Consequently, behavior like obedience would remain mysterious if not inexplicable were we not to take account of the subject's active and not merely passive role—and "active" includes conscious and unconscious processes—in retroactively (*Nachträglichkeit*) integrating the event into an enjoyable sense of self.

Cultural studies wants to attend to the full range of human experience in culture. It has achieved a useful and progressive synthesis of approaches, theories, and methodologies. Since I have utilized many of them in this book, obviously I am not hoping to "supplant" or "negate" cultural studies. Cultural studies has opened up too much new and fertile terrain, and I would like nothing more than for it to continue to do so. Certainly, in terms of the conservative ideology of the aesthetic so common to literature, cultural studies is a real advance. Nevertheless, in its classroom articulations, whether in literature, composition, or elsewhere, cultural studies has put forward its liberationist politics in ways that I hope I have made clear are quite problematic. Nor is it really a matter of its leftist political bent (at least for me—others may take extra umbrage here). Instead, it comes down to an issue of rhetoric: in the classroom, cultural studies has not been very persuasive to students (although we might note the exception of students who go on to humanities graduate programs, where other persuasive forms come into play, such as group identity formation and enjoyment). It has been my contention throughout the book that psychoanalysis can help cultural studies find a more effective practice. Indeed, it may be helpful to recall that, above all, Freud and Lacan were clinicians. Psychoanalysis is a praxis, designed to help people, and its theories were developed through interactions with patients (see Fink, *Clinical*; Dor). They were not spun out of air. They were not developed as forms of critique. They were not concerned primarily with cultural meaning. They had a very direct aim: to help people who were having problems learn to cope with them and get better. While psychoanalysis may not always have lived up to that goal, as Freud's sometimes bungled cases testify, that does not belie the attempt. And perhaps on this point, psychoanalysis can learn from cultural studies the importance of attending to the wider socio-political implications of practice.

In saying that I hope to supplement cultural studies, or make it a more effective practice, I need to emphasize that this does not mean inserting psychoanalysis into the main cultural studies project as it has been articulated and practiced pedagogically. In effect, I am questioning the very notion of what it means to have an effective practice, if that is commonly understood as the smooth, frictionless transfer of ideas and practices to others. What "effectiveness" might also convey is something messier, more complex. I am not offering psychoanalysis to help cultural studies achieve its goals in such a frictionless manner. Indeed, this is, I think, one of the problems with Alcorn's otherwise excellent book on cultural studies and psychoanalysis. In the end, Alcorn accepts cultural studies' guiding framework as also being that of psychoanalysis, which can be seen in his emphasis on the achievement of the free circulation of desire as a pedagogical/political goal. The result is that psychoanalysis becomes the means for cultural studies to operate better, with no attendant questioning of the various symptomatics it produces and how they might reflect on cultural studies. Thus, cultural studies' emphasis on social politics, its approaching/receding liberationist bent, and its practical applications are some of my primary targets in this book.

So, ideally, I mean more than that psychoanalysis can supplement cultural studies; I also mean it can transform cultural studies. Perhaps it might be said that the two need each other, but this is not enough either, as it just seems to indicate that bringing them together can mend their shortcomings. What is further needed is precisely the rhetorical dimension. In declining to accept that psychoanalysis can cure us, in the larger sense of dissolving human antagonism or getting us to the great good place, I have also declined to accept cultural studies' hopes to cure us—or, just as bad, to "liberate" us. Psychoanalysis wants to cure us of psychic pain and allow us to function in normal and productive ways, and it can do this to some extent. But it stops short of larger social cures. Cultural studies aims at precisely these larger social issues, desiring to cure us of our bad politics, our cynicism, our cultural perversities and petty hatreds. It wants to cure us of injustice. When cultural studies is conjoined with rhetoric in composition pedagogies, it is as if rhetoric were redefined in line with the goals of cultural studies. Rhetoric becomes the means to achieve a progressive, civically engaged citizenry. Rhetoric, in this view, can cure of us of injustice.

Certainly, rhetoric can help us overcome injustice. However, rhetoric does not want to cure us of anything. Indeed, if we listen to Aristotle, who assigns rhetoric to the realm of the probable, we can see that ultimately rhetoric is symptomatic. If we had the Truth qua cure, or if we had the Path to it, we would not need rhetoric. Rhetoric is for those who may hope for a cure, who may hope for the truth, but who find that in the long run, truth and cure are as metonymic as desire. Is this a problem to be surmounted or a beauty to be celebrated? Probably both. Certainly it suggests that the notions of freedom and liberation that circulate in cultural studies, functioning akin to the *objet petit a*, the object/cause of desire, are thoroughly enmeshed in fantasy; facing up to structural limits—the fissures that characterize the Real—can help us move through such phantasmatic notions. In giving to rhetoric this psychoanalytic twist, then, we advance our repertoire of themes and motifs, allowing our understanding of the relations between rhetoric and community to become still more intimate.

In any event, the rhetoric I have advocated here looks to psychoanalysis as providing a well-developed, if idiosyncratic, theory of affects. As Žižek suggests, "communication does not take place through subjects but through affects" (*Tarrying* 218). Our sense of ourselves and our others is achieved not only through the lenses of discourse and the socius but through our affective engagements. Thus, I have suggested throughout that identification, as useful as this concept is for rhetorical and psychoanalytic theory, reaches its limits right alongside representation itself. The fact that representation never "says it all" necessitates our positing a beyond to the symbolic field, a beyond that we fill in through fantasy. Yet fantasy also functions on the side of reality, protecting us from too traumatic an encounter with the Real. On the one hand, we need this phantasmatic dimension; for example, fantasy supplies the minimum idealization necessary for our everyday dealings with Others, the overbearing "presence" of whom we could not otherwise withstand. While our ethical systems almost universally proclaim golden rules about loving our neighbors and respecting Others, our everyday comportments and affective experiences suggest something opposite: there is only so much of the Other we can take. This says nothing about the other person per se, of course; it says something about how our intersubjective relations flow and evolve. More important, it says something crucial about the symptomatic emergence of rhetoric and how we might consider the rhetorical constitution of community in the face of cultural studies narratives about the "coming community" or "democracy-to-come."

Fantasy, however, is only one of several facets of psychoanalytic affect; the other I want to reflect on is *jouissance*. We have seen that *jouissance* is a libidinal glue tying us to the world, generating a sense of worthwhile-ness, but it is also a libidinal "sticking point" wedding us to patterns and behaviors. It can both reinforce and disturb forms of identification, thereby showing us that identification is "not all." What is particularly uncanny is that *jouissance* is always emerging. Repetition especially marks the spot of its emergence, a point that emphasizes the connection of *jouissance* to drive over desire. Shaking hands, for instance, is a simple ritual useful in social interaction. But someone who pumps your hand vigorously, for too long, disturbs. Shaking hands becomes perverse, sexualized, repellent not just on its own account but for the disgusting enjoyment the other wrings from it. We are strikingly attuned to such emergence. In a restaurant the other day, I saw someone eating quesadillas, and there was something in the ritualized manner in which the food was eaten, the relish with which it was chewed, that raised my hackles. Yes, you might say I am being irrational. But that is precisely the point. *Jouissance* emerges anywhere, everywhere, and it is something that eludes our conscious control. It inspires reactions in us about what we do and how we see ourselves, and it provokes reactions in us concerning others.

In terms of rhetoric, *jouissance* is ever present. *Jouissance* can be taken to mean, among its other meanings, joy-in-sense. Joy in the word. More pertinently, *jouissance* works at both ends of rhetoric. *Jouissance* suffuses our activity, even if it is often unconscious; yet at the same time, *jouissance* is posed. Again, one of the effects of entering the symbolic is that subjects retroactively posit a phantasmatic, presymbolic sense of primal *jouissance*. Desire emerges through the symbolic and has as one of its aims the achievement of this *jouissance* it never had. Perhaps more pernicious, we are sensitive to the emergence of *jouissance* in others, and frequently we find this disturbing. It calls to mind our narcissistic relation to our own *jouissance*, present, but never to the extent we retroactively posit, and hence always somehow insufficient. The Other's organization of *jouissance* pricks us, and as Žižek repeats frequently, this generates an intersubjective fissure that endlessly frustrates the great project of neighbor love. It is precisely this intersubjective fissure that cultural studies continually stumbles over, preferring the fantasy of a pluralist if conflictual democracy-to-come over the full recognition of the stain of particularity and its perverse if not violent irrepressibility. Cultural studies may study perverse subjects, but it will not embrace them nor see in them but particular manifestations of the perversity common to us all. To do that would require a change in cultural studies' modus vivendi.

This is true of rhetoric as well, if we see rhetoric in terms of its contemporary rearticulations as profoundly civic. Of course it is civic, but this does not mean it is inevitably community building or even democratic. Psychoanalysis calls attention to and attempts to describe some of the perversities inherent in human beings. Rhetoric, in its classical, modernist, or postmodernist formulations, has attempted to work with these perversities, largely pragmatically. When rhetoric is defined narrowly—as intentional persuasion, for instance (see Coles)—these functional pragmatics come to the fore. What emerges as a problem, however, is settling questions about rhetoric's effectiveness. If a rhetorical discourse proves insufficient, we are left with rhetoric's own commonplaces to explain why. Was it inattentive to some nuance of audience? Could it have been an issue of credibility? And so forth. Whatever answers we might derive from such inquiries, I hope to have shown that what Žižek has accomplished greatly expands our understanding of their limitations. As I hope is clear, this is not a dismissal; it is a call for expansion and augmentation, albeit one that challenges rhetoric to understand itself differently.

So human perversity introduces complications into what rhetoric is. This is not of itself a startlingly new claim, of course, as rhetorical theory has come to this insight before. I do not see such insights being pressed as far as they might be, however. For instance, Kenneth Burke's indirect use of Freud to theorize identification in A *Grammar of Motives* might well be seen as opening a door we have yet to step through. It is as if we stand on the threshold, leery of going beyond. In some ways, this is understandable as we leave behind an intentionality that frames most rhetorical theory, especially in its pedagogical expressions in composition classrooms. In working through the complexities of cultural studies pedagogies, we therefore also stumble upon a core fantasy underpinning rhetoric: the phantasmatic assumption that our intentions have the desired effects for the reasons we think they do. It is time to reconsider this assumption, although, as I have said, Burke has already opened that door, and postmodern theorists such as Victor Vitanza, D. Diane Davis, and others are also providing new and alternate paths moving us away from this conception of rhetoric. What I hope to have shown here is that neo-Lacanian psychoanalysis offers us its own path, one that, in its better moments, asks us to work with perverse subjects, not just perfectable ones. In the end, even civic rhetorics, those informed by cultural studies or those that simply look back to Isocrates and the classical tradition, have yet to work through the roadblocks and forking paths such perversities create. The suturing of "critical thinking" to civic rhetorical projects, especially when given pedagogical expression, presents still larger problems. Critique, as we have seen, can never escape fantasy or *jouissance*, and any civic project grounded on the hope critique offers is only setting up blinders to the looming clouds of human perversity.

In the face of such claims, it might be considered odd that there is very little that is prescriptive in this book. I cannot claim this was always intentional. But a lesson that has emerged during the course of writing is that classroom pedagogical content may matter less than we think. I am not saying that it does not matter: it matters a great deal. Nevertheless, the highly symptomatic pedagogy wars of the 1990s made pedagogical content a massive concern. One risked terrible damage to students in choosing the "wrong" pedagogy. Scholars stuffed journals and books with charges about how great their pedagogies were and how other teachers were somehow failing students in pursuing lesser, more problematic pedagogies. Expressivism in particular got a bad rap. But the performative and symbolic aspects of pedagogy are as important, if not sometimes more so, than the specific content. Or, better, the performative/symbolic aspects generate a short circuit with the content, thereby transforming what that content will "mean" for others, how it will be used, how it might be reacted to. This is especially true of the emergence of authoritarian positions, or the reemergence of authority through the symbolic precisely where it seems to have been evacuated. Thus, while the content of one's class may aspire to be directly liberatory, the pedagogy may perform in an authoritarian manner directly at odds with the content. Students will recognize this conflict and react to it in a variety of ways, and often that will mean forms of resistance or rejection. Perhaps even more significant, students will learn those selfsame authoritarian behaviors, even replicate them, to the extent that a teacher has legitimated them in performance.

So phenomena like resistance, power flows and shifts, enjoyment, and dis/identification can lead us toward fresh rhetorical understandings—they function as concepts and heuristics, explanatory frameworks and analytical terminology. But as I have said, they do not necessarily prescribe a particular pedagogy or assignment, much less tell us what to do on Monday morning. This is as it should be. I maintain that a plurality of pedagogies is positive for the field. What a psychoanalytic rhetoric does provide us with are vocabularies, theories, and insights that can aid us in expanding, honing, or otherwise further developing whatever we are working with; alternatively, it can be used to diagnose problems, pose challenges, or otherwise help us become cognizant of troubling aspects in our pedagogies. A psychoanalytic rhetoric should be suitable for wherever one is, with whatever one is prepared to work through. What it expressly does not do is insist that one must change the pedagogical road one is on. However, it may suggest that one could inhabit that pedagogy differently, or that one could come to a new appreciation or level of sophistication regarding how that pedagogy works, what it does, and how it affects students and the achievement of goals.

The above is not to suggest that only a psychoanalytic rhetoric can save us. I do not think this is the case, and psychoanalysis might best be considered in relation to a number of approaches. This means, among other things, that the conjoinment of cultural studies, rhetoric, and writing pedagogy has done much to revitalize our relation to the liberal arts tradition, something I consider to be of great import today as the corporate university comes into its own and finds ways to curtail that tradition. Cultural studies is highly attuned to our cultural landscape and its productions, in all their wondrous vitality and diversity. If it gravitates toward a negating criticality, asking us to be suspicious and hyperaware of how culture constructs us and reproduces social injustice, it nevertheless still attends to the conjunction of aesthetic and rhetorical production and, perhaps just as important, supplies strong rationales for why we need to do so. For me, cultural studies remains an important resource for conceiving rhetoric and developing writing pedagogies.

As I have argued, however, the negativity inherent in establishing critique as the ultimate sign of a student-citizen-rhetor remains problematic, if not actively detrimental. The reduction of writing to this kind of criticality is a disservice. Alcorn suggests that this focus on critique is a problem, too, but ultimately he remains under the sway of cultural studies' political project, arguing that a better way to fulfill what cultural studies wants is the free circulation of desire (*Changing* 8). Alcorn is more cognizant than many that the free circulation of desire is not an innocent project and that its achievement brings with it the work of mourning. This seems right to me, and Alcorn's book is quite useful for exploring how this is so. Certainly, I see the work of mourning as Alcorn describes it played out in my classes (intriguingly, in my graduate classes more than my undergraduate classes). But what if we want to counter-supplement what Alcorn has to say? *Countersupplement* here means "to build on and with," but to do so in a way that transforms the entire project. I would begin by going back to psychoanalysis and seeing what else it might offer us. That is, where else does it suggest we might go? In large part, this book springs from precisely this question, and as we now take a retrospective look, I think some directions have been offered.

Lacan was well-known for his pithy locutions, and I have used many of them. Up to now, however, I have not emphasized Lacan's ethic, which is also captured in a zinging phrase: do not give ground on your desire (*Seminar VII* 319). What might this mean?

One way to consider what Lacan might have meant is to consider his talk to rebellious French students in 1968, "Impromptu at Vincennes," which is gathered with other material in *Television*. As he indicated in a later televisual broadcast, they were getting "on his back" and he "had to take a stand" (*Television* 32). This can be seen in the interruptions of the students transcribed in "Impromptu." In one case, Lacan moves to put one of his infamous equations on the board, and a student shouts out, "Man cannot be solved like an equation" (118). The students continue in this vein. Certainly, Lacan baits them in places, mocking them with a falsetto voice, insulting them obliquely, carrying on coolly. (Lacan clearly did not have to worry about course evaluations.) But finally he has had enough and tells them: "If you had a little patience, and if you were willing for our impromptus to continue, I would tell you that the aspiration to revolution has but one conceivable issue, always, the discourse of the master. That is what experience has proved. What you, as revolutionaries, aspire to is a Master. You will have one" (126). This passage has always given me pause. Lacan sometimes exhibited a true gift for nastiness. Nevertheless, while it is not immediately obvious what lurks beneath his statement, the basic outlines of his position are clear: revolution may posit liberation as its goal, but in actuality its goal is simply a new master, which, of course, means that the liberation being sought is phantasmatic. Lacan makes this even more explicit with his closing lines, calling the students *ilotes* (rebel-slaves, as in the Spartican rebellion) whose real function is not revolution but a starring role in the socio-symbolic as surplus *jouissance* inevitably recuperated by the powers that be (128). That is, in presenting themselves as easy targets against which the social order can rally, they are in collusion with the forces they think they resist insofar as they make it easy for their own eventual recuperation, by either the current or a future master. In any case, the liberation that they ostensibly claim as their goal will not be forthcoming.

I suggest that one might see the so-called culture wars of the 1990s as functioning in a similar manner. As cultural studies academics and the movement for political correctness came into the spotlight, the public reaction could hardly be characterized as a Habermasian dream of proper debate through media channels or even as a Foucauldian war of forces/positions. Rather, the dominant powers, which of course controlled or had privileged access to the major media channels, put everything they could on prime-time display and in so doing won over the bulk of the populace against now suddenly "dangerous" liberal academics brainwashing young minds. In my everyday life with family and friends outside academia, I am regularly confronted with this narrative. While I would not want to claim that my personal experience demonstrates de facto proof of my suggestion, I find that I share this perspective with many fellow academics who could add their own abundant examples. I would even submit that an event like Linda Brodkey's "troubles at Texas," where her attempts to design a cultural studies first-year writing curriculum based on controversial court cases met with what eventually became a national and highly successful smear campaign, is absolutely paradigmatic of my point. Indeed, the sheer overreaction, malice, and unfairness that characterized the affair already indicate the powerful role *jouissance* played in initiating and fueling the actions of Brodkey's opponents (see Brodkey, *Writing*).

Against this background, in what sense can we understand the ethic of not giving way on one's desire? As this book suggests, we can navigate by a few, rather nebulous although quite useful coordinates. Žižek argues that while we can never attain the magic "it," the sublime object granting us full satisfaction (primordial *jouissance*), we are nevertheless structured via the "backwards glance" of fantasy that suggests it is still attainable. Desire, framed and organized via fantasy, has such *jouissance* as its object. Even in the case of simple need, subjects also reach for and derive surplus symbolic enjoyment. Put succinctly, and in contrast to scholars like Teresa Ebert, there is no "pure" need. The belatedness of the subject is caught in this snare, and Žižek argues that the best we can do is manage with the symbolic forms and objects we do have and give up the belief that we can ever attain the magical "it." About this alienation Žižek says, "there is no solution, no escape from it; the thing to do is not to 'overcome,' to 'abolish' it, but to come to terms with it, to learn to recognize it in its terrifying dimensions and then, on the basis of this fundamental recognition, to try to articulate a *modus vivendi* with it" (*Sublime* 5). This is the lesson psychoanalysis has for cultural studies, but if cultural studies could go through the fantasy (of achieving the next good place through its good works, of curing students and citizens of injustice, of rectifying political wrongs and inducing students to join in on such good works), it would no longer be cultural studies as we know it. This might be the very best thing that could happen to cultural studies.

And yet, we are left with this nagging suggestion: do not give ground on your desire. Adrian Johnson argues that this ethic is often understood as being anti-Kantian if not outright Nietzschean. Kant's categorical imperative has as its goal the elimination of any particularity, any pathological stain, in its elevation of an ethical injunction to a universal. Nietzsche, in contradistinction, might be read as elevating the eternal return in opposition to Kant: making one's most individual particularity precisely what one devoutly wishes for all time. Johnson suggests that Lacan fits neither of these ethical positions (411–12). Earlier, I explained that the subject seeks a primordial but lost *jouissance*, but, again, desire and *jouissance* are not simply originary, free-floating entities. The sense of loss is phantasmatic, a condition of entry into the symbolic. Desire and *jouissance*, then, are in a sense manufactured. Desire, however, is less about the particular object than about the metonymic progression. The Law and the Other play key roles in providing the coordinates allowing desire to escape its deadlock (i.e., giving desire direction so that choices can be made). The function of Law, as symbolic prohibitions and injunctions, is to educate and produce desire. In this regard, for example, we should not see the incest prohibition as curtailing a real desire. Instead, the incest prohibition produces the desire. Thus, desire and Law are intimately connected. Law helps inculcate desire, and, in a reversal, obedience to Law can also function to aid in defending the subject from an excess of desires.

What this suggests is that the psychoanalytic ethic not to give ground on one's desire should not be turned into an imperative (Johnson 417). That is, Lacan is not saying that one should pursue one's desires as an absolute. He is instead suggesting that when one gives way on desire, one pays for it with guilt. We might recognize here a permutation of the "injunction to enjoy" discussed earlier. Guilt emerges as the superego's aggressivity toward the subject's adherence to Law, which functions to educate and coordinate desire. Insofar as the subject posits a lost but hypothetically still attainable *jouissance*, and continues to make sacrifices in accordance with Law, the subject experiences guilt. Not giving way on one's desire, then, means that *jouissance* must also be accorded a limit. As Lacan says, "desire is a defense, a prohibition against going beyond a certain limit in *jouissance*" (*Ecrits* 322). Not giving way on one's desire means not that *jouissance* should be one's ultimate pursuit but that when one's desire is jeopardized, giving way will result in a masochistic economy of guilt. The emergence of guilt coincides with the superego's injunction to enjoy, reinforcing the masochistic recuperation of *jouissance*. Further, if the incident at Vincennes is any indication, this logic plays out at the social level as well; the aspiration to revolution as the injunction to pursue desire manifests a surplus *jouissance* easily recoverable by society, thereby setting the stage for the emergence of another form of control, another new master. Such pursuits, in short, do not produce liberation. Furthermore, ignoring these libidinalized intricacies is what allows for the emergence and easy circulation of phantasmatic narratives of liberation and freedom — me and you and a dog named Boo, travelin' and livin' off the land, indeed.

It may be noted that all this can seem anticlimactic when presented as an ethic. Indeed, as Johnson notes, it may be that this only prepares us to think more carefully about ethics (420) (and, I might add, the relation between ethics and ideas of liberation). At least it provides sophisticated tools for understanding other ethics we might advance. Again, some of the social freedoms we push for—the multiplicity of subject positions qua lifestyles, the proliferation and perfection of technologies of the self—may advance startling new forms of violence and obedience. If Lacan is leery of embracing the Nietzschean position and elevating *jouissance* to an imperative, he is equally skeptical of Kant's elevation of the universal into ethical duty. Certainly, however, this points to problems with the ethics characteristic of cultural studies, especially cultural studies pedagogies. Suffusing countless first-year composition textbooks, for example, is the implicit ethical injunction to always respect Others, if not actively to take on responsibility toward those Others. Such an ethic, Lacan seems to suggest—and certainly this is Žižek's interpretation— amounts to a willful disregard of the inevitable encounter with the *jouissance* of the Other, which, as often as not, we will find traumatic.

In terms of our collective psychic economy, this results in conditions typical of today, when the public face of tolerance and positive multiculturalism is upheld, but in political activity at every end of the spectrum we see cynical apathy and/or emergent hatreds. Sharon Crowley's book *Toward a Civil Discourse: Rhetoric and Fundamentalism* is replete with examples of the angry intolerance in wide circulation today. Such surging animosity was also keenly exemplified during the 2004 presidential election, when, as part of the media parade of faces showcasing the ongoing Bush versus Kerry battle, *Daily Show* comedian Jon Stewart was invited to appear on the CNN "hard talk" show *Crossfire*. The gambit of *Crossfire* was to have one representative of the right (Tucker Carlson) and one from the left (Paul Begala) duke it out. Stewart mocked both of them mercilessly, claiming that they were hurting America. The show, in effect, spelled the death of real political discourse in favor of feeding hostile polemics. There can only be two sides and one winner, the show implicitly argued, and if you happen to be the loser, you are entitled to hate the winner. In the psychic economy outlined by Lacan, such a spectacle gives free rein to hatreds that constitute the seamy underside of benign tolerance and Other-love. Stewart's genius was to make this seamy underside palpable during the course of a brief fifteen-minute guest stint.

The notion of Other-love is, of course, religious and Christian: "love your neighbor as you love yourself." The injunction to bear responsibility and respect for the Other just as you would your own self therefore bears traces of narcissism. But insofar as we are incomplete, fissured subjects, the Other confronts us with that incompleteness. As Žižek never tires of telling us in his books, this is precisely the logic of racism. In anti-Semitism, Jews come to function as the traumatic symbol of the impossibility of social wholeness; in eliminating Jews, society can phantasmatically achieve the social cohesion it so desperately desires. The *jouissance* attributed to Jews—or Blacks, Balkans, Iraqis, or some other Other—feeds the fantasy and thereby exacerbates the hatred. This logic is endlessly resurgent and very potent; it will not be "cured." As I write this now, I see the latest version played out in the media: if we can just close the borders to illegal aliens, especially from Mexico, then America will finally regain some security . . .

Jouissance and desire do not, then, directly give us an ethics. They do not tell us what it is we should do. I earlier discussed Avital Ronell's "ethics of decision," and I bring this notion up again here to show that ultimately, a psychoanalytic rhetoric cannot supply us with "it," a sublime answer or injunction, telling us either how to decide or whether, in anticipation or retrospection, some decision is ethical. Neither the free circulation of desire—although some freeing of desire may help—nor the free circulation of *jouissance*—although, again, some freedom may help—will suffice to bring "it." Fantasies of social wholeness and subjective satisfaction may spur us on, but they can also be perilous. This, then, is where psychoanalysis leaves us: with the advice, the urging, to go through the fantasy that these things are achievable. This, I think, leaves us firmly in the realm of the probable, which is to say, on the ground where language and rhetoric come together. Nothing prevents us from working toward social justice, from eliminating pathological social unrest and violence, from pursuing good works, and there is nothing in going through the fantasy that suggests that we would stop desiring these things or that we should stop trying. But it does admit to a certain partiality. It suggests that our rhetorical work is never done and that rhetoric will never be done with us; it suggests that our attempts will be simultaneously furthered, hindered, and led awry by our own psychical structures; it suggests that subjectivity is tenacious, simultaneously dispersed and fissured, and entirely caught up with symbolic structures, Law, and dis/identifications with the Other; and it teaches us that reality is a composite of the world-as-it-is and fantasy, and the composite will not be undone. Finally, it suggests that our great desirings, as they come to be practices driven by expectations, might be tempered by relinquishing the belief that such works will return us to the great good place where *jouissance* thrills with potent purity.

NOTES

PROSPECTIVE

1. I would point out that in terms of the La Louvière wine example, while the direct enjoyment I receive from it is not *jouissance*, the enjoyment I may derive from collecting fine Bordeaux, relishing rituals such as popping the cork and swirling the glass, may very well be. For instance, in a PBS wine program called *Wine, Food, and Friends*, the host, Karen MacNeil, displays an overheated, controlling investment in pairing the perfect wine with food for her guests. Her palpable sense of *jouissance* is both compelling and disturbing, captivating and disgusting. Indeed, this is one of the more uncanny aspects of *jouissance*: we crave it for ourselves but can find it repellant in others.

ON BELATEDNESS AND THE RETURN OF THE SUBJECT

1. The literature on this subject is vast and diverse. The following is only a partial list of material. For diagnoses of the contemporary university, see Bloom; Readings; Aronowitz. For more discipline-specific perspectives, see Scholes; Giroux and Myrsiades; Downing; R. Miller, *As If*; Crowley, *Composition*.

2. In this regard, early, more historically oriented works like those of Robert Scholes and Richard Ohmann stand as harbingers of what was to emerge in the 1990s. Indeed, it might be profitable to frame Allan Bloom in this way; certainly, doing so gives his work a keener edge, though it also demonstrates how misplaced many of his charges were.

3. We will leave aside for the moment the idea that composition studies is already permeated by postmodernism, as argued, for example, in Phelps. Phelps, incidentally, traces the sense of crisis to the 1960s (5).

4. At least one caution is in order here: Crowley labels her suggestion "a modest proposal," indicating a degree of irony if not satire. But the length of time spent on the proposal, as well as the overall thrust of the book, which suggests that first-year

composition is of limited usefulness, indicate that the irony can only go so far. At some level she appears serious, even if rather sanguine about the real possibility of making first-year composition optional. As she points out, first-year composition is a perennial favorite.

5. See Kant. Also of interest is Schmidt, which includes a different translation of Kant's essay.

6. See, e.g., Fitts and France; Berlin and Vivion; Gere; Morton and Zavarzadah; France, *Composition*; Bizzell; and Schilb.

7. See Vitanza, "Wasteland,'" the plenary address Vitanza gave at the Research Network Forum at the 1998 Conference on College Composition and Communication. Also see his reader response to Julie Drew, and her response to him, in *JAC* 19.4 (1999): 699–706.

8. *Critical thinking* has become a ubiquitous if often empty term, akin to how Readings describes *excellence* as used in the contemporary university. Its meaning is strictly coterminous with whatever instruments of accountability one brings to it (Readings 21–43).

9. Wall provides a rigorous and rich exploration of this idea in the thought of Levinas, Blanchot, and Agamben. Wall accepts that Lacan too was exploring a radically passive understanding of the self but remains critical on certain points: Lacan was invested in lack, which Wall finds problematic, and Lacan retained a notion of the self or ego, however vestigial (40, 44). While Wall is essentially correct, he avoids the complications of Lacan's qualifications concerning lack, such as "nothing is lacking in the Real." I take up these questions in more detail later, but it might be useful to add that such criticisms help to demonstrate psychoanalysis's limits. Indeed, a key theme in this book is that no discourse can say everything, and this should of course include psychoanalysis.

10. It is doubly ironic that in an analysis about *Nachträglichkeit*, the key dream was itself only recognized after the fact; that is, the analytic encounter was also caught in a structure of belatedness.

11. In omitting the reason, I am following Barthes's lead when he omitted the picture of his mother in *Camera Lucida*. This further underscores the intricate networks, or chains of signifiers, through which writing weaves. Of course, most people would not catch such an oblique allusion, given that they are not me, that they are not the singularly unique patchwork of experiences that constitutes my "Thomas-ness." Thus, the absolute, singular finitude of the subject—always materialized in some little detail or object, what Žižek calls playing off the abstract purity of transcendence, a miserable piece of the Real. I might also add that the CD was Morphine, *Cure for Pain*.

12. This return to the discussion of Hegel found at the beginning of this chapter performatively enacts the very structure of transformation I am describing here.

13. Žižek, taking an example from Lacan, describes this idea of reality functioning as an escape from trauma with the example of Zhuang Zi, who, upon awakening from a dream that he was a butterfly, considered the possibility that he was

actually a butterfly dreaming he was a human. In the Real of his desire, suggests Žižek, Zhuang Zi *was* a butterfly, and Zhuang Zi as his symbolic sense of self was merely the comforting reality he inhabited (*Sublime* 45–46).

TOWARD A NEO-LACANIAN THEORY OF DISCOURSE

1. A crucial exception to this statement is Grossberg, an early and insightful theorist of the role of affect in culture, especially in music. Another cultural theorist who points to the importance of affect is Massumi. The work of Deleuze, on his own and with Guattari, is also concerned with affect; the problem here is that Deleuze's work has, with a few exceptions, only recently begun to be addressed in cultural studies and rhetoric.

2. Heidegger's work on language is extensive and suffuses nearly all his work, especially his later work; see in particular *On the Way* and "Letter on Humanism," in *Basic Writings*. Also of use is Taylor, "Heidegger, Language, and Ecology," in *Philosophical Arguments*. In these works and others, it is clear that Heidegger is breaking with representationalist models of language and moving toward what Taylor characterizes as an "expressive-constitutive" model (101). Lacan and Žižek, it should be clear, are also working out of a constitutive and not a representationalist understanding of language. For more on the relations between Lacan and Heidegger, and the constitutive role of metaphoric language, see Chaitin.

3. See in particular *Theory* 58–59, where Kinneavy presents the sources of the triangle and charts its development.

4. There have been other critiques of Kinneavy and the triangle since Fulkerson, Hunter, and Crusius. Vitanza also takes on the triangle in a number of essays, most notably "Three Countertheses" and "Two Propositions." In addition, two collections have appeared that deal extensively with Kinneavy: see Gabin; Witte, Nakadate, and Cherry.

5. For Lacan's outline of the four discourses, see *L'envers de la psychanalyse*. An English translation by Russell Grigg is forthcoming as *The Other Side of Psychoanalysis*.

6. It should be noted that Vitanza finds poststructuralist and postmodern theories useful to the extent that they demonstrate the unfeasibility of a totalizing framework or all-encompassing theory; see, e.g., Vitanza, "Three" 148.

7. I again refer to Macdonell. For Macdonell, poststructuralist thought can be characterized as a collection of related (although not the same) theories of discourse emphasizing the political and constructed nature of the world as mediated through language, especially what is historical, relational (positional), productive, limiting, and resistant in discourse.

8. See, e.g., Berlin and Inkster.

9. Berlin was continually revising and elaborating this taxonomy. For example, in *Rhetoric and Reality*, he reduces the major categories to three—objective, subjective, and transactional—with finer subdivisions accounting for the specific pedagogies. Thus, expressivism is categorized as subjective, and classical rhetoric

is considered transactional. However, these revisions are all based on the triangle; as Berlin puts it, "Every rhetorical system is based on epistemological assumptions about the nature of reality . . . [and] these matters, of course, converge with the elements of the rhetorical triangle: reality, interlocutor, audience, and language" (4).

10. My understanding of the usefulness of a psychoanalytic contribution to discourse theory here relies on Bracher et al. The thesis uniting this disparate collection of essays is that Lacanian psychoanalysis can aid in producing a theory of discourse that offers "unique possibilities for understanding both the constitutive and the transformative functions of discourse in human affairs" (1).

11. For a thorough analysis of Laclau and Mouffe's theory of discourse, and its further refinement by Žižek, see Torfing. What unites Laclau, Mouffe, and Žižek is an understanding of discourse that is predicated on the notion of social antagonism.

12. The work of Deleuze and Guattari critiques this notion of lack. Although Lacan, Deleuze, and Guattari all agree that nothing is lacking in the Real, Lacan emphasizes in his work the structural role of language for producing lack; Deleuze and Guattari, on the contrary, emphasize the real fulsomeness of desire in the face of the production of lack. For them, desire is always present in social assemblages, not as an originary principle but as something that emerges in activity or performance. In short, Deleuze and Guattari's understanding of discourse is substantially different from most other poststructuralist conceptions. Unlike Foucault, whose analyses of power and the process of subjectivization remain largely at the level of the disciplined body, Deleuze and Guattari attempt to explain in more concrete terms the connections between discourse and the internal psyche. I would argue that in part this stems from their encounter with Lacan. Ultimately, however, Deleuze and Guattari's work produces a substantially different understanding of discourse from neo-Lacanian theory or other poststructuralist theories coming out of Derrida, Foucault, Barthes, Lyotard, and others. Unfortunately, I do not have the space to explore this quite promising material here, and it will have to wait until a later project.

13. Alcorn cites Fredric Jameson as being characteristic of those who read Lacan as a poststructuralist. For example, Jameson writes that "the polemic thrust of Lacanian theory, with its decentering of the ego, the conscious subject of activity, the personality, or the 'subject' of the Cartesian cogito—all now grasped as something like an 'effect' of subjectivity . . . poses useful new problems for any narrative analysis" (*Political* 153). The subject is here understood as being a discursive (narrative) effect, a kind of subjectivization achieved through the marshalling of discourses as opposed to a subject that would be in excess of any solely discursive containment.

14. The term *essentialism* is embroiled in many, diverse debates. Fuss provides a close reading of the term and the motivations behind its deployment, on the one hand, and the attacks that are made against it, on the other. Fuss concludes that essentialism, even when it is attacked, is "effectively doing its work elsewhere"

(1). Not only is a reliance on essentialism difficult to avoid, but it often underpins antiessentialist positions. That said, I understand there to be a difference between assigning essential characteristics to a person or thing in an effort to naturalize that person or thing (the attempt to define sex categories of man and woman is a typical example) and attempting to theorize language in its functioning as having certain inherent limitations. Of course, my position is that concepts like "limitation" and "impasse" are often coded negatively, at the expense of their productive possibility. Like Fuss, I am interested less in assigning a categorical assessment to such terms as *essentialist* and *limited* than in problematizing the received wisdom that would deny them their usefulness, if not necessity. What is most important, as Fuss notes, is "*who* is utilizing [the term], *how* it is deployed, and *where* its effects are concentrated" (20).

15. Žižek understands trauma to be our response to an impossible limit or radical antagonism; it is an experience of constitutive anxiety or unease at the terrifying prospect of the impossibility of achieving harmonious resolutions to personal and social conflicts. Furthermore, trauma is intensified by the fact that it also "resists symbolization, totalization, symbolic integration" (*Sublime* 6). For Žižek, then, not only do we experience trauma when confronted with various forms of antagonism, but we also experience supplementary trauma due to our inability to find an adequate expression for it. For other views on trauma, see Caruth.

16. This aspect of discourse calls to mind the sublime, and just as speculative reading could not find its place on the communications triangle, neither can the sublime. A further advantage of neo-Lacanian discourse theory, then, is precisely that it includes in its understanding of discourse the uncanny, sublime element that seems easily lost in pragmatics. This would be useful not only in terms of Žižek's theory of ideology, which involves the transmutation of the desired object into a sublime object (see chap. 4), but in terms of aesthetic theory, which has for long now alternately tarried with and been enraptured by theories of the sublime. Indeed, if literature itself, in the ideology of the aesthetic, is held to be a sublime object capable of generating liberation and resistance, what is at stake in a theory of discourse that can only map literature's "literariness" and not its sublimity? This is not to suggest that literature is in fact a sublime object; it is only to point out the difficulties of attempting to come to grips with such debates via the communications triangle.

IN THE FUNHOUSE

1. Copjec notes that there are added complications on this point because Foucault is sometimes at odds with the implicit immanence of his theory of power. She offers as an example his discussion of the subjectivity of the "pleb" as something structurally unknowable and lacking content—an understanding that has similarities to Lacan's theory of the subject. For further details, see Copjec 1–3.

2. Miller's use of the metaphor of "the carnival" is based on Stallybrass and White. Stallybrass and White, in turn, work out of Bakhtin, whose book *Rabelais*

and His World first investigated the meaning and implications of carnival. At stake in Stallybrass and White's investigation is the idea of carnival as a "mode of understanding" or "cultural analytic," especially for investigating the intermixture of high and low culture (6). My use of the metaphor of the "funhouse" is not so much an attack on the use of carnival as a cultural analytic as a supplement that can extend its usefulness. We might say that every carnival has its funhouse.

3. Vitanza states, "I want everything that has been excluded, now reincluded, put back into The History of Rhetoric" (*Negation* 13).

4. See Derrida, "'To Do Justice to Freud': The History of Madness in the Age of Psychoanalysis" (*Resistances* 103).

5. Recall how Coles responds to his students who ask him what he wants from them in class. He reverses their plea, essentially saying that he wants what they want when they know what they want—which, in a sense, is no response at all. What Coles accomplishes with this dialectical play is first to throw the students back on their own fantasy scenes (e.g., the holy grail of a perfectly grammatical paper) but next to force them to modify their fantasy scenes in accordance with the precepts of the class—which, in some sense, dislodges precisely the desire of students to please their (fantasy construction of) the teacher. See Coles 34–35.

6. See Žižek, *Sublime* 173–78; Fink, *Lacanian* 3–13.

7. I will note in passing how Miller's words say far more here than she intends. The intrusion of the "real" into discourse that she mentions is paralleled by the intrusion of what Lacan calls the "Other" tongue into the very midst of our own speech. Thus, Miller unintentionally performs the very disruption that psycho-analysis makes a practice of analyzing. As we shall see, this eruption of an "Other" discourse is precisely what makes Miller's stated goal—"seeing things for what they are"—so difficult. If fantasy and desire suffuse all our relations and practices, then we never *really* see things for what they are. This does not in the least threaten the reality of the world, which carries on quite well; but it does suggest that our *experience* of the world is always bound up with our subjectivity.

8. Kojève's *Introduction* examines this dialectic of recognition in detail through an analysis of Hegel's description of the Master and Bondsman in *Phenomenology of Mind*; see esp. "In Place of an Introduction" (3–30).

POLITICA PHANTASMAGORIA

1. Yet another perspective that could be taken is that "ideology" does not really exist. This is a point made by Deleuze and Guattari when they claim, "There is no ideology and never has been" (*Thousand* 4). They go on to argue that there are only flows, assemblages, multiplicities, lines of flight, and linkages. I will make a rather bold claim and state that in some ways this is a very useful way to consider ideology—it does not exist except insofar as we can use the concept as a kind of "quilting point" that will gather together otherwise disparate signifying chains. Or, as Eagleton puts it in *Ideology*, the concept of ideology is useful to distinguish between power struggles that are "somehow central to a whole form of social life,

and those which are not" (8). That said, it should also be emphasized that Deleuze and Guattari's sense of "does not exist" is nevertheless quite different from that used in neo-Lacanian theory. Specifically, Deleuze and Guattari mean "does not exist" in a real, materialist sense, whereas for neo-Lacanian theory, "does not exist" describes the discrepancy between symbolic effects and the Real. Ideology is not of the Real, but its *effects* can be of the Real, and its primary impetus stems from an engagement with fundamental antagonisms that are in the realm of the Real.

2. See Althusser's "Ideology and Ideological State Apparatuses," in *Lenin*.

3. This is Žižek's version of Marx's phrase "Sie wissen das nicht, aber sie tun es," rendered as "They do this without being aware of it" in the English version of *Capital* translated by Ben Fowkes (166–67).

4. For another perspective on Žižek's emphasis on the external, performative dimension of ideology, see Sánchez.

5. For another way to conceive this problem, see Vitanza's discussion of economies in *Negation*. The separation of needs and desires, argues Vitanza, is the product of a restricted economy based on specific deployments of the negative. A general economy would attempt to move beyond this reliance on the negative and seek alternative, nonoppositional ways to conceive need and desire.

6. Drawing on Sloterdijk, Žižek, and especially Baudrillard, Vitanza addresses this problem of cynicism arising from critique in cultural studies–based pedagogies. See "Hermeneutics" and the exchange between Vitanza and Julie Drew in *JAC* 19.4. For other views on the negative effects of critique, see Elbow, *Embracing*; North.

7. For a more thorough explanation of this understanding of interpellation, see Krips's "Interpellation, Antagonism, Repetition" (*Fetish* 73–95).

8. For more on the notion of the truth-dimension, see chap. 2.

9. I owe this insight to Hans Kellner. During class one day in the mid-1990s, he began commenting on the odd ubiquity of the phrase "making a difference." It was not until revising this manuscript in 2006 that I made the connection between this phrase and the idea of a performative commitment. This looks like another case of deferred action (*Nachträglichkeit*).

10. For more on retroactivity and subjectivity, see chap. 1.

11. Žižek discusses the way in which a speaker receives a message back in inverted form: "It is in the 'essential by-products' of his activity, in its unintended results, that his message's true, effective meaning is returned to the subject" (*Looking* 78). We are typically disconcerted by such inversions and defend ourselves with ever ready excuses such as "That is not what I mean at all. That is not it at all."

12. Lacan defines the Master as one who so identifies with a given matrix of Master Signifiers that s/he believes her/himself to be whole, undivided, and self-identical. Bracher et al., *Lacanian* is a useful overview of this key aspect of Lacan. See also Lacan, *Four* 230–43.

13. Ballif sharply criticizes production-oriented pedagogies: "This is the process of *production*, a process that has control as its goal: mastery of the world, of the

word, and of the self. The will to mastery and its attendant violence ensures that all things are fixed with 'true' representations, that all signifieds are fixed with 'corresponding' signifiers, as a means of guaranteeing Identity, Truth, and Presence" (86). In Jay's case, then, we see that the ultimate *telos* of his pedagogy is a particular subjective Identity for the student—s/he becomes the "subject who is supposed to know."

14. Another way to think of this is that the symbolic order itself—what Lacan and Žižek refer to as the big Other—is "precisely the agency that decides instead of us, in our place" (Žižek, *Looking* 77). When we are confronted with a symbolic mandate—what appears as being in us, as being us, from the perspective of the Other—it is actually the effect of our position in the symbolic field.

15. While it lies outside the scope of this book, it would certainly be interesting to compare Jay's classroom strategy of making students active learners with Socrates's strategy of awakening latent knowledge in a slave boy in the *Meno*. Plato, like Jay, is attempting to demonstrate agency on the part of the learner that is not tied to the teacher.

16. One is reminded here of Baudrillard's famous pun (derived from Hegel's notion of the "cunning of reason") about the "cunning of capital"; all consumption within capital is already tainted by complicity with the workings of capital (*Mirror* 31).

17. This is not to suggest that no problems emerge with Ulmer's attempt to retain a critical sensibility. After all, the subtitle is of his essay is "On Deprogramming Freshmen Platonists"; the term *deprogramming*, in combination with other metaphors for the classroom, including *textshop* and *laboratory*, suggests an authoritarian and clinical feel. This is further underscored by Ulmer's attitude toward resistance itself; he claims that "once the resistance has manifested itself we can recognize it for what it is—ideology—and deal with it in a constructive way" ("Textshop" 763). Ideology manifests itself through resistance and discussion, not just invention, and ultimately it is the teacher who will "deal" with it.

18. This traumatic conflict, as previously explained, can take any number of forms, as examples of social antagonism, anti-Semitism, etc., have suggested. I want to add that such conflict can also be internal, what Lacan calls the deadlock of desire. That is, fantasy and ideology can help us break through the indecision of determining which of our many desires we actually want to pursue. The allure of breaking this deadlock should not be underestimated.

19. It is for this reason that Žižek claims that "politics exists because 'society doesn't exist'" (*Ticklish* 177). In other words, there is always an empty signifier that will designate the content of this impossibility of society—"democracy" does so because the term can as easily designate a welfare state as laissez-faire capitalism, even though these are two totally different versions of capitalism. Which is to say, "democracy" as a concept is fundamentally unstable; its meaning fills out when a political body attempts to make the concept its own or achieve hegemony. Of

course, *politics* is the term used for the struggle to determine which content will fill out that empty signifier; see Laclau and Mouffe.

20. For more on this issue, see my discussion of psychoanalytic discourse theory in chap. 1.

21. Žižek provides detailed readings of this concept throughout *Sublime*; see esp. 74–75, 124–29.

22. My use of the term *abandonment* stems directly from a reading of Vitanza, "Hermeneutics." However, it should be noted that Vitanza is coming to this term from a radically different theoretical perspective that will necessarily provide a quite different inflection. That said, as my use of the term indicates, a parallel remains insofar as abandonment traces an ethical "giving over" (of the need to control, master, deny, or vilify) to what will in any event occur precisely because it is beyond the boundaries of human control or intervention. This is not passivity: it is an active choice staging an ethical orientation that would reconfigure or reimagine the forms, goals, and economies within which socio-political activities occur.

23. I derive the term *fast capital* from Agger, who proposes that the stage of "late capital" is best understood in terms of speed—the rapid shift of positions and ideas such that no hold can be maintained and one is swiftly swept along. In such an epoch, argues Agger, the possibility of critique is jeopardized and must be regained.

BREAKING THE LAW

1. The work in rhetoric and composition that deals with resistance is vast, but I would like to note a few important texts: Boyd; Fitts and France; X. Gale; Hurlbert and Blitz, *Composition*; Miraglia; Murphy; Paine; Shor.

2. It should be noted that this notion of law is not simply a manifestation of the internalized, symbolic force of law. Rather, it speaks to the fact that law has a structural component that lies beyond the plane of social and historical immanence. This point is developed more fully below. It might be added that this argument has relevance for debates concerning the limits (or not) of social constructivism, but it is beyond the present scope to enter those debates.

3. For a more thorough critique of Foucault from a Lacanian position, see Copjec. Copjec notes that her project is complicated by the fact there is no one "Foucault," that "Foucault" also designates those who work out of him, and even that his position is at times strikingly close to the one she is upholding (see, e.g., 3–4). The difficulties Copjec describes are also applicable to my own arguments concerning Foucault. That is, his name should be taken to signify an aspect of his work or how his work has been utilized by others. Of further interest is Copjec's final chapter, in which she defends Lacan's formulas of sex division against Butler's deconstructive critiques.

4. Butler dryly describes the rationale for her new focus: "Actually, in the recent past, the question was repeatedly formulated to me this way: 'What about the materiality of the body, Judy?'" (*Bodies* ix). *Bodies That Matter*, then, should be

seen as a response to charges that her conception of performativity ignored material "reality."

5. See, e.g., Žižek, *Sublime* 165–69, in which Žižek relates the story of the Yugoslavian soldier who refused to "freely" sign a loyalty oath unless ordered to do so, in which case, of course, the signature would no longer be freely given. The problem was solved, and a prison sentence for the young soldier avoided, by the paradoxical solution given by the military court of a formal order to sign a free oath.

6. My reference to "Signature, Event, Context" is from *Margins*.

7. In accordance with the conventions established in Lacan and Žižek, *Real* is capitalized. For perhaps obvious reasons, Butler declines to follow this practice, preferring lowercase usages. In the text, when I am following Butler's arguments, I will also use lowercase.

8. See the excerpt from "On Truth and Lying in an Extramoral Sense," in *The Portable Nietzsche*. For a full version, see Nietzsche, *Philosophy*, which also includes selections from Nietzsche's earlier drafts.

9. Nietzsche never makes this statement directly, and in actuality, his position is much more complex than Solomon suggests, as an examination of *The Gay Science* or "On Truth and Lying in an Extramoral Sense" will reveal.

10. For more on this understanding of the truth-dimension in discourse, see the discussion of the painting *Lenin in Warsaw* in Žižek, *Sublime*.

11. For further examples of such scenarios, see the special issue of *Dialogue* on contrapower harassment (5 [Spring 1999]). Of relevance here is Bay. In contrast to Crowley, who sees student resistance as stemming from her symbolic position as an older, culturally devalued woman, Bay emphasizes the body and how culturally sanctioned codes of attractiveness can lead to problematic behavior from male students toward female instructors.

12. It should be kept in mind that my discussion is filtered through the representations of them supplied by Fetterley and Crowley, with all the qualifications and limitations this implies. I would further add that despite my criticisms, Fetterley and Crowley should be applauded for taking the risk of relating such classroom incidents and thereby giving us the opportunity to learn with them. Nor should we forget that these kinds of classroom incidents are genuinely troubling and sometimes tramatic.

13. Of course, as one reader has pointed out, we overlook female agency if we do not grant that it is just as plausible that some or all of the female students took this position with no consideration of what the male students thought. It should be noted that Fetterley and Crowley do present their cases as involving male persuasion of the other students. Nevertheless, even if it is true that the female students came to their conclusions independently of the male students, this does not change my argument concerning the emergence of the fissure, which does not ultimately depend on the gender of the resister.

"HANDS UP! YOU'RE FREE"

An earlier version of this chapter appeared as "'Hands Up, You're Free': Composition in a Post-Oedipal World," *JAC* 21.2 (2001): 287–320. It is reprinted here with permission from the publisher.

1. See Bewes; Craig and Bennett; Sloterdijk.

2. Howe and Strauss collect a substantial body of quotes from the media that disparage Generation X (*13th*). See also Bloom; Craig and Bennett.

3. For more on the possible media exaggeration of cynicism, see Craig and Bennett.

4. My use of the prefix *post-* serves multiple purposes. First, it is useful as a signifier of the shift in pedagogical orientation for which I am arguing. Second, given that academia is itself increasingly permeated by the logic of the market, it is useful to brand the concepts one deploys in academic writing. Third, at the performative level, my use of a popular prefix — perhaps it might even be called ubiquitous — replicates to a certain degree the waning effectiveness of critique. Although many academics, especially those aligned politically on the left, are critical of the infiltration of market logic into academia, nevertheless the pressure to produce something new that will "sell" in the marketplace of ideas is extremely high. Thus, my use of *post-* should also be taken as an ironic comment on my own entry into this market terrain, since I am to some degree also critical of this infiltration, but for all that just as caught at the material level in its logic. Fourth, *post-* establishes a thematic resonance among some of the key terms deployed in this essay, such as postpedagogy, post-Oedipal, and postmodern, which reinforces my argument that the postmodern age requires strategies, tactics, and concepts specially suited to it. Last, postpedagogy resonates with the same or similar usages of the term (such as post[e]-pedagogy) in other works; see Ulmer; D. Davis.

5. Baudrillard writes: "At the fourth, the fractal (or viral, or radiant) stage of value, there is no point of reference at all, and value radiates in all directions, occupying all interstices, without reference to anything whatsoever, by virtue of pure contiguity. At the fractal stage there is no longer any equivalence, whether natural or general. . . . Good is no longer the opposite of evil, nothing can now be plotted on a graph or [analyzed] in terms of abscissas and ordinates" (*Transparency* 5–6). The irony for Baudrillard is that "things" (signs or actions) not only continue to function in this state but function better.

6. Mann connects the "critical drive" to interpretation in general, arguing that interpretation is the disease and that therefore critics and interpreters are not immune to the pathology; he further adds that every critical gesture is a sign of infection. As he sums it up, "one's very insistence on critical distance might be a sort of hermeneutic *Verneinung* or denial, and the most salient symptom of all" (ix). For example, in terms of the avant-garde's "death," Mann extrapolates from Baudrillard, claiming, "The death of the avant-garde is not an end to its production, which continues unabated, but a theory-death, the indifferent circulation

of its products in a critical atmosphere in which the very idea of cultural opposition is increasingly problematic, and no less so for being ever more shrilly proclaimed" (xi).

7. I have in mind here a statement on liberation made by Foucault: "I do not think that there is anything that is functionally—by its very nature—absolutely liberating. Liberty is a *practice*. So there may, in fact, always be a certain number of projects whose aim is to modify some constraints, to loosen, or even to break them, but none of these projects can, simply by its nature, assure that people will have liberty automatically, that it will be established by the project itself. The liberty of men [*sic*] is never assured by the institutions and laws that are intended to guarantee them. This is why almost all of these laws and institutions are quite capable of being turned around" ("Space" 245). Foucault's argument, I think, is an indication that concepts like "freedom" and "liberation," insofar as they mean anything at all, refer to ongoing practices; they refer to the trajectory of actions to which we give our hopes (futurity) or our assessments (posterity).

8. The "bad" class, of course, is usually the class of the Other (pedagogue). Sifting through a few years' worth of *College English* and *College Composition and Communication*, one gets the impression that the favorite pastime of composition scholars is to demonstrate how "bad" some other kind of pedagogy is. The "other" pedagogy is always failing, oppressing, inadequately preparing, brainwashing, or otherwise doing something wrong to students—at the very least not producing good writing—while the "new" pedagogy being offered is always "better." My own work risks reproducing this structure of critical one-upping on one level, but I acknowledge this tendency and attempt to incorporate it into a pedagogy that would extricate itself from these kinds of simple binary reversals. One should not so much transform one's pedagogy as perhaps inhabit one's pedagogy freshly, allowing change, if it is to occur, to emerge out of the intersection of reading and thinking and actual classroom interactions.

9. As Vitanza explains, negative deconstructions stay in the binary; thus, he proposes an affirmative deconstruction, which "calls out to the other so as perhaps to pass out of the binary" (*Negative* 219). I derive the term *excriptive* from D. Diane Davis; as she puts it, "We will hope, rather, to EXcribe ourselves, to locate a postpedagogy, a pedagogy that would be other/wise" (*Breaking* 213). Note the double meaning of "other/wise": to be different than previously, and to be wise in our comportment toward (our) others. See also *Breaking* 13–14, for further elaboration on excription.

10. Deleuze explains: "In Nietzsche's terminology the reversal of values means the active in place of the reactive (strictly speaking it is the reversal of a reversal, since the reactive began by taking the place of action). But *transmutation* of values, or *transvaluation*, means affirmation instead of negation—negation transformed into a power of affirmation, the supreme Dionysian metamorphosis" (*Nietzsche* 71). I understand Deleuze to be describing the attempt to move beyond reactive, oppositional strategies that, due to their dependence on what they are reacting

against, are precisely not *action*. Instead, they are in a sense always subsidiary because what they oppose provides their raison d'être. A transvaluation, on the other hand, would no longer seek a trajectory within the circumscribed path of an oppositional object and would therefore no longer be secondary and reactive. I later discuss Lacan's objection to direct opposition as being socially foolhardy.

11. Although many theorists argue that disciplinary society is undergoing a transition, this should not be taken to mean that the institutions, discourses, and mechanisms of a disciplinary society are being replaced. The emergence of new strategies results in reconfigurations and realignments in the extant logics of control, not the advent of something entirely different.

12. See also Butler; D. Davis.

13. See Segal.

14. See Jameson; Lasch; Pfeil; Worsham.

15. See Vitanza.

16. The WBTV network's success in the 1990s was predicated on a batch of new, youth-oriented shows, such as *Felicity* and *Dawson's Creek*, which illustrated this need to feel deeply and not a little sentimentally. In these shows, teens are shown to be wracked with powerful feelings, passionately reaching out to each other along the tumid creek and street. We can read this need for powerful emotions as symptomatic of a general waning of affect finding its "other scene" in televised spectacle. This further suggests that the "waning of affect" may simply be code for alternate modalities and distributions, a new structure of feeling that does not show up for us as we are accustomed through our dominant vocabularies and theories.

17. Žižek would claim further that in a sense this constitutes the fundamental fantasy that serves as the support of a (liberatory) pedagogue's subjectivity. Army life, for example, requires a certain homoerotic male bonding that must be disavowed in order to remain effective (*Ticklish* 266). Similarly, the liberatory pedagogue ultimately enjoys his/her service to the state (and the benefits that accrue from such service) but must disavow this attachment in order to maintain enjoyment. This adds to our understanding of academics who "hate capital" but nevertheless profit from its benefits: job, salary, validation, vacations, publishing, and all the other defining practices of the working academic.

18. On a personal note, I recall my summers off from college in the mid-1980s, working on a salmon-processing boat around the Aleutian Islands. Seven people were responsible for operating a machine that cut off the heads and gutted the salmon—approximately one fish every two seconds, sixteen hours a day, seven days a week. I still recall the delicious joy we experienced when someone managed—always deliberately—to jam the machine. There was nothing quite like a five-minute respite from production.

19. See Dean.

20. See Vitanza, *Negations*.

Agger, Ben. *Fast Capitalism: A Critical Theory of Significance*. Urbana: U of Illinois P, 1989.

Alcorn, Marshall W., Jr. *Changing the Subject in English Class*. Carbondale: Southern Illinois U P, 2002.

———. "Changing the Subject of Postmodernist Theory: Discourse, Ideology, and Therapy in the Classroom." *Rhetoric Review* 13.2 (1995): 331–49.

———. "The Subject of Discourse: Reading Lacan through (and beyond) Poststructuralist Contexts." *Lacanian Theory of Discourse: Subject, Structure, and Society*. Ed. Mark Bracher, Marshall W. Alcorn Jr., Ronald J. Corthell, and François Massardier-Kenney. New York: New York U P, 1994. 19–45.

Althusser, Louis. *Lenin and Philosophy and Other Essays*. Trans. Ben Brewster. London: New Left Books, 1971.

Arnold, Gina. *Route 666: On the Road to Nirvana*. New York: St. Martin's, 1993.

Aronowitz, Stanley. *The Knowledge Factory*. Boston: Beacon P, 2000.

Axelrod, Rise, and Charles Cooper. *The St. Martin's Guide to Writing*. 2nd ed. New York: St. Martin's, 1988.

Bahri, Deepika. "Marginally Off-Center: Postcolonialism in the Teaching Machine." *College English* 59 (March 1997): 277–98.

Bakhtin, Mikhail. *Rabelais and His World*. Bloomington: Indiana U P, 1984.

Ballif, Michelle. "Seducing Composition: A Challenge to Identity-Disclosing Pedagogies." *Rhetoric Review* 16.1 (1997): 76–91.

Barth, John. *Lost in the Funhouse*. New York: Anchor, 1988.

Bartholomae, David. "The Tidy House: Basic Writing in the American Curriculum." *Journal of Basic Writing* 12.1 (1993): 4–21.

Barton, Ellen, and Gail Stygall. *Discourse Studies in Composition*. New Jersey: Hampton, 2002.

Baudrillard, Jean. *The Mirror of Production*. Trans. Mark Poster. St. Louis: Telos P, 1975.

———. *Seduction*. Trans. Brian Singer. New York: St. Martin's, 1990.

———. *Simulacra and Simulation*. Trans. Sheila Glazer. Ann Arbor: U of Michigan P, 1994.

———. *The Transparency of Evil*. Trans. James Benedict. New York: Verso, 1993.

Bay, Jennifer. "Who's Afraid of Their Male Students?" *Dialogue* 5.1 (1999): 31–45.

Bazerman, Charles. "Theories That Help Us Read and Write Better." Witte, Nakadate, and Cherry 103–12.

Beale, Walter. "Rhetoric in the Vortex of Cultural Studies." *Proceedings of the Fifth Biennial Conference of the Rhetoric Society of America*. Minneapolis: Avairom Burgess, 1992. 1–22.

Berlin, James A. "Composition and Cultural Studies." Hurlbert and Blitz 47–55.

———. "Composition Studies and Cultural Studies: Collapsing Boundaries." *Into the Field: Sites of Composition Studies*. Ed. Anne Ruggles Gere. New York: MLA, 1993. 99–116.

———. "Contemporary Composition: The Major Pedagogical Theories." *College English* 44 (December 1982): 765–77.

———. "James Berlin Responds: 'Rhetoric and Ideology in the Writing Class.'" *College English* 51 (November 1989): 770–77.

———. "Postmodernism, Politics, and Histories of Rhetoric." *Pre/Text* 11.3–4 (1990): 169–87.

———. "Poststructuralism, Cultural Studies, and the Composition Classroom: Postmodern Theory in Practice." *Rhetoric Review* 11.1 (1992): 16–33.

———. "Revisionary Histories of Rhetoric: Politics, Power, and Plurality." Vitanza, *Writing* 112–27.

———. "Revisionary History: The Dialectical Method." *Pre/Text* 8.3–4 (1987): 47–61.

———. "Rhetoric and Ideology in the Writing Class." *College English* 50 (September 1988): 477–94.

———. *Rhetoric and Reality: Writing Instruction in American Colleges, 1900–1985*. Carbondale: Southern Illinois U P, 1987.

———. *Rhetorics, Poetics, and Cultures: Refiguring College English Studies*. Urbana: NCTE, 1996.

———. *Writing Instruction in Nineteenth-Century American Colleges*. Carbondale: Southern Illinois U P, 1984.

Berlin, James A., and Robert P. Inkster. "Current-Traditional Rhetoric: Paradigm and Practice." *Freshman English News* 8 (1980): 1–14.

Berlin, James A., and Michael J. Vivion. "Introduction: A Provisional Definition." *Cultural Studies in the English Classroom*. Ed. James A. Berlin and Michael J. Vivion. Portsmouth: Boynton/Cook, 1992. vii–xv.

Bewes, Timothy. *Cynicism and Postmodernity*. New York: Verso, 1997.

Biesecker, Barbara A. "Rhetorical Studies and the 'New' Psychoanalysis: What's the Real Problem? or, Framing the Problem of the Real." *Quarterly Journal of Speech* 84 (1998): 222–59.

Bizzell, Patricia, and Bruce Herzberg. *Negotiating Difference: Cultural Case Studies for Composition.* Boston: Bedford, 1996.

Blitz, Michael, and C. Mark Hurlbert. *Letters for the Living: Teaching Writing in a Violent Age.* Urbana: NCTE, 1998.

Bloom, Allan. *The Closing of the American Mind.* New York: Touchstone, 1988.

Boyd, Robert. "Reading Student Resistance: The Case of the Missing Other." *JAC* 19.4 (1999): 589–605.

Boynton, Robert S. "Enjoy Your Žižek!" *Lingua Franca* (October 1998): 41–50.

Bracher, Mark. *Lacan, Discourse, and Social Change: A Psychoanalytic Cultural Criticism.* Ithaca: Cornell U P, 1993.

——. *The Writing Cure: Psychoanalysis, Composition, and the Aims of Education.* Carbondale: Southern Illinois U P, 1999.

Bracher, Mark, Marshall W. Alcorn Jr., Ronald J. Corthell, and François Massardier-Kenney, eds. *Lacanian Theory of Discourse: Subject, Structure, and Society.* New York: New York U P, 1994.

Brereton, John C. "Review: *As If Learning Mattered: Reforming Higher Education,* by Richard E. Miller." *CCC* 51.3 (2000): 494–97.

Brodkey, Linda. "Remembering Writing Pedagogy." *JAC* 17.3 (1997): 489–93.

——. *Writing Permitted in Designated Areas Only.* Minneapolis: U of Minnesota P, 1996.

Brooke, Robert. "Lacan, Transference, and Writing Instruction." *College English* 49 (October 1987): 679–91.

Brooke, Robert, Judith Levin, and Joy Ritchie. "Teaching Composition and Reading Lacan: An Exploration in Wild Analysis." *Writing Theory and Critical Theory.* Ed. John Clifford and John Schilb. New York: MLA, 1994. 159–75.

Burke, Kenneth. *A Grammar of Motives.* Berkeley: U of California P, 1969.

Butler, Judith. *Bodies That Matter: On the Discursive Limits of Sex.* New York: Routledge, 1993.

——. "For a Careful Reading." *Feminist Contentions: A Philosophical Exchange.* Seyla Benhabib, Judith Butler, Drucilla Cornell, and Nancy Frasier. New York: Routledge, 1995. 127–43.

——. *Gender Trouble: Feminism and the Subversion of Identity.* New York: Routledge, 1990.

——. *The Psychic Life of Power: Theories in Subjection.* Stanford: Stanford U P, 1997.

——. *Subjects of Desire: Hegelian Reflections in Twentieth-Century France.* New York: Columbia U P, 1987.

Butler, Judith, Ernest Laclau, and Slavoj Žižek. *Contingency, Hegemony, Universality.* New York: Verso, 2000.

Carter, Michael. *Where Writing Begins: A Postmodern Reconstruction.* Carbondale: Southern Illinois U P, 2003.

Caruth, Cathy. *Trauma: Explorations in Memory.* Baltimore: Johns Hopkins U P, 1995.

———. *Unclaimed Experience: Trauma, Narrative, and History.* Baltimore: Johns Hopkins U P, 1996.

Chaitin, Gilbert D. *Rhetoric and Culture in Lacan.* Cambridge: Cambridge U P, 1996.

Clifford, John. "Review: Discerning Theory and Politics." *College English* 51 (September 1989): 517–32.

———. "The Subject of Discourse." Harkin and Schilb 38–51.

Clifford, John, and John Schilb, eds. *Writing Theory and Critical Theory.* New York: MLA, 1994.

Coles, William E., Jr. *The Plural I—and After.* Portsmouth: Boynton/Cook, 1988.

Collins, Ronald K. L., and David M. Skover. "The Death of Discourse." *Signs of Life: Readings on Popular Culture for Writers.* 2nd ed. Ed. Sonia Massik and Jack Solomon. Boston: Bedford Books, 1997. 171–77.

Copjec, Joan. *Read My Desire: Lacan against the Historicists.* Cambridge: MIT P, 1994.

Craig, Stephen C., and Stephen Earl Bennett. *After the Boom: The Politics of Generation X.* Lanham: Rowan and Littlefield, 1997.

Crowley, Sharon. *Composition in the University: Historical and Polemical Essays.* Pittsburgh: U of Pittsburgh P, 1998.

———. *The Methodical Memory: Invention in Current-Traditional Rhetoric.* Carbondale: Southern Illinois U P, 1990.

———. *Toward a Civil Discourse: Rhetoric and Fundamentalism.* Pittsburgh: U of Pittsburgh P, 2006.

Crusius, Timothy W. *Discourse: A Critique and Synthesis of Major Theories.* New York: MLA, 1989.

———. "James L. Kinneavy: A Bibliographical Essay." Witte, Nakadate, and Cherry 351–70.

Davis, D. Diane. *Breaking Up [at] Totality: A Rhetoric of Laughter.* Carbondale: Southern Illinois U P, 2000.

———. "Confessions of an Anacoluthon: Avital Ronell on Writing, Technology, Pedagogy, Politics." *JAC* 20.2 (2000): 243–81.

Davis, Robert Con. "Pedagogy, Lacan, and the Freudian Subject." *College English* 49 (November 1987): 749–55.

Dean, Tim. "Bodies That Mutter: Rhetoric and Sexuality." *Pre/Text* 15.1–2 (1994): 80–117.

Deleuze, Gilles. *Negotiations: 1972–1990.* Trans. Martin Joughin. New York: Columbia U P, 1995.

———. *Nietzsche and Philosophy.* Trans. Hugh Tomlinson. New York: Columbia U P, 1983.

Deleuze, Gilles, and Felix Guattari. *Anti-Oedipus: Capitalism and Schizophrenia.* Trans. Robert Hurley, Mark Seem, and Helen R. Lane. Minneapolis: U of Minnesota P, 1983.

———. *Kafka: Toward a Minor Literature.* Trans. Dana Polan. Minneapolis: U of Minnesota P, 1986.

———. *A Thousand Plateaus: Capitalism and Schizophrenia.* Trans. Brian Massumi. Minneapolis: U of Minnesota P, 1987.

Derrida, Jacques. *Dissemination.* Trans. Barbara Johnson. Chicago: U of Chicago P, 1981.

———. *Margins of Philosophy.* Trans. Alan Bass. Chicago: U of Chicago P, 1982.

———. *Of Grammatology.* Trans. Gayatri Spivak. Baltimore: Johns Hopkins U P, 1974.

———. *Of Spirit: Heidegger and the Question.* Trans. Geoffrey Bennington and Rachel Bowlby. Chicago: U of Chicago P, 1989.

———. *Resistances to Psychoanalysis.* Trans. Peggy Kamuf, Pascale-Anne Brault, and Michael Naas. Stanford: Stanford U P, 1996.

———. *Spectres of Marx: The State of the Debt, the Work of Mourning, and the New International.* Trans. Peggy Kamuf. New York: Routledge, 1994.

Dews, Peter. *The Limits of Disenchantment.* New York: Verso, 1995.

Doors, The. *The Complete Lyrics.* Ed. Danny Sugarman. New York: Delta, 1992.

Dor, Joël. *Introduction to the Reading of Lacan: The Unconscious Structured Like a Language.* Ed. Judith Feher-Gurewich, in collaboration with Susan Fairfield. New York: Other P, 1998.

Drew, Julie. "(Teaching) Writing: Composition, Cultural Studies, Production." *JAC* 19.4 (1999): 411–29.

Eagleton, Terry. *Ideology: An Introduction.* New York: Verso, 1991.

———. *Literary Theory: An Introduction.* Minneapolis: U of Minnesota P, 1983.

Ebert, Teresa. "For a Red Pedagogy: Feminism, Desire, and Need." *College English* 58 (November 1996): 795–819.

Elbow, Peter. *Embracing Contraries: Explorations in Learning and Teaching.* New York: Oxford U P, 1987.

Elliot, Anthony. *Subject to Ourselves: Social Theory, Psychoanalysis, and Postmodernity.* Cambridge: Polity P, 1996.

Faigley, Lester. *Fragments of Rationality: Postmodernity and the Subject of Composition.* Pittsburgh: U of Pittsburgh P, 1992.

———. "Literacy after the Revolution." *CCC* 48.1 (1997): 30–43.

Fairclough, Norman. *Critical Discourse Analysis: The Critical Study of Language.* London: Longman, 1995.

Felman, Shoshana. "Psychoanalysis and Education: Teaching Terminable and Interminable." *Yale French Studies* 63 (1982): 21–44.

Fetterley, Judith. "Foreword." Hurlbert and Blitz ix–xii.

———. *The Resisting Reader: A Feminist Approach to American Diction.* Bloomington: Indiana U P, 1978.

Fink, Bruce. *A Clinical Introduction to Lacanian Psychoanalysis: Theory and Technique.* Cambridge: Harvard U P, 1997.

——. *The Lacanian Subject: Between Language and Jouissance.* Princeton: Princeton U P, 1995.

Finke, Laurie. "Knowledge as Bait: Feminism, Voice, and the Pedagogical Unconscious." *College English* 55 (January 1993): 7–27.

Fish, Stanley. *Doing What Comes Naturally: Change, Rhetoric, and the Practice of Theory in Literary and Legal Studies.* Durham: Duke U P, 1989.

Fitts, Karen, and Alan W. France, eds. *Left Margins: Cultural Studies and Composition Pedagogy.* New York: SUNY P, 1995.

Forrester, John. *The Seductions of Psychoanalysis: Freud, Lacan, Derrida.* New York: Cambridge U P, 1990.

Foster, Hal, ed. *The Anti-Aesthetic: Essays on Postmodern Culture.* Seattle: Bay P, 1983.

Foucault, Michel. *Discipline and Punish: The Birth of the Prison.* Trans. Alan Sheridan. New York: Vintage, 1979.

——. *The History of Sexuality.* Vol. 1, *An Introduction.* Trans. Robert Hurley. New York: Vintage, 1978.

——. "Space, Knowledge, Power." *The Foucault Reader.* Ed. Paul Rabinow. New York: Pantheon, 1984. 239–56.

France, Alan W. "Assigning Places: The Function of Introductory Composition as a Cultural Discourse." *College English* 55 (November 1993): 593–609.

——. *Composition as a Cultural Practice.* Westport: Bergin and Garvey, 1994.

Frank, Thomas. *The Conquest of Cool: Business Culture, Counterculture, and the Rise of Hip Consumerism.* Chicago: Chicago U P, 1997.

Freud, Sigmund. "From the History of an Infantile Neurosis." *The Standard Edition of the Complete Psychological Works of Sigmund Freud.* Trans. James Strachey. London: Hogarth, 1964. 17: 7–122.

——. *The Interpretation of Dreams.* Trans. James Strachey. New York: Avon, 1965.

Fulkerson, Richard P. "Composition at the Turn of the Twenty-First Century." *CCC* 56.4 (2005): 654–87.

——. "Four Philosophies of Composition." *CCC* 30.4 (1979): 343–48.

——. "Kinneavy on Referential and Persuasive Discourse: A Critique." *CCC* 35.1 (1984): 43–56.

Fuss, Diana. *Essentially Speaking: Feminism, Nature, and Difference.* New York: Routledge, 1989.

Gabin, Rosalind J., ed. *Discourse Studies in Honor of James L. Kinneavy.* Potomac: Scripta Humanistica, 1995.

Gale, Fredric G., and Michael W. Kleine. "Speaking of Rhetoric: A Conversation with James Kinneavy." *Rhetoric Society Quarterly* 27.3 (1997): 31–50.

Gale, Xin Liu. *Teachers, Discourses, and Authority in the Postmodern Composition Classroom.* Albany: SUNY P, 1996.

Gere, Anne Ruggles, ed. *Into the Field: Sites of Composition Studies.* New York: MLA, 1993.

Giroux, Henry A. "Cultural Studies and the Culture of Politics: Beyond Polemics and Cynicism." *JAC* 20.3 (2000): 505–40.

———. *Fugitive Cultures: Race, Violence, and Youth.* New York: Routledge, 1996.

———. *Pedagogy and the Politics of Hope: Theory, Culture, and Schooling.* Boulder: Westview P, 1997.

Giroux, Henry A., and Peter L. McLaren. "Radical Pedagogy as Cultural Politics: Beyond the Discourse of Critique and Anti-Utopianism." *Theory/Pedagogy/Politics: Texts for Change.* Ed. Donald Morton and Mas'ud Zavarzadeh. Urbana: U of Illinois P, 1991. 152–86.

Giroux, Henry A., and Kostas Myrsiades, eds. *Beyond the Corporate University.* Lanham: Rowman and Littlefield, 2001.

Goleman, Judith. *Working Theory: Critical Composition Studies for Students and Teachers.* Westport: Bergin and Garvey, 1995.

Gramsci, Antonio. *Selections from the Prison Notebooks.* Ed. and trans. Quintin Hoare and Geoffre Nowell Smith. New York: International, 1971.

Grossberg, Lawrence. *We Gotta Get Out of This Place: Popular Conservatism and Postmodern Culture.* New York: Routledge, 1992.

Grossberg, Lawrence, Cary Nelson, and Paula Treichler, eds. *Cultural Studies.* New York: Routledge, 1992.

Habermas, Jürgen. "Modernity—An Incomplete Project." Foster 3–15.

———. *The Philosophical Discourse of Modernity.* Trans. Frederick G. Lawrence. Cambridge: MIT P, 1990.

———. *The Theory of Communicative Action.* Vol. 1, *Reason and the Rationalization of Society.* Boston: Beacon P, 1985.

Hairston, Maxine. "Diversity, Ideology, and Teaching Writing." *CCC* 43.2 (1992): 179–93.

Halberstam, Judith. *Female Masculinity.* Durham: Duke U P, 1998.

Haraway, Donna. *Simians, Cyborg, and Women: The Reinvention of Nature.* New York, Routledge, 1991.

Hardt, Michael. "The Global Society of Control." *Discourse* 20.3 (1998): 139–52.

Harkin, Patricia. *Rhetorics, Poetics, and Cultures* as an Articulation Project." *JAC* 17.3 (1997): 494–97.

Harkin, Patricia, and John Schilb, eds. *Contending with Words: Composition and Rhetoric in a Postmodern Age.* New York: MLA, 1991.

Harris, Joseph, and Jay Rosen. "Teaching Writing as Cultural Criticism." Hurlbert and Blitz 58–69.

Hegel, G. W. F. *Phenomenology of Spirit.* Trans. A. V. Miller. New York: Oxford U P, 1977.

———. *Philosophy of Right.* Trans. T. M. Knox. New York: Oxford U P, 1952.

Heidegger, Martin. *Basic Writings.* 2nd ed. Ed. David Farell Krell. New York: HarperCollins, 1993.

———. *Being and Time.* Trans. John Macquarrie and Edward Robinson. New York: Harper and Row, 1962.

——. *An Introduction to Metaphysics*. Trans. Ralph Manheim. New Haven: Yale U P, 1959.

——. *On the Way to Language*. Trans. Peter D. Hertz. New York: Perennial, 1971.

——. *Poetry, Language, Thought*. Trans. Albert Hofstadter. New York: Perennial, 1971.

Horkheimer, Max, and Theodor Adorno. *Dialectic of Enlightenment*. Trans. Edmund Jephcott. Stanford: Stanford U P, 2002.

Howe, Neil, and Bill Strauss. "The New Generation Gap." *Atlantic Monthly* (December 1992): 67–89.

——. *13th Generation: Abort, Retry, Ignore, Fail?* New York: Vintage, 1993.

Hunter, Paul. "'That We Have Divided / In Three Our Kingdom': The Communication Triangle and A *Theory of Discourse*." *College English* 48 (March 1986): 279–87.

Hurlbert, C. Mark, and Michael Blitz, eds. *Composition and Resistance*. Portsmouth, NH: Boynton/Cook, 1991.

——. "Resisting Composure." Hurlbert and Blitz 1–11.

Jameson, Fredric. *The Political Unconscious*. Ithaca: Cornell U P, 1981.

——. "Postmodernism and Consumer Society." Foster 111–25.

——. *Postmodernism; or, The Cultural Logic of Late Capitalism*. Durham: Duke U P, 1991.

Jaworski, Adam, and Nikolas Coupland, eds. *The Discourse Reader*. New York: Routledge, 1999.

Jay, Gregory S. "The Subject of Pedagogy: Lessons in Psychoanalysis and Politics." *College English* 49 (November 1987): 785–800.

Johnson, Adrian. "The Vicious Circle of the Super-Ego: The Pathological Trap of Guilt and the Beginning of Ethics." *Psychoanalytic Studies* 3.3–4 (2001): 411–24.

Kafka, Franz. "The Emperor." *The Basic Kafka*. Trans. Richard Winston and Clara Winston. New York: Pocket, 1979. 183.

——. *The Trial*. Trans. Willa Muir and Edwin Muir. New York: Schocken Books, 1995.

Kant, Immanuel. "An Answer to the Question: What Is Enlightenment?" *Perpetual Peace and Other Essays*. Trans. Ted Humphrey. Indianapolis: Hackett, 1983. 41–46.

Katz, Adam. "Pedagogy, Resistance, and Critique in the Composition Class." *Left Margins: Cultural Studies and Composition Pedagogy*. Ed. Karen Fitts and Alan W. France. New York: SUNY P, 1995. 209–18.

Kellner, Hans. "After the Fall: Reflections on Histories of Rhetoric." Vitanza, *Writing* 20–37.

Kincaid, James R. "Resist Me, You Sweet Resistible You." *PMLA* 118.5 (2003): 1325–33.

Kinneavy, James L. "The Basic Aims of Discourse." *CCC* 20.5 (1969): 297–304.

——. *A Theory of Discourse: The Aims of Discourse*. New York: Norton, 1971.

BIBLIOGRAPHY

Kojève, Alexandre. *Introduction to the Reading of Hegel: Lectures on the Phenomenology of Spirit.* Trans. James H. Nichols Jr. Ithaca: Cornell U P, 1969.

Krips, Henry. *Fetish: An Erotics of Culture.* Ithaca: Cornell U P, 1999.

Lacan, Jacques. *Ecrits: A Selection.* Trans. Alan Sheridan. New York: Norton, 1977.

——. *The Four Fundamental Concepts of Psychoanalysis.* Ed. Jacques-Alain Miller. Trans. Alan Sheridan. New York: Norton, 1977.

——. "Position of the Unconscious." Trans. Bruce Fink. *Reading Seminar XI: Lacan's Four Fundamental Concepts of Psychoanalysis.* Ed. Richard Feldstein, Bruce Fink, and Maire Jaanus. New York: SUNY P, 1995. 259–82.

——. *Le séminaire, livre XVII: L'envers de la psychanalyse.* Text established by Jacques-Alain Miller. Paris: Seuil, 1991.

——. *The Seminar of Jacques Lacan, Book VII: The Ethics of Psychoanalysis, 1959–1960.* Ed. Jacques-Alain Miller. Trans. Dennis Porter. New York: Norton, 1992.

——. *The Seminar of Jacques Lacan, Book XX: Encore: On Feminine Sexuality, The Limits of Love and Knowledge, 1972–1973.* Ed. Jacques-Alain Miller. Trans. Bruce Fink. New York: Norton, 1998.

——. *Television: A Challenge to the Psychoanalytic Establishment.* Trans. Denis Hollier, Rosalind Krauss, and Annette Michelson. New York: Norton, 1990.

Laclau, Ernesto. *Emancipations.* New York: Verso, 1996.

Laclau, Ernesto, and Chantal Mouffe. *Hegemony and Socialist Strategy: Towards a Radical Democratic Politics.* New York: Verso, 1985.

Land, Nick. *A Thirst for Annihilation: Georges Bataille and Virulent Nihilism.* New York: Routledge, 1992.

Landry, Donna, and Gerald MacLean. *Materialist Feminisms.* Cambridge: Blackwell, 1993.

Laplanche, Jean. *New Foundations for Psychoanalysis.* Trans. David Macey. Cambridge: Basil Blackwell, 1989.

Lasch, Christopher. *The Culture of Narcissism.* Rev. ed. New York: Norton, 1996.

Lurie, Susan. *Unsettled Subjects: Restoring Feminist Politics to Poststructuralist Critique.* Durham: Duke U P, 1997.

Lynch, Dennis, and Stephen Jukuri. "Beyond Master and Slave: Reconciling Our Fears of Power in the Writing Classroom." *Rhetoric Review* 16.2 (1998): 270–88.

Lyotard, Jean-François. *Heidegger and "the Jews."* Trans. Andreas Michel and Mark Roberts. Minneapolis: U of Minnesota P, 1990.

——. *Libidinal Economy.* Trans. Iain Hamilton Grant. Bloomington: Indiana U P, 1993.

——. *The Postmodern Condition: A Report on Knowledge.* Trans. Geoff Bennington and Brian Massumi. Minneapolis: Minnesota U P, 1984.

Maasic, Sonia, and Jack Solomon, eds. *Signs of Life: Readings on Popular Culture for Writers.* 2nd ed. Boston: Bedford, 1997.

Macdonell, Diane. *Theories of Discourse.* New York: Blackwell, 1986.

Mahoney, Patrick. *Psychoanalysis and Discourse.* New York: Tavistock, 1987.

Mann, Paul. *Masocriticism.* New York: SUNY P, 1999.

Marcus, Greil. *Lipstick Traces: A Secret History of the Twentieth Century.* Cambridge: Harvard U P, 1989.

Marx, Karl. *Capital.* Vol. 1. Trans. Ben Fowkes. New York: Vintage, 1977.

Marx, Karl, and Frederick Engels. *The German Ideology.* Moscow: Progress Publishers, 1976.

Massumi, Brian. *Parables for the Virtual: Movement, Affect, Sensation.* Durham: Duke U P: 2003.

McComiskey, Bruce. "Composing Postmodern Subjectivities in the Aporia between Identity and Difference." *Rhetoric Review* 15.2 (1997): 350–64.

——. *Teaching Composition as a Social Process.* Logan: Utah State U P, 2000.

Mensch, Richard James. *Knowing and Being: A Postmodern Reversal.* University Park: Pennsylvania State U P, 1996.

Metzger, David. "Let's Give Them Something to Talk About: (Guest Editor's Introduction to) 'Lacan and the Question of Writing.'" *PreText* 15.1–2 (1994): 8–26.

——. "Writing as Symptom and Desire: A Lacanian Perspective on the Emergence of Popular Culture in the Composition Classroom." *Writing Instructor* 13.3 (1994): 101–10.

Miller, Richard E. *As If Learning Mattered: Reforming Higher Education.* Ithaca: Cornell U P, 1998.

——. "Fault Lines in the Contact Zone." *College English* 56 (April 1994): 389–408.

Miller, Susan. "Jim Berlin's Last Work: Future Perfect, Tense: Technologies of Self?-Formation." *JAC* 17.3 (1997): 497–500.

——. *Textual Carnivals: The Politics of Composition.* Carbondale: Southern Illinois U P, 1991.

Miller, Thomas P. "Memorial Tribute to James L. Kinneavy, 1920–1999." *College English* 62 (January 2000): 313–16.

Mills, Catherine. "Efficacy and Vulnerability: Judith Butler on Reiteration and Resistance." *Australian Feminist Studies* 15.32 (2000): 265–79.

Miraglia, Eric. "Resistance and the Writing Teacher." *JAC* 17.3 (1997): 415–35.

Morton, Donald, and Mas'ud Zavarzadeh. *Theory/Pedagogy/Politics: Texts for Change.* Urbana: U of Illinois P, 1991.

Muckelbauer, John. "On Reading Differently: Through Foucault's Resistance." *College English* 63 (September 2000): 71–94.

Mullarkey, John. *Bergson and Philosophy.* Notre Dame: U of Notre Dame P, 1999.

Murphy, Ann. "Transference and Resistance in the Basic Writing Classroom: Problematics and Praxis." *CCC* 40.2 (1989): 175–87.

Nealon, Jeffrey. *Alterity Politics: Ethics and Performative Subjectivity.* Durham: Duke U P, 1998.

Nicol, Bran. "Reading Paranoia: Paranoia, Epistemophilia, and the Postmodern Crisis of Interpretation." *Literature and Psychology* 45.1–2 (1999): 44–62.

Nietzsche, Friedrich. *Beyond Good and Evil.* Trans. Walter Kaufman. New York: Vintage, 1966.

———. *The Gay Science.* Trans. Walter Kaufman. New York: Vintage, 1974.

———. "On the Uses and Disadvantages of History for Life." *Untimely Meditations.* Trans. R. J. Hollingdale. New York: Cambridge U P, 1983.

———. *Philosophy and Truth: Selections from Nietzsche's Notebooks of the Early 1980's.* Trans. Daniel Breazeale. Atlantic Highlands: Humanities P, 1979.

———. *The Portable Nietzsche.* Trans. Walter Kaufman. New York: Vintage, 1968.

North, Stephen M. "Rhetoric, Responsibility, and the 'Language of the Left.'" Hurlbert and Blitz 127–38.

O'Banion, John D. "*A Theory of Discourse*: A Retrospective." *CCC* 33.2 (1982): 196–201.

Ohmann, Richard. *English in America: A Radical View of the Profession.* Hanover: Wesleyan U P, 1976.

Osborne, Peter, ed. *A Critical Sense: Interviews with Intellectuals.* New York: Routledge, 1996.

Paine, Charles. *The Resistant Writer: Rhetoric as Immunity, 1850 to the Present.* Albany: SUNY P, 1999.

Pascal, Blaise. *Pensées.* Trans. Isaac Taylor. New York: Penguin, 1995.

Pell, Derek. "The Elements of Style." *Pre/Text* 15.3–4 (1994): 218–46.

Pepper, Thomas. *Singularities: Extremes of Theory in the Twentieth Century.* Cambridge: Cambridge U P, 1997.

Pfeil, Fred. *Another Tale to Tell: Politics and Narrative in Postmodern Culture.* New York: Verso, 1990.

Phelps, Louise Wetherbee. *Composition as a Human Science.* New York: Oxford U P, 1988.

Plato. *Gorgias.* Trans. W. C. Helmbold. New York: Bobbs-Merrill, 1952.

Ragland, Ellie. "Psychoanalysis and Pedagogy: What Are Mastery and Love Doing in the Classroom?" *Pre/Text* 15.1–2 (1994): 46–77.

Readings, Bill. *The University in Ruins.* Cambridge: Harvard U P, 1996.

Ronell, Avital. *Crack Wars: Literature Addiction Mania.* Lincoln: U of Nebraska P, 1993.

———. *Dictations: On Haunted Writing.* Lincoln: U of Nebraska P, 1986.

———. "Our Narcotic Modernity." *ReThinking Technologies.* Ed. Verena Conley. Minneapolis: U of Minnesota P, 1993. 59–73.

Rose, Nikolas. *Powers of Freedom: Reframing Political Thought.* Cambridge: Cambridge U P, 1999.

Ross, Andrew. "The Rock 'n' Roll Ghost." *October* 53 (Summer 1990): 108–17.

Sacks, Peter. *Generation X Goes to College: An Eye-Opening Account of Teaching in Postmodern America.* Chicago: Open Court, 1996.

Sánchez, Rául. "Composition's Ideology Apparatus: A Critique." *JAC* 21.4 (2001): 741–59.

Schiffrin, Deborah. *Approaches to Discourse*. Cambridge: Blackwell, 1994.

Schilb, John. *Between the Lines: Relating Composition Theory and Literary Theory*. Portsmouth, NH: Boynton/Cook, 1996.

———. "Comment on James Berlin, 'Rhetoric and Ideology in the Writing Class.'" *College English* 51 (November 1989): 769–70.

———. "Cultural Studies, Postmodernism, and Composition." Harkin and Schilb 173–88.

Schmidt, James, ed. *What Is Enlightenment? Eighteenth-Century Answers and Twentieth-Century Questions*. Berkeley: U of California P, 1996.

Scholes, Robert. *The Rise and Fall of English*. New Haven: Yale U P, 1998.

Segal, Judy. "Pedagogies of Decentering and a Discourse of Failure." *Rhetoric Review* 15.1 (1996): 174–91.

Serres, Michel. *Hermes: Literature, Science, Philosophy*. Baltimore: Johns Hopkins U P, 1982.

Shor, Ira. *When Students Have Power: Negotiating Authority in a Critical Pedagogy*. Chicago: U of Chicago P, 1996.

Sidler, Michelle, and Richard Morris. "Writing in a Post-Berlinian Landscape: Cultural Composition in the Classroom." *JAC* 18.2 (1998): 275–91.

Sirc, Geoffrey. "The Difficult Politics of the Popular." *JAC* 21.2 (2001): 421–33.

———. "English Composition as a Happening II (Part One)." *Pre/Text* 15.3–4 (1994): 264–93.

———. "Godless Composition, Tormented Writing." *JAC* 15.3 (1995): 543–64.

———. "Never Mind the Tagmemics, Where's the Sex Pistols?" *CCC* 48.1 (1997): 9–29.

———. "Writing Classroom as an A&P Parking Lot." *Pre/Text* 14.1–2 (1993): 27–70.

Sloterdijk, Peter. *Critique of Cynical Reason*. Minneapolis: U of Minnesota P, 1987.

Smith, Paul. *Discerning the Subject*. Minneapolis: U of Minnesota P, 1988.

Solomon, Robert C., and Kathleen M. Higgins. *Reading Nietzsche*. New York: Oxford U P, 1988.

Stallybrass, Peter, and Allon White. *The Politics and Poetics of Transgression*. Ithaca: Cornell U P, 1986.

Strunk, William, Jr., and E. B. White. *The Elements of Style*. 4th ed. New York: Longman, 1999.

Taylor, Charles. *Philosophical Arguments*. Cambridge: Harvard U P, 1995.

Therborn, Göran. *The Ideology of Power and the Power of Ideology*. London: Verso, 1980.

Threadgold, Terry. *Feminist Poetics: Poiesis, Performance, Histories*. New York: Routledge, 1997.

Torfing, Jacob. *New Theories of Discourse: Laclau, Mouffe, and Žižek*. Malden: Blackwell, 1999.

Trimbur, John. "Agency and the Death of the Author: A Partial Defense of Modernism." *JAC* 20.2 (2000): 283–98.

Ulmer, Gregory L. *Applied Grammatology: Post(e)-Pedagogy from Jacques Derrida to Joseph Beuys.* Baltimore: Johns Hopkins U P, 1985.

———. *Heuretics: On the Logic of Invention.* Baltimore: Johns Hopkins U P, 1994.

———. *Internet Invention: From Literacy to Electracy.* New York: Longman, 2002.

———. "Textshop for Psychoanalysis: On Deconstructing Freshman Platonists." *College English* 49 (November 1987): 756–69.

Vasterling, Veronica. "Butler's Sophisticated Constructivism: A Critical Assessment." *Hypatia* 14.3 (1999): 17–38.

Vitanza, Victor J. "The Hermeneutics of Abandonment." *Parallax* 4.4 (1998): 123–39.

———. *Negation, Subjectivity, and the History of Rhetoric.* Albany: SUNY P, 1997.

———. "'Some More' Notes, Toward a 'Third' Sophistic." *Argumentation* 5 (1991): 117–39.

———. "Taking A-Count of a (Future-Anterior) History of Rhetoric as 'Libidinalized Marxism'" (A PM Pastiche)." Vitanza, *Writing* 180–216.

———. "Three Countertheses; or, A Critical In(ter)vention into Composition Theories and Pedagogies." Harkin and Schilb 139–72.

———. "Threes." *Composition in Context: Essays in Honor of Donald C. Stewart.* Ed. W. Ross Winterowd and Vincent Gillespie. Carbondale: Southern Illinois U P, 1994. 196–218.

———. "Two Propositions: On the Hermeneutics of Suspicion and on Writing the History of Rhetoric." *Discourse Studies in Honor of James L. Kinneavy.* Ed. Rosalind J. Grabin. Potomac: Scripta Humanistica, 1995. 55–72.

———. "'The Wasteland Grows'; or, What Is 'Cultural Studies for Composition' and Why Must We Always Speak Good of It?: ParaResponse to Julie Drew." *JAC* 19.4 (1999): 699–703.

———, ed. *Writing Histories of Rhetoric.* Carbondale: Southern Illinois U P, 1994.

Vries, Hent de, and Samuel Weber, eds. *Violence, Identity, and Self-Determination.* Stanford: Stanford U P, 1997.

Wall, Thomas Carl. *Radical Passivity: Levinas, Blanchot, and Agamben.* Albany: SUNY P, 1999.

Whitebook, Joel. *Perversion and Utopia: A Study in Psychoanalysis and Critical Theory.* Cambridge: MIT P, 1995.

Widder, Nathan. "What's Lacking in the Lack: A Comment on the Virtual." *Angelaki* 5.3 (2000): 117–38.

Witte, Stephen P., Neil Nakadate, and Roger D. Cherry, eds. *A Rhetoric of Doing: Essays on Written Discourse in Honor of James L. Kinneavy.* Carbondale: Southern Illinois U P, 1992.

Worsham, Lynn. "Going Postal: Pedagogic Violence and the Schooling of Emotion." *JAC* 18.2 (1998): 213–45.

Yagelski, Robert P. "The Ambivalence of Reflection: Critical Pedagogies, Identity, and the Writing Teacher." *CCC* 51.1 (1999): 32–50.

Young, Iris Marion. *Justice and the Politics of Difference.* Princeton: Princeton U P, 1991.

Zavarzadeh, Mas'ud. "Pun(k)deconstruction and the Postmodern Political Imaginary." *Cultural Critique* (Fall 1992): 5–45.

Žižek, Slavoj. *The Abyss of Freedom.* Ann Arbor: U of Michigan P, 1997.

——. "The Depraved Heroes of 24 are the Himmlers of Hollywood." *Guardian,* 10 January 2006. <http://www.tikkun.org/rabbi_lerner/news_item.2006-01-16.9282463496>. Accessed 19 July 2006.

——. *Enjoy Your Symptom!: Jacques Lacan in Hollywood and Out.* New York: Routledge, 1992.

——. "Fantasy as a Political Category: A Lacanian Approach." *Journal for the Psychoanalysis of Culture and Society* 1.2 (1996): 77–85.

——. *For They Know Not What They Do: Enjoyment as a Political Factor.* New York: Verso, 1991.

——. *The Indivisible Remainder: An Essay on Schelling and Related Matters.* New York: Verso, 1996.

——. "Is There a Cause of the Subject?" *Supposing the Subject.* Ed. Joan Copjec. New York: Verso, 1994. 84–105.

——. "A Leftist Plea for Eurocentrism." *Critical Inquiry* 24 (Summer 1998): 988–1009.

——. *Looking Awry: An Introduction to Jacques Lacan through Popular Culture.* Cambridge: MIT P, 1993.

——. *The Metastases of Enjoyment: Six Essays on Women and Enjoyment.* New York: Verso, 1994.

——. "Multiculturalism; or, the Cultural Logic of Multinational Capitalism." *New Left Review* 225 (1997): 29–52.

——. *The Plague of Fantasies.* New York: Verso, 1997.

——. "Postscript." Osborne 36–44.

——. *The Sublime Object of Ideology.* New York: Verso, 1989.

——. *Tarrying with the Negative: Kant, Hegel, and the Critique of Ideology.* Durham: Duke U P, 1993.

——. *The Ticklish Subject: The Absent Centre of Political Ontology.* New York: Verso, 1999.

Žižek, Slavoj, and Geert Lovink. "Civil Society, Fanaticism, and Digital Reality: An Interview with Slavoj Žižek." *Digital Delirium.* Ed. Arthur Kroker and Marilouise Kroker. New York: St. Martin's, 1997. 64–72.

Žižek, Slavoj, and Renata Salecl. "Lacan in Slovenia." Osborne 20–35.

BIBLIOGRAPHY

influence of, 177; as social/symbolic edifice, 47

132–33; critiques of, 6–7, 26–27, 108–9, 129–30, 139, 165, 202–3, 206; and decentered classroom, 109–10; as enlightenment project, 12; ethics and, 108–9, 132, 136, 212; ideology and, 117; institutionalization of, 136–39; poststructuralism and, 13, 55; psychoanalysis and, 4, 202–4, 210; rationality as basis of, 4–5; responsibility and, 19–20; rhetoric and, 13–14, 204; rise of, 120; value of, 208. *See also* composition studies

Cultural Studies (Grossberg, Nelson, and Treichler), 12

culture wars, 209–10

cynicism: Baudrillard and, 166–67; in contemporary culture, 160–61; critical pedagogy and, 183; ideology critique and, 101–3; media and, 162; modernism and, 11–12; pedagogy and, 162–63; student resistance and, 192; temporal factors in, 14

Davis, D. Diane, 10, 30, 170–73, 175, 183, 206

Dean, Timothy, 156–57

"Death of Discourse, The" (Collins and Skover), 168

decentered classroom, 109–14

decisions: and crucible of undecidability, 30–31; lack of agency in, 19, 21, 29–30; nature of, 18–19

deferred action. *See* belatedness

Deleuze, Gilles, 162, 174, 176, 178–79, 184, 185, 187, 190–91, 197, 200, 218n12, 220n1

democratic consciousness, 131–32

de-Oedipalization, 162–63, 170, 174–81, 185, 187. *See also* Oedipalization

Derrida, Jacques, 127; and belatedness, 15, 16–17; and citationality, 143; and discourse, 45; on Foucault, 85; and language, 35

desire: fantasy and, 63, 89; and injunction to enjoy, 188; intersubjective, 87–88; *jouissance* and, 211; Law and, 211; modes of, 87; need and, 102–3; as nondiscursive element, 46; of the Other, 60–61, 88–89, 114, 201; symbolization and, 63; Žižek on, 210

Dialectic of Enlightenment (Horkheimer and Adorno), 11–12, 101

discourse: communications triangle model of, 37–39; conflict in, 53; Deleuze and Guattari on, 218n12; distortion in, 58; and fissure, 45–46; Lacan on, 40, 44, 48, 58; linguistic approach to, 34; as mirror versus screen, 61–62; neo-Lacanian theory of, 45–53, 64–66; openness of, 45; poststructuralism and, 35–37, 40–41, 45–46; psychoanalytic approach to, 34–35, 44, 46; reality and, 52–53; rhetoric/composition studies and, 36–37; study of, 33–37, 52–53; subjectivity and, 61–62; sublime and, 219n16; types of, 40; Žižek on, 45, 52, 57–58. *See also* language

Discourse Studies in Composition (Barton and Stygall), 34

Dissemination (Derrida), 16

dissensus, social, 32

DIY (do it yourself), 195

doubt, working-through and, 20

dreams, interpretation of, 199–200

Drew, Julie, 13

Eagleton, Terry, 14, 117

Ebert, Teresa, 79, 102–3, 107–8, 111, 210

education. *See* pedagogy

Elements of Style, The (Strunk and White), 98–99

emotion. *See* affective realm

empowerment, pedagogy not designed for, 119

enjoy, injunction to, 186, 188–89, 193, 211

enjoyment. *See jouissance*

enlightened false consciousness, 12, 101–2, 125, 136

Enlightenment, 120

enlightenment projects: end of, 11–12; limitations of, 2, 4, 6. *See also* critique; social transformation

eternal return, 31

ethics, 19–20; cultural studies and, 108–9, 132, 136, 212; Lacan and, 209, 211–12; rhetoric and, 174

ethos, 202

Faigley, Lester, 10, 11, 41, 49–50, 71–73, 89, 119, 133–36, 144, 161, 166–69, 173–74

false consciousness: enlightened, 12, 101–2, 125, 136; ideology as, 101; limitations of concept of, 2, 4, 100

Family Ties (television show), 123

fantasy: concept of, 2–3, 58–59; desire and, 63, 89; going through, 213; ideology and, 126; *jouissance* and, 62–64; as nondiscursive element, 46; opposition and, 196; Other and, 60; pedagogy and, 111; reality and, 59, 126, 128, 204–5; Žižek on, 33, 59–60, 62

Felman, Shoshana, 113

feminist classrooms, 152–54

Fetterley, Judith, 151–54

Fink, Bruce, 91

Finke, Laurie, 118, 171

First Amendment, 168

fissure: in big Other, 56; discourse and, 45–46; intersubjective, 205–6; irreducibility of, 155; in Other, 91; racism and, 213; in society, 126–27; subjectivity and, 76, 90–91, 92, 157–58; of symbolic order, 47. *See also* fundamental antagonism

foreclosure, 147

Foster, Hal, 15, 26

Foucault, Michel, 105; and agency, 68–69; and disciplinary society, 176, 177; and discourse, 34–36; and power, 68–69, 140–41, 151; and resistance, 141; and subjectivity, 24, 61, 67–68, 84–85, 89–90; work of, 223n3

France, Alan, 13, 55

Frank, Thomas, 189

Frankfurt School, 101

Freud, Sigmund: as clinician, 203; and deferred action, 15, 22–23, 25; Foucault and, 85; on interpretation, 199–200; Lacan and, 200; and revision, 27; and rhetoric, 206; and temporality, 23

Fulkerson, Richard, 6, 38, 41

fundamental antagonism: irreducibility of, 51, 129, 148–49; meaning of, 47; pedagogy and, 110–12; in the Real, 59; in the social, 45, 106; Žižek's work as addressing, 151. *See also* fissure

funhouse metaphor, 70, 91–92, 94–95

Funkadelic, 115

Gadamer, Hans Georg, 36

Gale, Fredric G., 39

Gender Trouble (Butler), 143

Giroux, Henry, 101, 102, 160, 175–76, 182

Goleman, Judith, 105

good, the, 17–18, 31

"good writing," 98–99

Gorgias (Plato), 174

grades, 180

Gramsci, Antonio, 105

Grossberg, Lawrence, 12

Guattari, Felix, 178–79, 185, 187, 200, 218n12, 220n1

guilt, 211

Habermas, Jürgen, 10, 34, 58, 187
habit, 114–15
Hairston, Maxine, 13
Halberstam, Judith, 145
Hardt, Michael, 176, 184
Harris, Eric, 184
Hegel, G. W. F., 15, 16–17, 25–26, 74–75
Heidegger, Martin, 17, 23, 25, 36
Hindess, Barry, 35
Hirsch, E. D., 171
Hirst, Paul, 35
Holocaust, 201
Holzer, Jenny, 188
Horkheimer, Max, 12, 101, 160
Horowitz, David, 139
House of Love, 160
Howe, Neil, 161
humanities. *See* liberal arts
Hurlbert, C. Mark, 163

identity, 75–76, 92, 147
ideology: active engagement in, 100;
    alternative theory of, 116–18; appeal
    of, 125–26, 128–29; Berlin on, 122–23;
    definition of, 100; fantasy and, 126;
    jouissance and, 106, 125, 128–29;
    Marxist perspective on, 101–4;
    materialization of, 117; nonexistence
    of, 220n1; pedagogy and, 118–19;
    postmodern perspective on, 104;
    Real and, 104; rhetoric and, 121;
    shortcomings of critique of, 99–100;
    subjectivity and, 105–6; Žižek on,
    100, 102–5, 117–18, 125–26, 128–29
institutions, declining power of, 176
interpellation, 100, 105–6
interpretation: correctness of, 112–13; of
    dreams, 199–200
intersubjectivity: desire and, 87–88;
    fissure in, 205–6; Other and, 204–5;
    rhetoric and, 29, 91
invention: Act as, 31–32; pedagogy and,
    116, 195

Jakobson, Roman, 37
Jaworski, Adam, 34
Jay, Gregory, 112–16
Johnson, Adrian, 210–12
jouissance: concept of, 3, 20, 62, 205;
    critique and, 170; in culture wars,
    210; desire and, 211; effects of, 20–21,
    215n1; *Elements of Style* and, 98–99;
    emergence of, 205; evil and, 201;
    as excess, 20; fantasy and, 62–64;
    ideology and, 106, 125, 128–29; as
    nondiscursive element, 46; rhetoric
    and, 205; and the Thing, 64; writing
    and, 28; Žižek on, 62, 64

Kafka, Franz, 138, 141
Kant, Immanuel, 11, 74–75, 120, 210
"kernel of enjoyment," 64, 125, 128–29
Kincaid, James, 139
King, Stephen, 27, 28
Kinneavy, James, 7, 36–39, 53
Klebold, Dylan, 184
Kleine, Michael W., 39
knowledge: crisis of, 11–12; temporality
    and, 17, 21, 25. *See also* truth
Kristeva, Julia, 93

Lacan, Jacques: on agency, 69; and
    belatedness, 15; on big Other, 47;
    as clinician, 203; on discourse, 40,
    44, 48, 58; ethic of, 209, 211–12; and
    Freud, 200; on interpretation, 199;
    and language, 35; poststructuralism
    versus, 49–50; on Real, 46; and
    rhetoric, 21; in rhetoric/composition
    studies, 84–85; on sexual relations,
    111; and subjectivity, 24, 61, 79–80,
    84–85, 89–91; and truth, 37
lack: concept of, 47; in Other, 60;
    reality and, 55; in subject, 61, 149.
    See also fissure
Laclau, Ernesto, 45, 56, 126–27

INDEX

patriarchy, 147–48

Pêcheux, Michel, 35

pedagogy: challenges in contemporary, 166–70, 174–75, 184–85; complicity of, 107–9, 180, 189–90, 193; in composition studies, 12–13, 42, 81, 130–31; content of, 207; control as issue in, 171, 172, 180, 195–96; controversies over, 207, 226n8; and cynicism, 162–63; in decentered classroom, 109–14; democratic consciousness as goal of, 131–32; desire of the Other in, 114; empowerment not the goal of, 119; fantasy and, 111; fundamental antagonism in, 110–12; ideology and, 118–19; Law and, 193; liberal, 107–9, 120–22, 126, 183, 193; performance of, 109–12, 207; power/authority and, 109–14, 118, 151–59, 170–71, 182–83, 186; production-oriented, 114, 221n13; promise of, 119–20; as resignification, 154–58; resistance and, 151–54; rethinking of, 164–65, 170, 172, 175, 203; and risk, 194–96; subjectivity and, 81–83; undecidability of, 111–12; utopian view of, 171; and violence, 162–63, 181–84. *See also* postpedagogy

Pell, Derek, 98–99

Pensées (Pascal), 115

Pepper, Thomas, 17–18

performance: of gender, 143–45; of pedagogy, 109–12, 207

persuasion: complexity of, 202; cultural studies versus psychoanalytic perspectives on, 4–5

perversity, rhetoric and, 206–7

Pfeil, Fred, 174, 177–79, 186

Phenomenology of Spirit (Hegel), 16, 74

philosophy, rhetoric and, 2

Pierce, Quentin, 191–97

Plato, 111, 174

plausible deniability, 3

pleasure. *See jouissance*

politics: agency and, 89–91; poststructuralism and, 48–49; social construction of reality and, 89–90; subjectivity and, 89–90

positionality, identity and, 76

Postmodern Condition, The (Lyotard), 10

postmodernism: and affect, 175, 181–82; challenges of, 8–9; commodification and, 184; as de-Oedpialization, 174–75; as incomplete project, 187; politics and, 48–49; psychoanalysis and, 5; and subjectivity, 10, 22, 71–74, 135–36, 182

postpedagogy: abandonment in, 196; as Act, 195, 197–98; meaning of "critical" for, 173, 175; surprise as element of, 172–73, 195

poststructuralism: cultural studies and, 13; and discourse, 35–37, 40–41, 45–46; and language, 48; politics and, 48–49; psychoanalysis versus, 49–50

power: agency and, 90; in classrooms, 109–14, 118, 151–59, 170–71, 182–83, 186; Foucault on, 68–69, 140–41, 151; gender and, 152–53; institutional, decline of, 176; resistance and, 139–40, 154, 177

prefaces, 16–17

psychoanalysis: cultural studies and, 4, 202–4, 210; and discourse, 34–35, 44; pedagogical applications of, 4–5; postmodernism and, 5; poststructuralism versus, 49–50; purpose of, 203; rhetoric and, 200, 204–8, 213; and subjectivity, 21–22, 47; temporality and, 22–23; value of, 6, 7, 21, 207–8

punk rock, 192, 194, 197

Solomon, Robert C., 150
"spirit is a bone," 74–75
St. Martin's Guide to Writing, The
(Axelrod and Cooper), 82, 134–35
Stallybrass, Peter, 91
Stewart, Jon, 212
Strauss, Bill, 161
student resistance, 80, 113, 115, 120, 130,
133, 151–59, 171, 181, 191. *See also*
resistance
Stygall, Gail, 34
subjectivity: belatedness and, 15,
21–26; Berlin on, 70–71, 73, 77–83;
capitalism and, 135–36; composition
of, 26–27, 30; discourse and, 61–62;
dynamic quality of, 30; fissure in, 76,
90–91, 92, 157–58; Foucault and, 24,
61, 67–68, 84–85, 89–90; funhouse
metaphor for, 94–95; and identity,
75–76, 92; ideology and, 105–6; indeterminate aspects of, 81; Lacan and,
24, 61, 79–80, 84–85, 89–91; lack in,
61, 149; language and, 49, 77–78,
149; models of, 70; modernist, 22,
71, 94; multiplicity in, 170; and the
Negative, 185; negotiation of, 72,
73; Other and, 60–61, 88–89, 91;
postmodernism and, 10, 22, 71–74,
135–36, 182; post-Oedipal, 177–79,
185, 191–93, 195–96; production of,
67–68; psychoanalysis and, 21–22, 47;
and self-subjugation, 187; symbolic
order and, 84–87; temporality and,
14–15, 23–24; writing and, 28; Žižek
and, 15, 24, 73–76, 85, 88, 93–94,
135–36, 177, 187
subjectivization, 68
sublime: discourse and, 219n16;
Kantian, 74–75; Žižek on, 74–75
supplement, 86
surprise, as element of postpedagogy,
172–73, 195

symbolic order: concepts in, 98; desire
and, 63; finite/infinite nature of,
57–58; fissuring of, 47; pedagogy
and, 155–58; Real versus, 26, 31, 47,
54–55, 57; subjectivity and, 84–87
Symposium (Plato), 111

teaching. *See* pedagogy
*Teaching Composition as a Social
Process* (McComiskey), 42–43
temporality: cynicism and, 14; knowledge and, 17, 21, 25; psychoanalysis
and, 22–23; subjectivity and, 14–15,
23–24; truth and, 16–17. *See also*
belatedness
Teresa, Mother, 75
Theories of Discourse (Macdonnell), 35
Theory of Discourse, A (Kinneavy), 7,
37–38
Therborn, Göran, 104, 105, 122
Thing, 64
time. *See* temporality
Torfing, Jacob, 36, 45
tragedy, 29–30
transgressiveness, 191–96
transvaluation, 197, 226n10
trauma: in rhetoric/composition studies,
8–9; in writing, 27–28; Žižek on,
219n15
Treichler, Paula, 12
Trimbur, John, 13
truth: discourse and, 54–55; temporality
and, 16–17; theories of, 36–37. *See
also* knowledge

Ulmer, Gregory, 112, 115–16
unconscious, 25, 188
undecidability, crucible of, 30–31
universalization, overrapid, 148–50
university: corporate, 6, 9, 208; crisis of,
9–10; culture wars in, 209–10
University in Ruins, The (Readings), 10